Transgenerational Media Industries

Transgenerational Media Industries

Adults, Children, and the Reproduction of Culture

Derek Johnson

University of Michigan Press
Ann Arbor

Copyright © 2019 by Derek Johnson
All rights reserved

This book may not be reproduced, in whole or in part, including illustrations, in any form (beyond that copying permitted by Sections 107 and 108 of the US Copyright Law and except by reviewers for the public press), without written permission from the publisher.

Published in the United States of America by the
University of Michigan Press
Manufactured in the United States of America
Printed on acid-free paper

A CIP catalog record for this book is available from the British Library.

Library of Congress Cataloging-in-Publication data has been applied for.

First published November 2019

ISBN: 978-0-472-07431-0 (hardcover : alk. paper)
ISBN: 978-0-472-05431-2 (paper : alk. paper)
ISBN: 978-0-472-12613-2 (ebook)

Contents

Acknowledgments	vii
Introduction: The Next Generation	1
Chapter 1. Co-Viewing the Future: Transgenerational Marketing in Post-Network Television	23
Chapter 2. "Share Your Universe": Generation, Gender, and the Marvel Dad	53
Chapter 3. Junior Executives: Producing Adult Professionalism in Children's Media Industries	91
Chapter 4. "I've Got a Golden Ticket!" Adult Fans of LEGO in the Child-Centric Factory	123
Chapter 5. Child Labor: Testing the Limits of Transgenerational Media Industries	161
Conclusion: Reproducing the Future	197
Notes	211
Bibliography	217
Index	239

Digital materials related to this title can be found on the Fulcrum platform via the following citable URL: https://doi.org/10.3998/mpub.9894091

Acknowledgments

I found the second book much harder to write than the first, and it is only thanks to a long list of very reliable colleagues, friends, and family that this project could be imagined.

As part of the Media and Cultural Studies program at the University of Wisconsin, I am lucky to work with the best colleagues in the world. In the moments that I have felt lost in the direction of this project or unsure of its value, I could count on each of them to roll their eyes and remain confident on my behalf. Jonathan Gray continues to be the most generous friend and collaborator anyone could ask for. Lori Lopez is honest with her feedback, generous with her enthusiasm, and the best for sharing a laugh. Undoubtedly, the most hours of support were logged by Jeremy Morris, who musters wise responses to work and life issues alike, all while maintaining a good biking or running pace. Meanwhile, Jason Lopez plays many roles—philosopher, bartender, game master, therapist—always teaching me something in each of them. Eric Hoyt reminds me to be bold and not worry about the risks of trying something new. Very much missed in her retirement, Michele Hilmes remains my role model for intellectual sophistication and leadership. Whether it is discussing business over Wednesday lunches, engaging with our students' research, or inevitably revealing myself to be a Cylon, I treasure every moment with this group.

Even with all this support close by, I remain equally in debt to many colleagues beyond the city of Madison who have encouraged and inspired me—far more than I can list here. Sarah Banet-Weiser, John Caldwell, Michael Curtin, Tim Havens, Henry Jenkins, Amanda Lotz, and Serra Tinic have been invaluable in their brilliant advice and their willingness to help me find and pursue new opportunities. Just as he did during grad school,

Aswin Punathambekar continues to remind me what to focus on, what distractions to avoid, and how to enjoy life while doing so.

My graduate students have also been a crucial source of inspiration. Camilo Diaz-Pino, Caroline Leader, Wan-Jun Lu, Taylor Miller, Jenna Stoeber, Tony Tran, and Drew Zolides all contributed to my initial attempts to wrap my head around this project during our 2013 seminar on cultural studies and kids' media. Since then I have also benefited from rewarding collaboration with advisees like Nick Benson, Caroline Leader, and Jennifer Smith, who share many of the interests in this book. As research assistants, Caroline and Jennifer deserve special mention for helping to lay the foundation for much of chapter 2; without them that chapter would be far less rich in detail.

Research assistance is not free, however—nor are trips to industry events and international sites of fan tourism. I am therefore extremely grateful for research support provided by the University of Wisconsin-Madison Office of the Vice Chancellor for Research and Graduate Education with funding from the Wisconsin Alumni Research Foundation. I have also been lucky to be able to rely on the generosity of George and Pamela Hamel, whose commitment to supporting faculty research in the Department of Communication Arts made a huge difference to this project. So too have department chairs Mike Xenos and Kelley Conway been instrumental in helping me find resources. I am also grateful to Camilla Torpe, Ryan Greenwood, and many of their colleagues at The LEGO Group for permitting me to do on-site research in Billund and providing useful feedback.

Indeed I would not have been able to turn this research into a deliverable manuscript without *all* the helpful feedback I received along the way. My editor at University of Michigan Press, Mary Francis, patiently listened to me stumble through my ideas for this book over the course of many meetings and many years, but I left each one with more focus and direction. I appreciate her persistence, excitement, and confidence in what this book could be. Dan Herbert shared his expert thoughts on early drafts of this project, and I continue to enjoy every opportunity I get to collaborate with him. Opportunities I have had to share this work with colleagues across the globe also provided vital insights. I am especially grateful for Tim Havens from the University of Iowa, Ben Aslinger from Bentley University, Sébastien Francois from the CoCirPE Project at Université Paris 13, and Jianbin Guo from Yunnan University for generous invitations to deliver talks based on works in progress. My colleague Zhongdang Pan was also particularly instrumental in facilitating that latter trip. Each of these intellectual exchanges significantly evolved and refined my ideas.

All that said, a book about media and the transformative, overlapping identities of kids and parents obviously owes much to my family. As this book often focuses on the pleasures of sharing media with the next generation, I must acknowledge a debt to my grandmother, Liz Johnson; decades later, I still remember her zeal in enabling me and my siblings in our earliest explorations of consumer culture and in taking us to movies for which we were certainly too young. My grandparents Donald and Milly Swanson were the complete opposite of this, but they are missed just the same. I am also grateful for the considerable time spent with my two daughters by their own grandparents Carol Johnson, Jeff Johnson, Steve Blomgren, and Mardie Blomgren (without which this book still would not be done). It is with Colleen, however, that I share the pleasures and responsibilities of raising, loving, and sometimes just dealing with our girls; I am in awe of how much she does, not just to give our kids the world, but also to make that world a better place. In bringing our girls into that world, she has already given me the entire universe—and I love sharing it with her.

It is a rather odd and mediated universe, though: one full of LEGO bricks, family movie nights, trips to the comic book store, nightly *Harry Potter* chapters, and co-viewings of *Deep Space Nine* and *Full House* alike. And in that sense, my daughters Dahlia Lucille and Annika Roslin were collaborators in the research for this book, as well as co-producers of the experiences and identities in play for me as an author. I dedicated my last book to Dahlia, so it is perhaps fairest and most appropriate to give this one to Annika, who came into our lives just as this project began. The process of writing this book brought the twin joys of trying to share that universe with her and slowly realizing that it was her universe to share all along. I look forward to seeing what else this wild, strong, independent girl will do to change it.

Introduction

The Next Generation

Popular media and entertainment industries have a funny way of making us feel our age. The barrage of images, narratives, and products aimed at our growing educational and cultural needs as children comes clearly labeled according to a graduated age progression: television programming carries ratings like "TV-Y7," while toy packaging promises appropriateness for "Ages 3+." In this sequential logic, no one's childhood lasts forever, and upon reaching adolescence, then adulthood, we gain not just greater consumer freedom but also new value to the entertainment industries. In pursuit of our disposable incomes, marketers increasingly cater to our tastes between the ages of eighteen and thirty-four—particularly if our age demographics overlap with other privileges of race, gender, class, and reproductive status. Whether we eventually become parents or not, this industry attention will soon consider our potential to consume on behalf of a new generation, where age guidelines and ratings systems now serve as our allies in making age-appropriate choices for younger consumers. And as media industries turn their attention to those new children, we may suddenly find ourselves left behind as an aging market outside the corporate pursuit of the future.

However, despite this portrait of a linear succession of age-defined media experiences cultivated by industry from consumer birth to death, these boundaries are not always so stark or well-policed. Indeed our first exposure to more mature media content may come not from the authorized curation of parents, marketers, or regulatory mechanisms but from our active attempts to circumvent those systems. Young media users often refuse the marketing categories to which they have been assigned to seek out entertainment forms deemed age-inappropriate, engaging in complex "identity work" to take pleasure in that transgression (Buckingham 2008: 230). Many adults, too, resist the perpetually forward-looking orientation of these marketing logics. Like Peter Pan, some refuse to grow up—at least in the ways imagined by marketers—reading children's literature or collecting toys despite social and industrial encouragement to turn their attention elsewhere.

Beyond the possibilities of refusing generationally linear boundaries, these age-defined media industries and cultures also depend on interaction and participation *across* age categories. Adult readers of *Harry Potter*, for example, transmit their fandom to the younger consumers in their life, gifting the books at birthdays and otherwise imagining the story as something to be passed down. Entertainment industries rely upon these dynamics, moreover, banking on the work that adult fans will do to promote media brands to the next generation of consumers. At this level of industry practice and strategy, potential for participation across the boundaries of generation crystallizes into institutionalized articulations, rather than divisions, of childhood and adulthood. On one hand, media industries develop ways of involving (some) consumers in the work of reproducing popular entertainment across generational lines. On the other, the production of media understood as "for" children (or any other specific age category) typically requires an adult work culture that can bridge generational boundaries. Because children cannot speak for themselves in professionalized industry realms exclusive to adults with the economic and legal standing to participate in labor relations (Buckingham 2000), children's media producers must find a way to connect their own tastes, knowledge, and expertise with those of the audience they aim to reach. Their work defies age boundaries as much as it is defined by them, producing children's media culture from adult attempts to interpret and negotiate childhood. The challenge of working across generational boundaries also prompts industries to cultivate relationships with consumers who might serve as productive allies—including the adult consumers who continue to participate in children's culture, who often may be more accessible or practical collaborators than children themselves. In the process of bridging generation gaps, then, media industries prompt a simultaneous transgression of boundaries between production and consumption.

Attuned to how these generationally dynamic strategies operate at the intersections of production and consumption, *Transgenerational Media Industries* interrogates the politics of labor, participation, and age in the industries that produce animation, comics, toys, games, and other cultural objects often understood as "children's" media. Considering collisions of adult and child consumer categories—particularly as constructed and confronted within media production cultures—the book problematizes linear boundaries of age in the making, marketing, and lived experiences of contemporary media culture. Instead it theorizes these media industries transgenerationally: as emerging from a process of transformation across generational lines that invites professionals and consumers alike to move between age-defined arenas of cultural participation. Trade discourse concerned with marketing across age categories commonly invokes comparable language, imagining consumer groups in terms of their potential crossover or cross-generational appeal (Benedetti 2011; "Musical" 2014). Such attempts at crossover typically envision interactions among specific, discrete generational cohort categories like baby boomers, Generation X, and millennials—each with their own historically specific identities, experiences, and lifestyles (Chaney, Touzani, and Slimane 2017: 180–81). However, while an approach imagined as cross-generational or intergenerational would lend itself to examining relations between discrete age cohorts, the distinctly transgenerational perspective developed here emphasizes the potential for media industries to operate in a greater matrix of blurred boundaries between adulthood and childhood, professionalism and amateur, work and play. I choose to theorize these media industries in terms of the transgenerational because that *trans-* prefix captures that boundary crossing dynamic and above all transformative character of the cultural logics in play. Under examination are not discrete, isolatable generations that media industries construct and exploit, but instead more complex processes in which the production and consumption of popular culture bends boundaries around adulthood and childhood.

At stake is first our ability to understand how age categories are constructed, maintained, and challenged within media industries. While marketers frequently use identity categories like gender to invoke audiences for industry product, age remains far less explored but equally important in those processes of determining whom popular culture serves and whom it empowers. At the same time as age categories communicate who culture is and is not intended "for," they produce a sense of who can and should make culture for particular audiences. While adult producers imagine age-bounded child audiences into being, they also exceed those boundaries to build professional identities in relation to childhood in their workaday lives. The boundary crossings necessary in the work of constructing age categories make them a unique and productive site to explore complex entanglements between labor, consumption, adulthood, and childhood in the media industries.

As a result, this book also helps us to see how the blurring of age boundaries in transgenerational media industries relates to convergences of professionalism and amateurism in those spaces. Adult fans of media products targeted at younger consumers participate in industry as brand ambassadors and perform other forms of deputized work, while children perform labor as research and product test subjects as well as virtuoso amateur producers on YouTube and other social media sites. As media professionals gain access to childhood through the amateur, moreover, the age-defying dimensions of transgenerational media rework and redefine the very bounds of industry production cultures. By looking more closely at the construction of these age categories, we can see how necessary it is to think about production in closer relationship to consumption: where both are enmeshed in the industrial labor of building bridges across the boundaries between adulthood and childhood.

Transgenerational media industries offer powerful insight into those dynamics by requiring adult producers to look outside their immediate professional communities to construct knowledge and expertise about younger consumers, to enlist adult consumers as nonprofessional participants in the generational transfer of taste, and to develop strategies for incorporating and exploiting the cultural work of child amateurs. By focusing on this media work that crosses boundaries of generation and age—and with them, amateurism and professionalism—this book directly confronts in transgenerational labor the participation of the consumer "outside" in the production "inside" of the media industries. Furthermore, this focus on the transgenerational dynamics in which children and childhood intersect with adults and adulthood reveals age and generation as productive sites of exchange and categories of co-constitutive relations—not dividing lines. In this sense, it would not be strictly accurate to say this is a book about "children's media"; instead this project reveals how media industries' construction of age-based content and markets involves a negotiated interplay of identity dynamically positioned between childhood and adulthood as well as professionalism and amateurism. Although this analysis could focus on media for children, by children, about children, or even the way in which adult media producers shape the culture of childhood, such a project would miss how media industries' construction of age-defined cultures demands boundary crossings between inside and outside, young and old, expert and layman. Readers interested in the media we readily recognize as "for kids" will have a lot to gain from this book, but along the way they will also gain better insights for understanding media industries more widely.

Thinking Transgenerationally

While I aim to build new insights and theoretical perspectives around it, this book is not the first to deploy a transgenerational framework to analyze media industries. Heather Hendershot (2004) and Marsha Kinder (1995) both reflect on forms of transgenerational address in popular television and film content. Meanwhile, Ellen Seiter (1995) and David Buckingham (2000) thoroughly acknowledge how adults play a vital, vested role in the production and consumption of kids' media, helping media scholars to recognize that research on children's popular culture demands equal attention to the cultures of parents and industry experts—even if these scholars do not use the same specific terminology. The emphasis on the transgenerational in this book does not lay monopolistic claim to this term nor suggest that there is anything particularly new in and of itself about the potential for the blurred boundaries between adulthood and childhood.

However, the conditions facing media industries in the twenty-first century make it particularly useful to reconsider and to continue developing these transgenerational frameworks. The age of media convergence in which "old and new media collide" (Jenkins 2006) might be equally described as a relation of generation in which old and young collide. Legacy industries like television, comics, and toys grapple not just with the age of their target markets but also their own maturation as they increasingly compete with new digital technologies and platforms for market attention—particularly when vying for younger consumers perceived as eager to embrace myriad new devices and media practices. Industries seeking to adapt to media change thus increasingly look for strategies that might harness emerging forms of creativity and innovation in the digital space, blurring the lines between production and consumption in the process of building appeals to the next generation of media users. In this context, it makes sense for companies invested in the production of children's entertainment to reassess the value of adult parents and fans who might help build bridges to emerging child consumers. However, it also behooves media industries negotiating the challenges of digital culture to consider child audiences less as external end users and more as innovative participants in the creative economies previously occupied and controlled by adults. In addition, industries contemplate the forms of adult participation—professional or amateur—that might be required to manage any potential contributions (practically, culturally, legally) from this next generation of media users. Thus, while the transgenerational character of the media industries is not necessarily new in its own right, that potential takes on added significance amid digital transformations that demand negotiation of the borderlands between new and old, professional and amateur, past and future. Often, as several chapters to come explore, this blurring of labor and generational boundaries also involves a collision of work and play, operating through gamified logics of competition and contests. The aging of legacy media industries thus motivates a growing need for transgenerational strategies that can cross all these gulfs and reconfigure the relationships media industries offer for adults and children within the spheres of production and consumption alike. This growing industrial capacity for thinking across boundaries makes it particularly crucial to expand our attention to the function and power of transgenerational relations.

My redeployment of transgenerational perspectives to analyze contemporary culture industries also takes cues from existing work aimed at cultivating theories of transmedia and the transnational. In the case of the former, Henry Jenkins describes transmedia as the industrial art of world building, where the practices of storytelling cross media platforms via coordinated collaboration between creators and active, participatory consumers who move across those boundaries to experience such worlds (2006: 108, 133). Although this definition of transmedia communicates aesthetic significance, it nevertheless recognizes the industrial potential to build crossover audiences attracted to different uses and iterations of the world across multiple media. Moreover, this sense of transmedia encourages us to think about the products of industrial boundary crossing and the potential for consumers and producers to be held in relationship to one another in those intersections. Transmedia transforms participation in storytelling, and by extension, we might consider how transgenerational strategies encourage more flexible forms of participation (from producers and consumers alike) in the spaces of adulthood and childhood. Studies of transnational media industries can also provide inspiration for how transgenerational perspectives might be built. Historian Michele Hilmes argues that the cultural economy of broadcasting possesses an inherent transnationalism "constituted both by the demands of the nation and the equally compelling impulse to go beyond, to provide a conduit to speak to other nations and to let other influences stream into the national space" (2012: 2). Rather than theorize the nation as a stable, discrete territory, her account focuses on the transgression of national boundaries, emphasizing dependence of national broadcast institutions on a "continuous flow of mutual influence circulating between them" (3). Application of these principles to the idea of generation attunes us to the mutual influences between childhood and adulthood, particularly as they are held in tension through their transformative participation in the cultures of production and consumption examined here. Just as Hilmes argues that transnational relationships are productive, so too might we consider how media industries develop significant strategies and practices from the resulting dialogue across generational lines. The categories of adult and child are not merely separate generationally defined markets, but are instead divisions transformed and transgressed by media industries in productive ways.

Looking past the *trans-* prefix, this book also reflects upon generation in the more general sense of biological and cultural reproduction in addition to specific generations such as boomers and millennials that have been fixed as sociological and marketing categories through their naming (Chaney, Touzani, and Slimane: 182). The prevalence of these named generations within professional industry discourse makes it unwise to ignore them entirely: as trade journalist Thomas Umstead wrote in 2016, the demographic logics of media industries "parse the world into groups of boomers, Gen Xers and millennials" (2016b: 9). As part of the building blocks of marketing, these named age groups become part of the "industry lore" (Havens 2007) through which practitioners understand their industrial work and pursue particular strategies and practices as commonsense. As Charles Acland (2004) writes, named generations manifest as "temporally designated communities, and might be best thought of as a form of *vernacular knowledge of historical location*, one that speaks to the role of novelty in contemporary capitalism" (2004: 33). This production of novelty undoubtedly supports media industries as they navigate wide-scale technological, economic, and social changes in the digital culture of the twenty-first century, making discourses about Generations Y and Z salient significations of historical breaks with the industrial and cultural conditions producing their Generation X forbearers. We cannot understand transgenerational media industries without acknowledging the historically specific generational discourses shaping and shaped by institutional practices and strategies, where the difference between one designated generation and the next reflects perceived changes in tastes, technological use, participatory media practices, and more.

Nevertheless, this project takes as its greater focus an interest in the construction of adulthood and childhood—and the reproductive, generative relationship between them—at all levels beyond the assignment of names to juxtaposed consumer markets. I use the term generative deliberately, turning significant focus on the potential for the pleasures of consumption and the work of production to be generated from these transformations and transgressions of adult-child boundaries. Generation here implies production and especially reproduction (where adults create children, biologically and as social subjects), and in doing so, identifies a trajectory of ongoing consumer and producer relationships pointing into the future. Moreover, the generative relationship between adulthood and childhood bears the potential to regenerate markets and labor forces upon which media industries depend. In sum, then, the transgenerational framework embraced here invites exploration of the ways media industries figure relationships between adulthood and childhood as a means of institutionally reproducing themselves (and media capitalism more broadly) into the future.

By invoking the futurity of reproduction, a transgenerational approach must also confront the politics of gender and sexuality intersecting with this industrial investment in age. Notable Marxist media critics Ariel Dorfman and Armand Mattelart (1971/2012) quite long ago critiqued industrially generated exchanges between adulthood and childhood as a means of biologically reproducing the cultural status quo of capitalism.[1] More recently, however, queer theory has destabilized the conservative politics of reproductive futures. Theorizing the "orientations" between bodies and objects in space and time, Sara Ahmed explains how the "well-trodden" paths of the past congeal as inheritances and normative "life courses" oriented toward certain habits and future outcomes (2006: 16, 21). By following the path of the family line that came before, bodies orient toward inherited repetition of heterosexual desire and reproduction: this orientation toward reproduction and inheritance traces the paths or lines through which "the openness of the future gets closed down" (58). Lee Edelman similarly critiques as "reproductive futurism" the "unquestioned" value of heterosexual reproduction, positioning in opposition to futures organized around the terms of "the Child" a queer futurity centered on "the rejection of a here and now and an insistence on potentiality or concrete possibility for another world" (2004: 1). For José Muñoz (2009), utopian forms of queerness might then disrupt orientations toward family and inheritance to imagine those different futures, just as Jack Halberstam posits queer temporalities as nonlinear, alternative ways of being that disrupt the normative values of family, longevity, and wealth accumulation that otherwise organize the imagination of the future (2011: 70). Queer theory issues a powerful challenge to the imagination of futures oriented to the principles of reproduction.

As a capitalist project of producing, sustaining, and extending markets over time, transgenerational strategies appear decidedly counterposed to the queer politics these theorists envision, where relationships between adults and children help secure a normative reproductive future for media industries. To the extent that they privilege the reproductive values of family and inheritance, transgenerational media industries seek to push the past into the future. Therefore, while queer theory might help us interrogate the intersectional politics of age, gender, and sexuality underpinning transgenerational strategies, it does not reflect the actual discourse and logics circulating within media industries, which remain firmly oriented to the normative politics of reproductive futurism. As a means of studying media capitalism, attention to this reproductive futurity does not reveal the nonnormative utopian alternatives of queerness, but instead denaturalizes the institutionalized processes by which gendered, racialized, and sexualized orientations to the future get produced (Gibson-Graham 1996: 144; Limbrick 2012: 104). My invocation of transgenerational media industries as constituted in and through boundary crossing thus refuses to position these strategies as essentially queer, feminist, or otherwise progressive; just as we would not assume the boundary crossings of transmedia or transnationalism to be inherently liberating, the transgression of divides surrounding generation and labor does not automatically translate to any radical politics. Instead dialogue between critical media industry studies and queer theory can highlight the potential for social and cultural transgression to be harnessed and incorporated within institutional frameworks. Such a perspective can reveal how capitalist emphasis on reproduction often mires media industries in heteronormative assumptions about the future.

However, we should not wholly dismiss the potential usefulness of this approach as a way of starting to imagine industrial possibilities beyond the hegemony of reproductive futurism. Within the transgression and transformation of age categories that industries forward as distinct, discrete markets, we might be able to glimpse the moments of "failed" adulthood and childhood that, in their awkward correspondence to the markets industries seek to reproduce, resist normative temporalities and orientation to the reproductive future.[2] While transgenerational media strategies often depend on the ideologies of family, inheritance, and reproductive futurism, they simultaneously invite participation from producer and consumer subjects who disrupt lines of generational transmission or follow them in unintended directions. At the same time that transgenerational media industries reproduce orientations, they may also open up spaces to explore the childish, for example, outside the privilege accorded to the Child itself. Considered in this way, the transgenerationalism examined here surrounds the institutional practices and strategies of reproducing consumer and producer subjectivities across generational lines, examining how they invite, harness, and negotiate the transgression of boundaries between adulthood and childhood as part of the industrial management of the future.

The Matrix of Age and Industry Participation

Rooted in analysis of the media industries, this book offers limited focus on the identities and experiences of actual media audiences who live in the transgenerational media culture under construction by these institutions of entertainment. First and foremost, examination focuses on the institutional discourses and practices that aim to marshal diverse media users as participants in that cultural economy—all of which extend from industrial interests and priorities. As such, concern for consumers alongside the attention to producers more typical of media industries research can attend to the construction of transgenerational industry subjects, zeroing in on the ways media industries address, invite, and encourage participants to adopt transgenerational positions and inhabit the relational space between adulthood and children. In other words, transgenerational media industries offer frameworks for producers and consumers alike to take up positions as participatory subjects of those industries. This distinction between actual consumers and their industrial construction as subjects also allows this project to build upon existing knowledge about children's culture in relation to subjectivities defined in and through the power of media and other capitalist institutions. As David Buckingham argues, "the relationship between children and the media can only be fully understood in the context of a wider analysis of the ways in which both are constructed and defined" (2008: 227). Adopting an industrially focused approach to the historical construction of childhood, Daniel Thomas Cook reflects on the power of markets to produce our social selves: "markets make persons," he argues, "in their capacity as power structure to 'hail' or call into being particular subjects and subjectivities . . . addressing and indeed encouraging active, agentive beings . . ." (2004: 12). Childhood becomes in that view a "generative culture site" in which the market and consumer unfold in tandem (13).[3]

This foundation for understanding childhood as a consumer subjectivity enables but also leaves room for more sustained engagement with the industry formations that look beyond hailing kids as consumer subjects to situate participants in both production and consumption economies alike at the intersections between childhood and adulthood.[4] Beyond simple recognition of child and adult markets as intertwined categories produced by industry, this book makes a more distinctive contribution by theorizing the production of transgenerational consumer subjectivities that encourage participants to transmit, transform, and transgress across the boundaries dividing adulthood and childhood. Following Nicholas Sammond's (2005) theorization of childhood within a "discursive matrix," transgenerational subjects can be situated within industry strategies that position adults and children as sharers and co-participants in the reproduction of popular culture. Attention to the industrial construction of these subjectivities reveals how the economies of popular culture in the twenty-first-century digital economy cohere around idealized adult and child relations that turn less on demographic division and more on shared participation in cultural reproduction.

That shared participation thus distinguishes transgenerational subjectivities not as coterminous with childhood but instead as inclusive of adults envisioned to participate as parents or as professionals. Adults have, of course, previously figured as participants in childhood cultures. Sammond emphasizes that twentieth-century parents "were expected to regulate their children's consumption of popular media," raising offspring in concordance with hegemonic American ideals (2005: 129). Cook, on the other hand, demonstrates how those ideological expectations produced motherhood as an adult consumer category in orbit around and the idea of childhood (2004: 39). In more contemporary studies, these subjectivities of childhood consumption unfold in opposition to those of adulthood. Sarah Banet-Weiser stresses that branded youth identities often cultivate rebellious opposition to the idea of adulthood (2007: 5), whereas Mary Kearney similarly explores teen empowerment from positions of resistance to adulthood (2006: 164–65). Yet these oppositions hint at the transgenerational connections at work in the industrial construction of childhood. Banet-Weiser explicitly describes childhood rebellion as part of incorporative industry logic: "Within this consumer market," she argues, "the two seemingly oppositional forms of address—the generational divide and the transgenerational connection—function in tandem to . . . smooth over any kind of generationally based conflict" (2007: 5). Another way of bringing focus to the participation of adults in the production and theorization of children's media culture, however, foregrounds the subjectivities of adult professionals working to produce content for kids. As both John Caldwell (2008) and Timothy Havens (2007) argue, media professionals engage in a process of commonsense-making about their work that regulates their participation in industry practice. In the case of kids' media specifically, adult professionals theorize about making media for children from subject positions outside that market category. David Buckingham adds that "far from enjoying an absolute power to define the child audience, producers and policy-makers in fact display a considerable degree of uncertainty about it," particularly insofar as changing social, industrial, and technological conditions reshape their perceptions and lay theorizations of that audience (2008: 229). Adult producers thus occupy subjectivities positioning them as representatives for children within industry cultures.

As subsequent chapters will explore, we should not too easily dismiss the potential participation of children in these work worlds. Nevertheless, kids' media industries distinctly imagine their consumers as "extra-commercium" (Cook 2004: 8), structurally barred from participation in production cultures by child labor laws as well as the age-based norms of professionalism (Buckingham 2000: 194–95, 203). Women, people of color, and queer media professionals face their own structural exclusions from media production, too; but the exclusion of children from the production of children's media hardly, if ever, prompts journalistic exposés or investigation of the sort that the US Justice Department and Equal Employment Opportunity Commission launched in 2015 around gender discrimination in Hollywood (Robb 2015). Instead children's extra-industrial status reads as an assumed, commonsense state of affairs.[5] Yet, as I argue here, child perspectives remain crucial to any consideration of transgenerational subjectivities within media production. In his historical study of children's marketing, Cook finds the voice of the child to be "always already mediated through adults and organizations . . . Those who claim to speak for children or a child can usually be refuted only by other nonchildren (adults) who compete to make similar claims" (2004: 15). The need to speak for children incites an ongoing discourse in which adults compete to occupy the positionality of the child, creating a culture of "pediocularity" within the culture industries that decenters adult modes of being in order to see "with children's eyes" (5, 67).[6] Through this transgenerational way of seeing, children's voices are not so much absent as mediated by the professional subjectivities discursively constructed for adults.

The power of adults to adopt transgenerational subjectivities is thus paramount, demanding attention to the function of children's media production cultures as "imagined" communities (Caldwell 2008: 111; Anderson 1983). Adult producers of children's television unite around shared values, meanings, and ideologies that constitute their understandings of childhood and their roles within child-defined industrial work worlds. Timothy Havens (2007), Heather Hendershot (1998), Dafna Lemish (2010), and Jeanette Steemers (2010) have all considered children's television production as a discrete sector within the wider television industries, tracing the discourses about shared professional investment in childhood that separate these production ecologies from other industry spaces. In her book *The Children's Television Community*, in fact, scholar practitioner J. Alison Bryant argues that children are a "special" audience with different cognitive, developmental, and emotional needs that demand unique consideration and expertise from content creators, regulators, and others who grapple with those demands (2007: ix). Based in service to unique childhood needs, this theorization of adult media professionals foregrounds the transgenerational identity work behind their community, where adult participation demands professional negotiation of and investment in the meanings, values, and perceived needs of childhood. The child audience, in this sense, is an Other in relation to which the adult seeks proximity, a subject position that cannot be fully inhabited, but which can be drawn nearer through the adjacent positionality of transgenerational professionalism. Paradoxically, membership in these production communities depends on subjective relationality to childhood.

Investigation of these industries thus need not center solely on the construction of children as a special audience or the imagination of children's media producers as a bounded community. Instead these production sectors can be understood as generative sites for the formation of transgenerational subjectivities across communities of workers and consumers alike. The construction of transgenerational industry subjects provides an opportunity to consider not just transgressed boundaries between adulthood and childhood but also permeable relations between professionalism and amateurism at the bounds of the industry "inside" and "outside" (Ortner 2013: 27) where producers confront their relations to communities of consumers, often "taking on the role of the audience" (Zafirau 2009: 197).

Finally, this concern for industry subjects encourages interrogation of the boundaries between adulthood and childhood as they are constructed by marketers as well as the discourses through which that same marketing might purposely trouble those neat niches. In the markets constructed by media industries, it is easy to perceive a gulf separating children and adults—or as David Buckingham describes it, the social and industrial segregation barring children from cultural experiences deemed "not 'appropriate'" and distancing adults from "the appropriate domains of children" (2000: 14–15).[7] Yet in the industrial adaptation to changing markets and new forms of participatory culture in the digital age, those boundaries can be just as easily disrupted. In this context, "traditional distinctions are being eroded, while new gaps are opening up. Children are increasingly gaining access to 'adult' media, and being 'empowered' as consumers in their own right" (192). Helen Nixon (2002), for example, argues that age-based television marketing appeals have become persistent in an era defined by industry struggles for smaller and smaller audience shares; and yet the proliferation of personalized television viewing devices makes it easier for children to access (or circumvent restrictions on) highly visible mature programming from a position outside industry-designated niches. Looking at *South Park*, she argues that "part of its appeal for young viewers" rests in an edginess that signals and even encourages transgression of childhood boundaries (2002: 101–2, 116). In this context, adult-skewed programs actually operate "among the range of sites in which the social construction of contemporary childhood is played out" (2002: 117). With this in mind, the proper scope for this book includes media explicitly marked as "for kids" as well as media otherwise assumed to be "for adults"—which together act as the sites of construction for a variety of interlocking transgenerational subjectivities outside the binary frameworks of demographic age divisions.

Into the Future

In pursuit of these insights, the following five chapters rely upon a "critical media industry studies" approach attuned to the operation of organizations, agents, and practices within the institutions of cultural production and distribution. As described by Timothy Havens, Amanda Lotz, and Serra Tinic, this approach emphasizes quotidian practice and the role of human agents in "interpreting, focusing, and redirecting" the economic imperatives that drive major corporations within the media industries, matching macrolevel analysis of industry strategy with attention to tactical negotiation, ambivalence, contradiction, and struggle on the ground (2009: 236). Critical media industry studies conceptualize power not as a form of pure economic control but as a more "productive" force that operates through industry decision-making and creative practice to generate "specific ways of conceptualizing audiences, texts, and economics" (237). As a "critical" endeavor, this research approach explicitly aligns with the intellectual project of cultural studies that explores ordinary practices and ways of life (Williams 1958/2011: 59; Grossberg 2010: 13) to reveal the specific articulations and contextual conjunctures of power that shape them (Hall 1981/2011: 76; Grossberg 2010: 20, 25). From this perspective, the transgenerational media industries of the twenty-first century can be understood as operating within the specific conjuncture between producers and consumers engaged in the work of reproducing popular culture across those boundaries of adulthood and childhood. Transgenerational media industries are produced from dynamic and contextual construction of subjectivities across adulthood, childhood, production, and consumption, as well as the practices through which participants in these cultural economies navigate those meaningful linkages. Applied in this way, a critical media industry studies approach provides a conceptual umbrella under which to contribute to inward-looking "production studies" (Mayer, Banks, and Caldwell 2009) while integrating new outward-looking attention to the consumer cultures increasingly participating in industry discourses and practices in the digital age (Bruns 2008; Banks 2013; Jenkins 2006).[8] Rather than deploy participant observation fieldwork and analysis of industry discourse as part of a narrower investigation into production cultures, I have thus embraced the broader, midrange critical media industry studies approach as a means of exploring how transgenerational media industries operate through articulation of production *and* consumption cultures.

Although it embraces media studies, my approach also looks beyond screen media to consider other forms of popular culture like toys and merchandise in which narratives and representations take material form. As both a staple of children's consumer culture and a focus for the consumer practices of adult collectors (Geraghty 2014), toys represent an especially rich lens through which to explore transgenerational articulations at an industry level. With physical merchandise and screen media equally part of a larger "culture industry" examined by critical scholarship (Adorno 1963/2000; Horkheimer and Adorno 1944/2012; Miège 1989), I will frequently describe toys and screen media as interlinked industries that organize the reproduction of culture according to the strategies, priorities, and constraints of capital. Nevertheless, I do not exclude toys and other merchandise from consideration of "media" in their own right. On the contrary, I treat toys as a crucial and integrated component of a mediated and mediatized popular culture, where toy companies like LEGO increasingly imagine themselves as media companies trading in the culture of play, developing significant film and studio holdings of their own.[9] Even more traditional plastic action figures, dolls, and other playthings removed from the screen might also be productively considered as media. As assemblages of parts, joints, and paint, toys are a representational form of cultural expression that communicate specific ideas, values, and meanings and in doing so mediate our understanding of the practices of play.[10] Toys mediate meaning through practices of production and consumption that can (and should) support greater attention with critical media industry studies.

The first chapter, however, starts with television. "Co-Viewing the Future: Transgenerational Marketing in Post-Network Television" zeroes in on the strategies that programmers have increasingly embraced to coordinate adult and child viewership as part of their adaptation to the changing television economies of the digital era. In the bundled cable environment, subscribers had little choice but to pay for demographically distinct services for children's programming and adult programming; cable packages offered services like HBO for edgy, mature, adult programming and Nickelodeon to meet the needs of younger viewers, for example. Yet in the "over-the-top" environment of streaming television where consumers bypass the tiered channel packages of the cable industry to instead make à la carte selections between individual services, Netflix, Amazon Prime, HBO Now, and other subscription television channels increasingly build appeals across generational lines, developing broad subscriber bases through integrated service to parents and children. Most famously, HBO lured first-run episodes of *Sesame Street* away from PBS in 2015 to assert its potential primacy as a streaming destination for adults and kids alike. Meanwhile, channels that continue to operate in the cable environment, too, figure relationships between adults and legacy television franchises as a means of building stronger engagement from the next generation of viewers. Considering these recent developments alongside the rise of industry discourse on co-viewership, this chapter reveals a new institutional imperative to construct television audiences across generational lines. At stake in co-viewing is the imagined future for this channel landscape, where adults deliver their children to television marketers, and those children might become the loyal adult consumers of tomorrow. As constructed by industry strategies, these co-viewers are transforming consumer subjects, carrying brand loyalties from childhood to adulthood and later sharing them as part of child-rearing. These viewers are not conceived either as distinct demographics bound by age or as undifferentiated family audiences; instead these strategies extend from the recognition of viewers with dynamic generational identities and programming interests that can nevertheless be profitably integrated. In bridging appeals across market boundaries, co-viewing evokes the "multicasting" imperatives identified by Julia Himberg (2013); yet co-viewing distinguishes itself by virtue of its focus on relations *between* audiences, depending on older and younger viewers to participate in one another's relationships to the screen.

The second chapter, "'Share Your Universe': Generation, Gender, and the Marvel Dad," asks how media industries recruit parents (and other adults) to engage in this work of transmitting brand loyalties to the next generation. Yet it moves beyond market strategy to consider the identity work involved in cultivating transgenerational consumer subjectivities. Faced with an aging readership, comic book companies deploy their adult fan base as a means of outreach to younger readers, encouraging this promotional labor by acknowledging fan authority and cultural capital. Yet this invitation to pass the cultural inheritance of comic books down to the next generation does not extend equally to all older readers, as industry efforts privilege the gender and reproductive status of some fan subjects perceived to be more suited to the work of crossing generational boundaries. To make this case, the chapter examines the "Share Your Universe" campaign during which Marvel Comics encouraged adult readers to accept responsibility for exposing younger readers to comic book superheroes, responding to an ironic decline in youth appeal despite the popularity of superheroes in other twenty-first-century media. Contextualizing the campaign within similar industry efforts—such as Free Comic Book Day and Comic-Con Kids Days—analysis of press releases, news stories, published interviews, social media communication, and event programming demonstrates how and why a mature comics industry enlisted adults into the boundary work of generational outreach. Strategically, this case also reveals the interconnectedness of transgenerational media with the transmedia convergences of industries, where building appeals across generations meant leveraging relationships between different media. Politically, however, these articulations of generation, industry, and consumer identity turned on ideologies of heterosexual reproduction and patriarchal family relations in which the gendered, heteronormative figure of the Marvel Dad was empowered by industry to pass down this corporate cultural inheritance. Thus the chapter relates cultural reproduction in its industrial sense to heterosexual reproduction outside that industry space, considering how authority and privilege operate between the two.

The third chapter, "Junior Executives: Producing Adult Professionalism in Children's Media Industries," extends this reflection on authority by temporarily setting aside the adult consumer to consider how professionals occupy proximate positions relative to childhood in the course of navigating kids' media industries. At this intersection, the children's media professional coheres as a transgenerational subject, where professional power extends from adult performances of child-oriented, pediocular identities. Yet much like the Marvel sharer examined in chapter 2, this junior executive role is not universally experienced by or accessible to adult workers, revealing transgenerational subjectivity as a site of inequality and struggle over agency within media industries. Examining who can and cannot claim to speak for and as child consumers—and why—this third chapter considers how kids' media producers carefully manage their own professional performances of gender and reproductive potential to lay claim to professional authority and pediocular knowledge. These arguments rely upon participant observation fieldwork conducted at the annual Kidscreen Summit, considering its ritual function for the adults gathered there from across the television, gaming, and merchandising industries. Professionals in attendance must constantly speak on behalf of the absent child, and bids for authority and status within the community often depend on legitimating one's suitability as a proxy. As such, the event is not just a space for circulating industry lore about marketing to kids but is also an industrial conjuncture articulating professional power to transgenerational identity work. This chapter thus focuses on moments in which adult professionals claimed proximate relations to childhood in the course of communicating their expertise—as well as on the forces that often prevented them from accruing power by doing so. I triangulate these constructions of pediocular professionalism at Kidscreen with mediated representations that similarly award professional authority to transgenerational subjects: textual analysis of US reality television series *The Toy Box*, in which aspiring adult toy inventors are subjected to the creative authority and industrial expertise of children, confirms the symbolic power of childhood in arbitrating, contesting, and performing professionalism in this transgenerational industry space.

With this door to the professional work worlds opened, the fourth chapter, "'I've Got a Golden Ticket!' Adult Fans of LEGO in the Child-Centric Factory," brings adult consumers back across that threshold, asking what happens and why when they are invited to participate as tourists in this culture of pediocular production. The adult consumer subjectivities explored in chapters 1 and 2 offer to media industries a means of neatly bequeathing inheritance of popular media culture to younger audiences. The adult consumer of chapter 4, however, more explicitly troubles the neat lines of succession implied by this generational trajectory; instead adult fans manifest as a "surplus audience" (Jenkins, Ford, and Green 2013; Scott 2013) consuming childhood media as end users, and participating in the childish without any necessary relations to actual children. Although such fans trouble the age-based divides upon which industries construct their markets, their adult legal standing better suits them for incorporation as industry subjects. Building on research into tourism and fan pilgrimages, this chapter identifies media industry tourism as a form of highly managed consumer participation in production worlds, where the transgenerational subject's movement across the lines of production and consumption can serve industrial strategies built on carefully cultivated relationships between adulthood and childhood. To develop these ideas, this chapter considers the annual LEGO Inside Tour, which in 2005 began offering consumers a fantasy of participation in relations of production within the toy manufacturer's factory spaces. Through fieldwork as a Tour participant (and analysis of related corporate documents and press releases), I examine a matrix of interaction between adult tourism and pediocular industry space, where adult participation in childhood consumption becomes transformed and incorporated into a culture of production. The aspirational transgenerational subjectivity on offer repositions the surplus adult consumer as a more professionalized source of productivity in greater harmony with the company's pediocular brand culture.

The final chapter, "Child Labor: Testing the Limits of Transgenerational Media Industries," examines the roles that children might yet play as creative workers within these industries, despite extra-commercium status. While the analysis of *The Toy Box* in chapter 3 explores a fictionalized professional subjectivity extended to children, this fifth chapter examines more material opportunities for children to participate in media industry work. In this way, transgenerational subjectivities offer participation in the media industries not just to pediocular and childish adults, as in chapters 3 and 4, but also to children themselves. Although the chapter contextualizes child labor in relation to child stardom and other highly visible forms of onscreen media work, it is more concerned with the capacity of children to do the behind-the-scenes industrial work adults might otherwise do (as well as work alongside adults). To that end, it explores the creative media work that children do as "toy testers"—whether that happens as market research subjects, as online review contributors, or as producers of "unboxing videos" in the space of online video platforms like YouTube. Analysis of trade reports, published interviews, job postings and application forms, and other industry discourse reveals how frameworks imposed by executives, parents, and other adults filter the meanings and values of this child labor. This chapter highlights attempts to recast that work as something other than the commodified labor adults might perform by framing it instead as part of a game-oriented economy in which kids vie for fun and prizes in ways more compatible with the extra-commercium ideologies of childhood. In particular, these discourses assert parental figures as a form of adult managerial authority over the creative labor of toy testing to insulate the productivity of children from direct industry agency and participation. Providing consent, collaboration, influence, and commitment to good child-rearing, these parental media managers nest childhood productivity within a wider set of transgenerational relations based in the work of family. In these processes, the boundaries between child and adult, professional and amateur, inside and outside are both challenged and reasserted.

Before opening each of these windows into the transgenerational media industries, I should also take a moment to reflect on my own position within them—not just as an author with a critical interest in the topic but also as a consumer participant in the relationships, markets, and practices on offer. Throughout my life, I have benefited from marketers' recognition of me as part of an extremely valued audience of white men, with countless media products and brands seeking my attention. Because there has been no shortage of popular culture intended "for" me, it is unsurprising that I end up being a fan of many of the different media objects that sit at the center of the transgenerational strategies explored in the subsequent chapters. Livingstone and Drotner anticipate this relationship to the subject matter when they critique the impact of adult perspectives on children's media research: "when adults investigate children and childhood they are offered an opportunity to revisit their own past with a view to framing the future; and this trajectory seems to undermine the distance required to position oneself as researcher in relation to the object of research" (2008: 10). Rather than aspire to clinical distance and detachment, however, I embrace here an ethic of self-reflexive attention to how my own participation in transgenerational media phenomena shapes my perspective.

Just as important to acknowledge, then, is that my perspective on transgenerational media industries extends from my experiences as the parent of two young girls throughout the course of this research. In this dual role as parent and fan, I have taken significant pleasure in the ability to share my media interests with my children. While I would maintain that there is real value to all in the bonding time we carve out for father-daughter *Star Trek* viewing or LEGO building, for example, these dynamics continue to orient toward reproduction—where the biological reproduction of people gives way to the cultural reproduction of media consumption and its subjectivities. While parents like me can sometimes feel as if they have cultivated consumer subject positions for their children in opposition to the forces of media marketing, this fan cultivation continues to reproduce across generational lines the brand loyalties that media industries can leverage. It might feel progressive to provide fatherly encouragement of a female *Star Wars* fandom too often ignored by marketers, for example, but this parental cultivation of a new generation of consumers plays easily into the hands of adaptable culture industries (to say nothing about the self-congratulatory valorization of reproducing "Dad's" masculinized popular culture). Beyond developing franchise extensions like *Forces of Destiny* that newly aims *Star Wars* videos and merchandise at girl consumers, companies like Disney support this generational transmission of consumption by positioning fan parents like me as crucial allies in this industrial work. As chapter 2 explores, I occupy as both father and fan a subject position constructed by media industries to enlist me as an agent of transgenerational cultural reproduction who can do the work orienting and initiating children into branded media worlds. The privilege enjoyed in one generation of media marketing reproduces itself in these transgenerational media industries, targeted and imagined as the power to bequeath a cultural legacy upon the next generation. This makes me a knowledgeable participant in the industrial relationships under construction, but also requires explicit critical attention to the consumer subjects and forms of transgenerational exchange that the media industries do not so readily imagine into being—as I try to do throughout the book.

At the same time, my role in this transgenerational media economy does not neatly end at sharing my fan identities with my children. Instead of exclusively supporting the generation of a new, successive class of child consumers to supplant the old, my consumer practice as a transgenerational subject extends from continued transgression of age-based marketing categories. My relationships with media brands like Marvel Comics or LEGO began as a child, yet upon reaching adulthood, my interests did not automatically turn toward the cultivation of the next generation of fans. Quite the opposite, that participation intensified with age—surely fed by greater disposable income that could be devoted to fan practices. Though I read comics occasionally as a child and became a fan of *X-Men* through the animated television series and video games, it was only as an adult that I came to regularly consume comics too. Similarly, after having already set aside my toys like most adolescents, my time working in a Target toy department just before college rekindled that consumer interest. My passage into adulthood, in other words, counterintuitively deepened my own individual participation in media industries ostensibly targeted to children. Becoming a parent surely opened up the potential for acting as a brand ambassador to the next generation—but that role, too, deepened my own consumer engagement. Having kids seemed like a great time to take possession of the LEGO toys my mother had saved from my childhood in order to pass them down to the next generation; yet that reacquaintance rationalized new habits that would bring me consumer satisfaction as much if not more than my kids. Tellingly, after first placing an order to replace pieces lost over the years, I turned next to eBay to acquire the LEGO pirate ship that I had wanted back in Christmas of 1989. As an adult, I continued to participate in brands and consumer practices that I first embraced as a child, with both the economics and the meaningfulness of that participation transforming along the way.

My self-reflection is idiosyncratic. However, I suspect most consumer subjects exist somewhere in this transgenerational space, not exclusively childish or adult in their interests but transforming in complex and overlapping ways over the course of their changing participation in the media industries. It is thus the tension between the transgenerational character of media consumption more broadly and the nomination of a select few empowered to act as sharers and stewards of a cultural legacy that most effectively captures the focus of this book; at its center is a concern for who gets to participate in the transgenerational production and consumption of culture as managed by the media industries. Although many of the case studies and cultural products under investigation might typically be considered entertainment media "for kids," this project does not embrace a distinctly "adult" perspective that seeks to define, interpret, or evaluate a discrete children's culture from a position outside of it. This book does not seek to reveal the secret, inside world of kids' media for an audience of adults that might look upon it and see something weird, foreign, and unknown in need of revelation. Instead the project is centrally aimed at exploring how the age-defined media products generated by these industries depend paradoxically on the transgression of boundaries between adulthood and childhood at the levels of production and consumption both. Those boundary crossings, moreover, often seek to enable a generational reproduction and retransmission of culture built on hierarchies of gender and sexuality—and thus demand critical analysis rather than a reflexive celebration of that transgressive possibility. While the idea of transgenerational media industries invites us to think about how the reproduction of culture thrives from the blurring of boundaries, its limits reveal the persistence of gender norms, reproductive ideals, and reproduction of authority as media companies incorporate generational boundary crossing as strategy.

CHAPTER 1

Co-Viewing the Future

Transgenerational Marketing in Post-Network Television

In contemporary television economies that privilege on-demand experiences personalized across myriad digital devices and narrowcast services, the ongoing industrial significance of family relations offers a paradox. Long gone is the idealized electronic hearth in which television provided the centerpiece of a domestic tableau and for which companies like A. C. Nielsen measured live viewership with units like "household" ratings. Instead the proliferation of screens has decentralized those viewing relationships, where parents and children can enjoy individualized programming in times and places of their choosing. Streaming services such as Netflix construct discrete profiles and experiences for different family members, extending decades of efforts by the cable industry to offer generationally exclusive programming experiences, in which channels like Nickelodeon construct kid appeal in opposition to adulthood (Banet-Weiser 2007) and services like HBO build "quality" reputations through mature, adults-only fare (Nelson 2007). Meanwhile, in pursuit of the young millennial "becomers" it defined as its target audience, ABC Family rebranded itself as Freeform in 2016, downplaying its outward claim to shared family viewing in order to stake out a narrower demographic territory and differentiated mission as one of numerous Disney-owned cable holdings (Selznick 2018). Although programming with cross-generational appeal persisted, even companies like Disney sought to disaggregate their family television brands. Nevertheless, even as television industries divest in the prior strategic orientations of the broadcast and cable eras, the family reasserts itself in response to new delivery technologies and distribution competition.

23

Since approximately 2005, programmers have increasingly relied on the idea of "co-viewing" as a means of building bridges across age demographics to navigate the significant economic, technological, and social shifts facing television. For channels like Nickelodeon, The Disney Channel, and others that identify children as their prime point of demographic segmentation and distinction, co-viewing logics have increasingly promised a means of resecuring advertising revenue and newly extending legacy brands. At the same time, nonlinear services like Netflix and Amazon Prime Video envision co-viewing as a way to cement their growing industry dominance—evidencing their broad appeal and incentivizing continued subscription in an "over-the-top" environment where consumers can bypass long-term commitments to cable subscription packages and drop internet-delivered television services at any time. Operative across many different channels, markets, and brands, co-viewing is thus best considered an umbrella logic that describes numerous related strategies for cultivating crossover engagement by children and adults. In preschool television, co-viewing figures parents as viewers who watch programming alongside their children in real-time, serving as monitors for those younger audiences. For other industry sectors, co-viewing envisions pleasures more substantively constructed and experienced across generational lines, where content providers make simultaneous appeals to older and younger viewers. Co-viewing strategies also adapt to the nonlinear nature of streaming television and the practices whereby children and adults watch television on their own personalized devices at individualized times; in this sense, co-viewing need not happen simultaneously, but may speak to shared engagement with the same content across those different contexts. In these cases, the temporalities of co-viewing turn on relationships between what one audience may have watched then and what another audience watches now.

Even though this complex and multivalent term came into prominent usage more recently, the principles behind co-viewing point to a continuity of industrial investment in building television viewership across generational lines and the ways in which the markets for children's culture have long depended on the consumer involvement of parents (Seiter 1995; Buckingham 2000). However, the transgenerational potentials of co-viewing prove increasingly valuable as mature television industries grapple with change, as legacy institutions and emerging competitors alike seek to secure their respective futures in a disrupted market. As a bridge between television's past, present, and potential future, co-viewing thus emerges as an increasing site of investment for television content providers new and old as they navigate their competitive positions in the "post-network era" (Lotz 2014).

Co-viewing seeks to transform the engagement of consumers in the past and present into a platform for building future generations of viewers, embracing play across generational differences as a means of regenerating and reproducing television markets. In response to market forces of disruption, competition, and instability, transgenerational imaginations of the audience become newly valuable, where the idea of *family* promises to reproduce continuity while adapting to change, extending industrially *familiar* models of production and consumption into the future. As television becomes embedded in algorithmic interfaces and social media networks, and thereby experienced through individualized recommendations rather than uniform scheduling, this generational logic also figures family relations as a primary platform for sharing and reproducing television tastes and experiences. In this contemporary context, co-viewing invokes more than appeals and experiences shared across the lines of childhood and parental adulthood. Instead contemporary co-viewing strategies envision generationally defined consumption in terms of its capacity to support continuity through transformation and change. Parent monitors can transform into fans of children's programming in their own right. Franchises undergo transformation to be pitched anew to the next generation of children, with the adults who consumed them in their youth becoming agents of promotion charged with sharing those television legacies with their progeny. Even consumer designations like adult and child become something more than static, separate categories, recognized as part of viewers' dynamic transformation over the course of their lifetimes. In the transgenerational logics of co-viewing, age-based television markets work not as interacting segments but as overlapping, transformative entities that mutually construct one another—and in doing so promise to extend television industries into the future.

To explore these ideas, this chapter first draws upon trade reporting, market analysis, and other industry discourse to identify the economic, social, and technological forces that support contemporary co-viewing despite decades of strategic efforts designed to carve adults and children into discrete markets. In these negotiations, co-viewing represents more than a response to market conditions, for it is also a politically and culturally significant development in which cross-demographic exchange of popular culture accrues new value. From there, this chapter secondly examines co-viewing in the linear context of kids' television cable channels, explaining why the strategy serves the needs of this fragmented market. The Hub Network offers an instructive case study, using co-viewing strategy to break into a crowded kids market in 2010 but also coming to recognize the potential to better exploit co-viewing dynamics in digital venues. Thus the chapter turns lastly to nonlinear streaming services that have relied on co-viewing principles to support subscription-based business models for online television. Co-viewing helps contextualize the growing dominance of services like Netflix, Amazon Prime, and HBO Now, while revealing their broader reliance on a transgenerational culture of shared viewing to manage their own ongoing vulnerabilities in a volatile over-the-top market. While co-viewing illuminates key transformations in the business of kids' television specifically, it also provides a means for these industries to imagine the future of television more generally. Within that future, unruliness and abundance of programming choice can be organized within the relationships of family, the transmission of taste and value from adult to child, and the transformation of children into brand-loyal adults who might one day have children of their own.

The Rise of Co-Viewing

Co-viewing offers the opportunity to reflect upon the seismic shifts reshaping the television industry in the twenty-first century. Amanda Lotz (2014) describes this "post-network" moment as one in which the broadcast network regimes that used to dominate through their control of linear programming schedules has given way to an abundance of viewer choice outside those distribution bottlenecks.[1] This is not to argue that viewers hold all the power now; industry power instead rests increasingly with nonlinear platforms like Netflix that afford viewers the choice denied them in the network era. Preferring to emphasize the affordances of new distribution platforms rather than the decline of traditional network power, Aymar Jean Christian (2018) alternatively characterizes this post-network moment as a "networked" era supporting openness and participation.[2] From these dynamics of choice and participation comes increased focus on the social and relational nature of television as consumers' idiosyncratic pathways through all this content come to intersect and link with one another. As Lotz (2017) and Catherine Johnson (2012) argue, "portals" like Netflix and Hulu alter the relationships between viewers and industry by providing menus of options from which any number of programming experiences can be generated.[3] Those infinite pathways work together, however, when portals draw upon algorithmic analysis of past user data to offer customized programming recommendations, suggesting particular pathways through program offerings based on what others have already watched. Personal recommendations from friends and family (whether by social media or old-fashioned word-of-mouth) also contribute to increasingly social and relational television consumption. At the same time, the vast library holdings of nonlinear services enable different consumer groups to develop distinct pathways and interests even while drawing from the same pool of content. In this context, demographically distinct niche services become less imperative, with children's programming, for example, only one choice among many dynamic options provided by nonlinear services. As Tim Havens suggests, services like Netflix increasingly view themselves as "general entertainment" brands, similar to broadcast networks in their aim for broad, cross-demographic appeal, but distinct in the varied and dynamic ways they serve different viewers (2018: 329).

As media industries change, so too do ideas about the family, what it should be, and how it can be imagined to operate in relation to those industries. Since the Industrial Revolution and the changes to divisions of labor that came with it, the family has, in Western cultural contexts, been shaped in large part by the ideals of child-rearing, where parents shape children into healthy and productive social subjects as defined by hegemonic gender roles, domestic hierarchies, and heterosexual reproductive ideals (Berlant and Warner 1998; Buckingham 2000; Kline 1995; Sammond 2005). These family dynamics have influenced the emergence of popular media cultures and their embeddedness in everyday life. Television, in particular, emerged as a family medium, discursively constructed in congruence with postwar domestic ideals in the United States (Spigel 1992) and used within contexts of family viewing shaped by the gendered and generational relations of the domestic sphere (Morley 1986). The production of media cultures in direct relationship to the family has also reshaped the family in turn: examining how parents make decisions about media use within the home, Diane Alters and Lynn Schofield Clark identify media as a defining point of reference and negotiation in contemporary domestic life (2003: 6).

Yet this articulation between television, family, and domesticity has not proven static, adapting instead to new forms of market capitalism. As Michael Curtin argues, the "neo-network" era that destabilized broadcast television in the 1980s and 1990s traded in an alternative strategy of "edge" that carved distinct audience groups from one another; in this shift, mass audiences built on appeals to "universal" taste gave way to distinctive, fragmented niches (1996: 189). Joseph Turow describes this shift as one from "society-making" to "segment-making" media, as "primary media communities" tied to narrower identities and niche lifestyles divisively exploited by industry replace cross-demographic communication (1998: 3–4).[4] Although Turow and Curtin tend to focus on the consequences of these industrial shifts for shared national identities, these changes reshaped the contours of family media consumption as well. In this context, the industrial value of inclusive family television pales in comparison to the narrower and more defined segment of children's television. As Catherine Johnson (2012) argues, television has depended significantly on branding logics to construct these narrow segments. Sarah Banet-Weiser (2007) reveals how a television channel brand like Nickelodeon offers its child viewers a distinct consumer citizen identity by differentiating itself as a kids-only space opposed to the boring worldview of adults. Children's television has also differentiated itself through brand partnerships with toy companies targeting younger consumers (Pecora 1998) and through the worldviews of producers who imagine their child audiences as having specialized needs distinct from adults (Lemish 2010). Within this narrowcasting model, family relations are disintegrated, parsed into a series of distinct, bordered market appeals. As media industries look beyond narrowcasting to experiment with "flexible microcasting" strategies that transcend market categories to track and personalize content to individual users (V. Johnson 2009; Parks 2004), the idea of family viewing seems all that more outmoded. Moreover, despite their novel functions, nonlinear television services, continue to select and organize content according to what Amanda Lotz calls "the strategies of audience targeting—or channel branding—that have been characteristic of cable channels" (2017: 24).

Yet the decline of the family as a universalized target market does not make family relations irrelevant to industry strategy—particularly in consideration of the future and industrial attempts to strategize and manage it. Instead the family and family relations enter into a new set of transgenerational strategies working across these established demographic distinctions. As Caroline Leader (forthcoming) argues, our perceptions of children's media often follow branded logics to treat children as a distinct and independent identity category; but a critical perspective oriented to family can understand media markets intersectionally, where even individuated engagements operate within the family relations that continue to shape everyday life. To that end, we can consider post-network television industries' transgenerational strategies as a means of reasserting family within branded segmentation strategies.

In describing co-viewing strategies as transgenerational, I build upon existing efforts by Marsha Kinder (1995) and Heather Hendershot (2004) to theorize the "transgenerational address" with which media industries negotiate the gulf between adulthood and childhood. In her reading of *Home Alone* as an exaggeration of the generational conflict at the heart of Clinton-era US politics, Kinder argues that the film hails a "dual audience of infantilised adults and precocious children," enabling the same product to be targeted to different audiences even while emphasizing the gulfs between them (1995:

77). Hendershot, meanwhile, complicates the generational exclusivity of the Nickelodeon brand by detailing the narrative and stylistic qualities that make *SpongeBob SquarePants* equally pleasurable to adults. She argues that the brand depends less on strict division of adults and kids and more on a willingness to play with that boundary, where "adults and kids can play at being each other" (2004: 183). While Kinder and Hendershot examine transgenerational address at the level of the text, I propose shifting focus to industry strategy to consider how television programmers capitalize on the persistence of family relations in a world of fragmented audiences and individuated distribution services. This shift in perspective moves from the specific content of television series to television platforms circulating them (including new digital services but also legacy distribution sites on cable), where industry strategies position segmented television viewing within the relations of family, articulating branded content to practices of sharing and recommendation across generational lines. To explore this transgenerational industry strategy, co-viewing can be analyzed as a means of capitalizing on family relations amid the uncertainty of television's post-network era. Neither a return to the broadcast logics of universal family appeal nor blanket continuity with the strictly divided consumer niches of cable narrowcasting, co-viewing puts both into dialogue through dependence on transgenerational family relations that can circulate television across market categories. Instead of segment-making or segment-breaking media, co-viewing aims for segment-relating.

Although not new, the term "co-viewing" gained increased industry purchase between 2005 and 2010 amid increased interest in programming appeals "that cross over from kid viewing to reel in adults and young kids as well" (Pounsett 2005: 92). When explaining co-viewing to readers of *Kidscreen*, a children's entertainment trade journal, Geoffrey Pounsett acknowledged other similar concepts within industry knowledge-making communities, including "audience harmonics" and the less catchy "growing with the audience" (92). Perhaps more so than co-viewing, these alternative terms captured marketers' transgenerational imagination of their consumers, where kids' markets were not discrete but part of a dynamic and evolving strategy to reproduce consumer habits and identities into adulthood, harmonized across generational lines. Regardless of the term used, these co-viewing principles extended longstanding strategies for balancing appeals to multiple audiences. As Marc Robichaux remarked in *Multichannel News*, "Stuffing a few adult jokes into cartoons and kids' shows is an old trick" (2010: 8). While lavishing attention on programs like *Phineas and Ferb*, *SpongeBob SquarePants*, and *The Fairly OddParents* acclaimed for their ability to inject kids' programming with sly humor appreciable by adults, the industry discourse on co-viewing recognized that animated series including *The Flintstones*, *The Simpsons*, and anime imports had long provided "cross-generational" appeal (Grossman 2005: 16). Nevertheless, co-viewing had become by 2006 a new "buzzword making the rounds" within professional circles (Stewart 2006).

This expanded concern for co-viewing suggested an attempt to reclaim family viewing after decades of niche marketing premised on distinct cable channels for different age categories. No longer was co-viewing only a coping strategy concerned parents might use to monitor their children's television use, as a 2000 McCann-Erickson study of adult attitudes toward "family friendly" programming had framed it ("A Third" 2000). Co-viewing now encapsulated industry hopes for a "dual ratings stream of kids and parents" (Robichaux 2010). In a 2010 "Special Report" on kids' television programming, *Multichannel News* even foregrounded co-viewing prospects as one of seven key considerations in its primer on the main players in the kids' television business (alongside distribution reach, ratings data, programming mix, and advertising clients) ("Catering" 2010: 12–13). According to Cartoon Network president Stuart Snyder, "The attractiveness of co-viewing is that you are able to grow your audience and speak to brands who want to be in the family space versus just the kids space" ("Turner" 2014).

However, this reclamation of family marketing sat in opposition to cable branding still largely figured through the "divide to conquer" logics ("Catering" 2010: 12) that produced what *Phineas and Ferb* co-creator Dan Povenmire once described as "balkanized" audiences (Robichaux 2010: 8). As the cable market for kids' television grew more competitive, in fact, marketers had responded by further refining and articulating narrower categories of children. This finer differentiation of child markets followed programmers' unequal access to different age ranges at different times of day: with school-aged children out of the home, kids' cable channels typically targeted the preschool children left behind in late morning and early afternoon hours. Through this daypart refinement, Nickelodeon and Disney developed programming blocks like Nick Jr. and Playhouse Disney, and by 2005 even Cartoon Network targeted this space with its Tickle U programming block (Littlejohn 2005: 11). By the 2010s, this strategy expanded to support separate, twenty-four-hour services devoted to preschoolers, as well as other more specialized child segments. Instead of providing a single destination for all young viewers, for example, The Disney Channel embraced more specific appeals to tweens, while new channels like Disney XD and Disney Junior emerged between 2009 and 2010 to offer differentiated service for boys and preschoolers, respectively (Chávez 2018; Hunting and Gray 2018). Speaking of similar efforts to subdivide the Nickelodeon brand and support new channels like Nick Toons, executive Cyma Zarghami reported wanting to "make sure we find the best stuff for boys. . . . When we switched to targeting boys, it opened a lot of doors" ("Catering" 2010: 13). Meanwhile, Sprout executive Sandy Wax described this narrowed scope as an industrial imperative: identifying her channel's audience as preschoolers two to five years old, she reports having "stayed true to that commitment" while acknowledging, "It's a challenge to stay to [*sic*] true to your brand and define what you stand for, which all kids' networks face." Against the growing fragmentation of the kids' market, co-viewing appeals to kids and adults could seem inconceivable. In a 2002 editorial in *Broadcasting & Cable*, TLC Entertainment partner Maureen Smith cast her own interest in "family" entertainment against prevailing industry logic: "I've heard many television executives claim that the days of parents and kids sitting down together in front of the TV are gone forever" (2002: 20).

Nevertheless, new developments in the early twenty-first-century television economy worked against these generationally divisive industrial premises. First, digital television technologies increased the potential for cross-demographic interaction and viewer control over programming flows outside of the neat, demographically defined schedules that linear channels offered. Digital Video Recorders (DVR) enabled time shifting, a flexibility that industry analysts believed made members of the same household more willing to watch together. Although its reporting focused specifically on bridging gender gaps in viewing, rather than those of age, *Broadcasting & Cable* claimed in 2008 that the presence of DVR boxes in 20 percent of US homes had led to fewer fights over the remote control at specific, scheduled times. As TiVo vice president of audience research Todd Juenger explained, "You still have to choose who watches first, but you don't have to go into a separate room. It is a great compromising vehicle" (Atkinson 2008: 9). Similarly, new ratings measurement technologies introduced in 2010 directed more industry attention to potential viewership overlaps. Nielsen's new Portable People Meter technology—devices that recorded survey participants' viewing habits by registering hidden tones embedded in programming—showed analysts at *Kidscreen* that "parents are watching a lot more TV with their kids than the older metrics indicated" (Rusak 2010: 24).

Perhaps most crucially, the incentive to bridge any so-called generation gap increased amid the growth of social media and streaming television distribution. Researchers at Bain & Company described "Generation #hashtag" as an emerging consumer group that preferred "content designed and distributed exclusively through digital channels" (Colombani and Sanderson 2016: 2). Generation #hashtag was an explicitly transgenerational category, driven by younger media users but inclusive of "consumers of all ages" who embraced digital video content served to their personal devices by nonlinear services over traditional television channels (6). Central to this perceived consumer market was both a willingness to pay for digital content and an openness to recommendations provided by social networks, platform algorithms, and family members. With new technologies and consumer mindsets, television accrued value as a relational platform for shared, social engagement. Sesame Workshop executive Terry Fitzpatrick noted in 2011 that co-viewing "has always been the goal, but on the newer digital platforms it's important and dynamic" due to the enhanced role of the parent as a curator of content for children, even if not simultaneous participant in viewing (Albinak 2011). Echoing claims about "spreadable media" and the participatory power of consumers who increasingly decide what content will (and will not) be dispersed throughout the communication networks of social media (Jenkins, Ford, and Green 2013), Fitzpatrick portrayed the digital environment as one in which parents participate in programming decisions as much as channel executives. With parents increasingly imagined as active choosers from nonlinear program menus and, crucially, *sharers* of content with their families, co-viewing emerged as a strategy to rationalize parental participation in the process of constructing kids' consumer lifestyles. Even for public broadcasters operating outside these commercial considerations, co-viewing promised greater potential in meeting educational goals; by 2018, US public broadcasting station WETA-Washington offered its viewers explicit instructions on how to best co-view with their child or to "help them understand the information they receive" and "Make watching TV active!" ("Co-Viewing" n.d.).

This reliance on parental sharing in kids' television makes added sense in consideration of professional perceptions of growing competition between new digital platforms and traditional patterns of legacy television distribution. Research conducted by Common Sense Media circulating in industry trade reports found that child use of mobile devices tripled in the United States between 2013 and 2017, with children now more likely to have access to online subscription video services like Netflix than traditional cable television (Foster 2017a). With contemporary children increasingly viewed as the "first generation to grow up in a truly multiplatform universe" spanning traditional television sets, iPads, mobile phones, and computers, the ability of marketers to get content in front of kids' eyes increasingly came into question (Umstead 2016a: 6). On the one hand, on-demand environments that encouraged binge viewing needed more content than ever before to meet consumption patterns perceived as "voracious"; on the other, these conditions required experimentations with content format, which YouTube "family and learning" executive Malik Ducard described as no longer constrained by the time limits of linear scheduling and commercial breaks (Longwell 2015). Amid this abundance of competing channels, platforms, and formats, the engagement of a parent who might serve as an ally in cutting through the competition to connect children with content—or, vice versa, children who might bring consumer messages to their parents—would offer significant advantage.

Thus the rise of co-viewing extended from the promise of shared engagement between children and parents as a means of improving consumer messaging. Of course, marketers of children's products have always contended with the prospect of parental approval and their willingness to provide children with spending money. In 2000, research by McCann-Erickson found that almost a third of all US adults had concerns about "personally offensive or morally objectionable" content, a dynamic that resulted in "high levels of parental involvement in TV content issues" and "special effort" to watch programming with kids ("A Third" 2000). Some analysts speculated that co-viewing could cultivate implicit parental approval of kids programming and thus help defuse regulatory attention to any objectionable content (Grossman 2005: 17). In the context of co-viewing a decade later, however, parental relationships to children's television could be described in less potentially antagonistic terms. Amazon.com and Hart Research Associates publicized in 2017 findings that US parents, far from disapproving, had grown increasingly comfortable with their kids' relationship to many digital devices and platforms of consumer culture—an acceptance strongly tied to parents' own embeddedness in these connected viewing practices (Dickson 2017a). In 2018, Common Sense Media maintained that only 10 percent of users expected YouTube to take responsibility for any inappropriate videos children might watch on the platform, with most users believing they were already "extremely or very aware" of what their children were watching (Whyte 2018a). Beyond managing parental concerns, however, these potential shared connections between kid and adult consumers could also figure as a market opportunity, where each participant in the family relationship presented a gateway to reach the other.

Co-viewing strategy could be deployed in response to declines in the advertising economy, for example. In 2006, kids' cable channels reported a "slowdown" in advertising buys for toys and fast food aimed at their core demographic, so they pursued new sponsorships from car manufacturers, full-service restaurants, and tourism companies in the hopes of harnessing the power of children to influence family consumption more generally. Contemporaneous research for Disney by Strottman International found that 92 percent of children sampled influenced their families' everyday discount store purchases, while smaller but significant portions between 28 and 38 percent shaped major family purchases, including vacations, computers, cell phones, large electronics, and automobiles. In light of these findings, Starcom USA media director Dan Kopec claimed this "influence of kids on family purchases is what the [television advertising] vendors see as a stop-gap measure for losing revenue" (Downey 2006: 26). However, in this new competition for family advertising dollars, channels delivering not just kid influence but also the simultaneous attention of adults (the final decision-makers) would offer advertisers the best bargain. Already by 2005, reports indicated that advertisers actively sought out the highest possible overlap between adult and child viewers when buying ad time on channels aimed at children (Grossman 2005: 17). In addition to providing dual access to consumers, co-viewing also held the potential for deeper, relational, transgenerational engagement. As Disney advertising executive Tricia Wilbur explained, "We have always heard and know that kids influence parents in terms of purchases. . . . But when moms watch TV with their kids, they have a conversation about it. That means that advertising is resonating not only with the child but also with the mom" (Downey 2006: 28). Research commissioned by Corus Television similarly held that consumers' ability to recall advertising messages—whether for kids' toys or "adult-targeted" goods like travel and home electronics—increased when parents and kids watched together because of closer parental monitoring and potential for discussion across generational divides (Rusak 2010: 24). By 2011, Paige Albiniak argued in *Variety* that "Selling to Kids is a one-two punch," with US advertisers investing $1.7 billion annually to capture kids' direct spending money and influence on their mothers' estimated $4 trillion in annual discretionary household income. Yet parents—often gendered as shopping "mothers"—also possessed their own consumer desires and pleasures. Savvy marketers thus did not craft appeals to children in a vacuum, attending instead to kids' embeddedness in consumer relations with their parents.

As Disney's Nancy Cleary noted, "Finding content that appeals to both kid and adult sensibilities is not easy to do, otherwise everyone would produce this type of content" (Dickson 2013: 37). However, ratings data confirmed the potential to capitalize on adult interest in kids' programming. In 2004, Nickelodeon outperformed Comedy Central and History Channel in adult primetime viewership, suggesting that more adults watched kids and family programming than these services assumed to have a more exclusive adult appeal (Umstead 2004). In 2010, 47 percent of adult audiences who watched new episodes of Disney's *Phineas and Ferb* did so with a child aged two to fourteen, while 37 percent of adult viewers for Disney's *Good Luck Charlie* watched with a child between six and fourteen years old (Robichaux 2010: 9). While these numbers certainly spoke to the prevalence of simultaneous co-viewing between child and parents, they also belied a significant number of adult viewers who watched by themselves. Anecdotal examples selected to explain these numbers pointed to viewers who wondered, "I'm twenty-six and I watch *iCarly*—am I weird?" and "I'm forty and I watch *iCarly* when the kids aren't home. Am I crazy?" (9). As R. Thomas Umstead reported in *Multichannel News*, adults sometimes watch "unabashedly on their own . . . apparently not too old or ashamed to tune into kids programming" (2004). These voices demonstrated an adult interest in kids' programming that co-viewing could try to harness—but they also spoke to a larger disruption of generational boundaries in which adults consumed kids' entertainment on their own (a dynamic further explored in chapter 4).

In addition to these shifts in the ratings and advertising economy, co-viewing strategies followed new industry meditations on the factors that distinguished twenty-first-century children from previous generations. As described by researchers and analysts, these perceived differences made it more feasible to leverage child relationships with parents. Commenting on 2011 research, longtime children's television programmer Margaret Loesch characterized co-viewing not as a response to adult desires for more "wholesome" children's programming but instead as an answer to young viewers' new desire to share their television experiences with parents (Umstead 2011: 12). Nickelodeon research in 2010 similarly claimed that contemporary children felt closer to their parents than those parents had felt with their own mothers and fathers. Within these closer child-parent bonds, Nickelodeon claimed that boys and their fathers shared 45 percent of their television tastes, while girls and their mothers shared 64 percent—reproducing essentialisms about gendered taste even while acknowledging overlaps at the level of age. From this research, Nickelodeon executive Cyma Zarghami argued that "The generational gap is closing. . . . This new generation of kids . . . they like being with their families and they like to watch TV with their families" (Robichaux 2010: 8).

This sociologically inclined industry research also identified a new generation of parents similarly open to sharing television with their children. A 2011 US industry study called "Watching Gens X, Y, and i" stated that some 60 percent of parents also saw television as a valuable means of connecting with their teens. By 2016, David Quinn, a senior executive at digital marketing firm Beamly, surmised that twenty- and thirty-something millennials "really like reminiscing about their childhood," a desire that Nickelodeon executive Chris Viscardi believed made them more likely to share their former television favorites with their kids (Umstead 2016b: 8). Older millennials that had started families were also perceived to watch three hours of live television a day, over 50 percent more than their childless counterparts, suggesting a strong relationship between child-rearing and television consumption for this generation (9). This notion of an increasingly close-knit television-family unit persisted in Nickelodeon's 2013 "The Family GPS: The Global Family Study," which claimed that thanks to social media, parents and children functioned more as friends than ever before (Dickson 2013: 37). For Disney's Gary Marsh, such understandings of the audience emerged "sociologically, as well as from a business perspective" (Robichaux 2010: 8). From that sociological perspective, television professionals imagined their viewers as part of a new set of family relations among children, adults, and television—one that invited and required new business and content strategies.[5]

Given this interest in building transgenerational bonds between millennials and their children, programmers increasingly pursued content with built-in, long-running franchise appeal. Reruns, reboots, and revivals of legacy television series from the 1980s and 1990s put the transgenerational strategy of co-viewing in direct relationship with the regenerative production logics of media franchising that encourage creative iteration and multiplication across different markets and industrial contexts (Johnson 2013a). In 2005, the Canadian preschool channel Corus depended on such "franchise extensions" as the *Dora the Explorer* spin-off *Go Diego Go!* "to introduce a whole new generation of preschoolers to the properties, as well as the potential of attracting older kids who grew up on the originals and are now just slightly out of preschool range" (Pounsett 2005: 92). To reach adult millennials and engage them in the work of sharing television with their families, Disney Channel spun off the 1990s sitcom *Boy Meets World* as the new *Girl Meets World*, while Disney XD launched a reinterpretation of the animated series *DuckTales*. Cartoon Network revived *The Powerpuff Girls*, and Nickelodeon renewed production of *Hey Arnold*—a move that Chris Viscardi, senior vice president of content development for Nickelodeon Franchise Properties, believed would bring older viewers back to the network. "There is a huge millennial love for those series," he argued, "so we know that millennial fans who grew up on them will come back" (Umstead 2016b: 9). The 2014 global rebrand of Boomerang similarly turned on a generational premise, where Turner Broadcasting promised its library of animated series could support a transmission of fandom from one consumer group to another: "as kids who grew up on these time-tested shows, parents will be able to share their childhoods with their own kids" ("Turner" 2014).

The embrace of co-viewing by no means eliminated the market segmentation practices that divide kids from adults and further differentiate between preschoolers, young children, tweens, and teens. However, within a transgenerational strategy, segments like preschool television could interoperate with others within a longer trajectory of consumer transformation. Disney Junior, for example, figured its articulation of a preschool audience alongside efforts to connect with parents. Channel general manager Nancy Kanter explained that interstitials placed in breaks between programs sought to build strong connections with mothers who co-view with their children; these messages were "more sophisticated in humor and content" in order to "let her know we know she's out there—and give her a giggle" ("Disney" 2012: 94). At the same time, preschool television served as an important staging ground for the construction of a multistep, branded consumer lifespan—only the first stage in a longer process (Hunting and Gray 2018). As the preschool market fed into a later six-to-nine-year-old demographic served by another channel (and subsequently by tween, teen, and adult channels), consumers' brand loyalties could be sustained and solidified over a lifetime, where they might be shared with the next generation in turn. Moreover, with preschoolers most likely to view television with a parent, that particular market niche represented a promising opportunity to start this construction at the very beginning of the consumer life cycle. In the words of Horizon Media's Brad Adgate, preschool marketing strategies functioned as part of an effort to capture consumers "from cradle to grave" (Littlejohn 2005: 11). In this light, the segmentation of preschool viewers represents something more than intensification of niche marketing strategies, directly related instead to the television industries growing interest in the relationship between kids' services and those for adults. When operating across these different age demographics, co-viewing helps to build a life-spanning sequence of consumption that transforms along with the consumer and provides opportunities to be shared with other consumers at different points in that trajectory.

Ultimately, the emergence of co-viewing suggests that the television industries' interests in narrow demographic categories like children have changed, with niche markets still very relevant but now figured relationally in a process of building bridges to other audiences. Such dynamics track with the suspicions of Amanda Lotz, who in a study of Spike TV and its struggles to sustain itself as a channel for men, doubts that twenty-first-century cable television can continue to support narrow appeals when facing new challenges from online subscription services (2018: 173). For kids' cable channels in the post-network era, however, co-viewing provided a means of cultivating multiple audiences and deploying those segments relationally. Of course, industry strategies do not always correspond to actual viewers' tastes, experiences, and relationship to one another, and as such the relational logics of co-viewing were not always successful in this context. When Nick Jr. introduced late night NickMom programming in an effort to hold on to the existing audience of co-viewing parents after children went to bed, for example, the irreverent and edgy appeals clashed with viewers' perceptions of its wholesome daytime image (Copple Smith 2018). However, Nickelodeon more broadly recognized the value of co-viewing in contrast to previous branding strategies that opposed kid tastes to those of adults. Explaining the channel's change in outlook, Nickelodeon advertising executive Jim Perry claimed in 2006 that "It's more than a kids' market to us, it's a family market, and it's a parents market as well" (Downey 2006: 26). In 2008, Nickelodeon tried to attract more parents and adults to its 8 p.m. eastern programming hour in order to have these older viewers already in place when the more family-skewing Nick at Nite service began at 9 p.m. (Umstead 2008: 12). Beyond supporting a bridge between the Nickelodeon and Nick at Nite markets, however, this family-focused co-viewing strategy opened the door to new potential revenue streams. As executive Cyma Zarghami explained, "The more kids who bring their parents to Nick and Nick at Nite, the more it helps Nickelodeon become more of a family brand and propels some of our other off-channel things we do, like our cruise business" (12). If the Nickelodeon brand was previously premised on the principle of kids rule (Banet-Weiser 2007), then the emergence of co-viewing increasingly reinscribed that child power within the transgenerational dynamics of family.

Cable's Co-Viewing Hub

Nevertheless, because cable branding strategies continued to turn on this identification of demographic cores, many executives often qualified their channels' investment in co-viewing—especially early on. Just a few years earlier in 2005, Nickelodeon personnel described co-viewing as only a "happy byproduct" of niche marketing strategies, with executive vice president of programming Marjorie Cohn juxtaposing it to the channel's primary objective: "We are a kids' network. . . . If we turn our eyes toward the parents and pander, we're removing our eyes from the prize" (Grossman 2005: 17). Similarly, Disney Channel president Rich Ross qualified strong co-viewing numbers in 2004 with a defensive insistence that the channel still represented "the kids' point of view" (Umstead 2004). Nickelodeon's Cyma Zarghami also denied any conscious aim of catering to adults. Adults might watch, but her objective was to be "kid first" without co-viewing becoming part of the "business plan" (Umstead 2004). Even as co-viewing strategy became more dominant, Disney Channel chief creative officer Gary Marsh clarified in 2010 that his programs were "kid-driven" even while being "family inclusive." Meanwhile, Zarghami continued to downplay co-viewing as the simple effect of quality programming: "Good writing works for everybody," she said, citing co-viewing as the "unbelievable benefit" of excellence rather than a purposeful strategic aim (Robichaux 2010: 8). Channels deploying animation to construct appeals to more mature, adult tastes qualified co-viewing from another perspective, pushing against crossover interest from younger viewers contrary to that branding. Concerned with maintaining the "purity" of the brand and its eighteen-to-twenty-four-year-old demographic, Adult Swim executive Jack Wakshlag claimed in 2005 that "Teens are the 18- to 24-year-olds of tomorrow, but we don't sell to them. The truth of the matter is we don't market to or advertise to teens. . . . We don't create cartoons for teens" (Grossman 2005: 17). Co-viewing was not without negotiation and resistance to its potential disruption of discrete niche markets.

By contrast, the story of the Discovery Kids channel—and its transformation into The Hub before a second rebrand as Discovery Family—turns more on a conscious, outward embrace of transgenerational co-viewing. When launched in 1996 by Discovery Communications, Discovery Kids emulated the company's flagship channel by pitching science and nature-themed content to younger cable viewers. In 2010, however, global toy manufacturer Hasbro acquired a 50 percent stake in the channel to relaunch it as The Hub. For Hasbro, this move offered the possibility of greater integration between its toy lines and the television narratives marketing them. As chief content officer Stephen Davis later explained, "Storytelling is really central to everything that Hasbro does" (Thielman 2015). While Hasbro had long depended on television to support perennial toy lines like Transformers, GI Joe, and My Little Pony (Johnson 2013a: 78–79), The Hub would provide a guaranteed outlet for any screen content produced in support of that toy business. Hasbro would no longer have to worry about securing favorable distribution terms for toy-based television shows from Disney, Cartoon Network, or Nickelodeon who might see such programming as competition for their own in-house media franchises. The Hub represented a secure pipeline to the television audience for the toy company, in which executives like Davis saw "an opportunity to reimagine, reignite, and reinvent Hasbro's brands for a contemporary audience" (Janoff 2011: 24).

Initially, however, cable industry analysts doubted The Hub's ability to compete with the many other established channels already targeting children. In the face of questions at launch from *Broadcasting & Cable* about the "crowded" market of "kid-targeted video content," CEO Margaret Loesch claimed that such concerns were an "adult perception" that would not be shared by her imagined viewers: "there are 40 or 50 channels appealing to adults 18–49. Why should there only be a half-dozen or fewer targeted at kids?" (Guthrie 2010: 12). Juxtaposing her new channel to those aimed at adults, Loesch argued that The Hub would find its footing by catering to the narrower six-to-nine-year-old range instead of a more generalized six-to-twelve-year-old appeal. Nevertheless, while Loesch endorsed further balkanization of the kids' market, some advertisers and industry analysts immediately saw another kind of potential, where built-in awareness of Hasbro's "legacy brands" could support co-viewing. With 25 percent of initial programming drawing from (and extending the market for) legacy Hasbro franchises already familiar to parents, The Hub had unique potential to support a transgenerational market outlook. As Horizon Media research vice president Brad Adgate argued, "They're targeting both groups; the parent and the child. To kids, it's new and to parents, particularly mothers, it's nostalgic" (Guthrie 2010: 12). By 2011, statements from Hub and Hasbro executives began to more explicitly embrace this co-viewing potential, with series like *My Little Pony: Friendship is Magic* described to *The New York Times* as aimed at "the three-to-six-year-old girl and her mom, who has fond memories of 'My Little Pony' from her childhood" (Vara and Zimmerman 2011). Hasbro programming like *Transformers* and *GI Joe* certainly encouraged paternal nostalgia as well—ultimately helping The Hub build strong male co-viewing numbers in contrast to the emphasis on "mom" at Disney Junior and other preschool channels (Dickson 2013: 37).

This reliance upon adult nostalgia for child brands measurably impacted Nielsen ratings for The Hub's toy-based animation programming. The channel reported "double digit" co-viewing numbers during its daytime afternoon schedule (suggesting more than 10 percent of children watched with their parents), while specific series like *My Little Pony* and *Pound Puppies* would deliver "nearly a 50–50 viewer split between adult women and girls" (Umstead 2011: 12). When asked about these returns, Hasbro Studios president Stephen Davis shrugged them off as the natural result of sound strategy: "If you tell me that as a dad you watch The Hub or play Hasbro games with your kids, that is not surprising" (Janoff 2011: 24). CEO Loesch likewise stated that this success owed to "the power of the nostalgic brands," adding, "These programs were beloved by older viewers, and now they're encouraging their kids to watch it and are watching with them" (Umstead 2011: 12).

Six months into the life of the new channel, programming at The Hub began to extend well beyond the company's toy franchises to include original and acquired series aimed at cultivating broader family appeals. Although the channel "primarily" served a demographic of young boys with its animated programming, it increasingly looked to classic syndicated live-action television series as well as original game show formats to cultivate broader family appeals across generational and gender lines (12). While The Hub's primetime schedule offered reruns of family-themed off-network series such as *Happy Days*, *Family Ties*, and *The Wonder Years* (evoking a Nick at Nite lineup), it also ordered original series like *Family Game Night* in which two nuclear families (invariably comprised of mother, father, and two children each) competed. *Family Game Night* continued the exploitation of "Hasbro's riches" on The Hub (Janoff 2011: 24), named after and drawing upon the brand umbrella shared by board games like Monopoly, Yahtzee, and Operation for its game show challenges. Plans in 2011 for more family game shows like *Scrabble*, *Clue*, and *The Game of Life* solidified this co-viewing approach to toy brand extension. At this point, 34 percent of kids aged two to eleven watching the channel did so with an adult aged eighteen to forty-nine, making it the most co-viewed of all networks airing children's programming in primetime (Umstead 2011: 12). Nickelodeon had previously ranked highest in 2010 with only a 22 percent primetime co-viewing overlap (Robichaux 2010: 8).[6]

Given this growth, Hub executives increasingly figured appeals to children and parents alike as the means to slowly but surely chip away at the market shares of established cable players like Nickelodeon and Cartoon Network (Janoff 2011: 24). Strategic commitment to co-viewing continued in 2012 with the acquisition of syndication classics like *The Facts of Life* and *Mork & Mindy* as well as the production of original series like *Care Bears: Welcome to Care-a-lot*, *Littlest Pet Shop*, and *Spooksville*—all based on toy franchises and literary series familiar to many parents who had been children in the 1980s and 1990s. According to Loesch, this strategic continuity reflected confidence that "The Hub is working. . . . When we started, we had this vision and thought that if we took nostalgic brands and we reimagined and re-presented them that there would be acceptance in the household among [parents] who remembered them, and kids who would embraced [sic] them and love them on their own. And that has happened"

(Umstead 2012: 16). By 2013, The Hub's vice president for ad sales, Nicole Cleary, could boast that competition for the channel's eight minutes of national commercial time per hour included clients from businesses such as insurance, auto, financial services, retail, and tourism ("Co-viewing" 2013: 38). The next year, The Hub extended its co-viewing outlook with the new network tagline, "Making Family Fun," and an order for *Parents Just Don't Understand*, a new series in which parents and children swapped roles in order to gain a better understanding of and connection with one another. Press releases described the series as only "the first in a slate of new series that reflects the Hub Network's expansion into programming for kids and their families to watch together" ("Musical" 2014).

This reliance on co-viewing can also be contextualized as a response to the obstacle that Hasbro's ownership of the channel created in the kids' advertising economy. Although The Hub offered Hasbro plenty of opportunity to market its own consumer products, Hasbro's ownership of the channel gave pause to the other toy advertisers one might expect to see on a narrowcast kids' cable channel. At launch, Margaret Loesch took extra care to frame the relationship between The Hub and Hasbro's proprietary franchises: "It's not the Hasbro channel . . . we have to be open for business. We can't show any favoritism. We have to buy shows from everybody. We have to take advertising from everybody. We have to be sort of like Switzerland" (Guthrie 2010: 12). Nevertheless, competitors like Mattel and LEGO never bought any ad time on The Hub; as one media buyer explained, until The Hub had built a viewership so large that it simply could not be ignored, these toy companies did not want their media budget to line the pockets of their competitor (Thielman 2015). As a platform for generating sales of Hasbro product, meanwhile, The Hub had not yet offered a direct and meaningful boost in toy revenue as reported by BMO Capital Market's Gerrick Johnson (Fisher 2014c). Furthermore, Hasbro's continued role as master toy licensee for Disney's *Star Wars*, Marvel, and Princess franchises created other industry conflicts. In 2014, analysts like Johnson reacted "skeptically" to rumors of a potential merger between Hasbro and DreamWorks Animation, worrying that such a partnership would complicate existing licensing relationships between Hasbro and Disney (Fisher 2014c). Indeed the rumor prompted a "nuclear-level reaction" (Masters 2014a) in which Disney "swiftly and angrily" threatened to dissolve contracts worth one-third of the toy manufacturer's total business (Thielman 2015). Given the obstacles that Hasbro's ownership of The Hub posed to relationship building with other companies in the kids' realm, co-viewing made more sense as a strategy to attract new advertising partners, such as insurance, tourism, automobiles, and others in the adult space.

This outlook beyond the toy market ultimately called into question the value of Hasbro's participation in The Hub. In 2014, Hasbro scaled back its ownership stake in the cable channel to 40 percent, ceding majority control back to Discovery amid the departure of channel CEO Margaret Loesch (Dickson 2014a; Getzler 2014). Going forward, Hasbro declined to maintain an exclusive relationship with the newly rebranded Discovery Family. Although Hasbro would continue to produce "a raft of shows for Discovery Family," including more episodes of *My Little Pony: Friendship is Magic*, it sought new outside distribution deals with Cartoon Network for content like *Transformers* with a "much broader, older-boy-skewed demo," according to Stephen Davis (Dickson 2014a; Thielman 2015). At the same time, Hasbro continued to pursue its storytelling and content production strategies by acquiring animation studios like Dublin-based Boulder Media ("Hasbro" 2016). By breaking off exclusive ties with Discovery, Hasbro also opened up greater possibility of pursuing distribution with Netflix and other emerging streaming video services for this self-produced content.

However, it was a failure to market toys narrowly to kids and not the transgenerational co-viewing strategy that stymied Hasbro's interest in The Hub. As identified in *Adweek*, the market that Hasbro still had "cornered" after its divestment in The Hub was the young parent who "grew up in the '80s" during the toy company's earliest efforts at crafting program-length marketing narratives (Thielman 2015). As it moved its kids' programming to Netflix and other digital spaces, Hasbro could continue to leverage the affective relationship it had built with the consumers of generations past. Meanwhile, even as its relationship with Hasbro loosened, the rebranded Discovery Family did not break with the co-viewing strategies that defined The Hub. Notably, the new channel name emphasized the potential for viewing across age ranges rather than a simple reversion to "Discovery Kids" as a narrower focus. *Variety* framed the reorganization of the channel as a growing recognition among both Discovery and Hasbro executives that in a market increasingly defined by on-demand viewing practices, "a linear channel squarely devoted to kidvid had limited growth potential" (Littleton 2014). A family channel pitched toward "multigenerational" co-viewing, however, promised a stronger way forward in this post-network cable environment, especially with the channel's co-viewing ratings continuing to increase at the time of the reorganization (Dickson 2014b). Meanwhile, competitors increasingly considered the viability of launching over-the-top online subscription services in which standalone channels could be unbundled from the broader cable environment and its narrowcasting logics. Nickelodeon, for example, announced in 2017 plans to enter the Japanese market with the launch of an over-the-top service (Foster 2017b), while Disney too promised to launch a proprietary streaming service of its own in the United States by 2019 (Spangler 2017). However, this move to online distribution put traditional cable channels into the space dominated by Netflix and other streaming services that had developed their own transgenerational logics and co-viewing strategies.

From Co-viewers to Co-evaluators to Co-subscribers

If online delivery channels like Netflix and Amazon Prime represented a next generation of production and distribution in the television industry, these emerging services just as often preoccupied themselves with the next generation of viewers. Of concern was not just the immediate goal of reaching a valuable young market but also shaping the spaces and practices in which the future of all television culture might unfold. As a result, these services invested heavily—sometimes disproportionately—in the development of series aimed at children. By 2014, the SNL Kagan research firm calculated that despite lack of critical and popular attention, kids' programming accounted for nearly a quarter of all content (original or acquired) available on Amazon Prime Video, and 17 percent by comparison on Netflix (Brustein 2015). As specialist trade publication *Kidscreen* described it, "Investing in kids content is becoming the new normal for streaming giants" (Fisher 2014b). US-based services were not unique in this regard; across the globe, thirteen different services aimed specifically at children launched between 2014 and 2015, including Hopster in the United Kingdom, TFOU Max in France, Kidoodle.TV in Canada, and Kividoo in Germany (Westcott and Stuart 2015: 9–15). The global market for on-demand kids' television was thus robust, growing, and competitive. As with cable, co-viewing emerged as a key strategy in that market—but in the nonlinear environment co-viewing served the specific function of engaging adults in the selection of kids' programming across a host of proliferating digital devices, as well as motivating consumers to maintain their subscriptions for general entertainment television services.

According to international television trade organization MIPCOM, Netflix became the "leading commissioner of original children's content" between 2013 and 2015, ordering over sixty-four hours of programming from suppliers during that period (Westcott and Stuart 2015: 8). Like The Hub's programming, this output relied heavily on adult nostalgia for specific media franchises to motivate co-viewing practices. In 2014, Netflix partnered with Saban Entertainment and Spin Master toys to remake *Popples*, an animated series first produced in conjunction with a 1986 line of plush animal toys (Fisher 2014e). A day after announcing *Popples*, Netflix acquired another toy-based animated series called *Winx Club WOW: World of Winx*, based on the long-running franchise of fairy-themed video productions and toy merchandising (Fisher 2014d).[7] By 2018, having newly invested in reboots of the 1990s series *Magic School Bus* and *Carmen Sandiego*, Netflix director of global kids content Andy Yeatman explained, "We think there's a huge benefit of having a program that parents remember fondly and grew up with. We are giving them the opportunity to introduce it to their kids and spark a conversation." As part of a careful calculus to bridge generations, Yeatman noted that Netflix carefully considered "how long it's been since the last version of the show aired" (Whyte 2018b). Instead of targeting franchises subject to constant rebooting every five to ten years, Netflix looked for untapped intellectual properties waiting to be rescued from a previous generation's memories past.

By comparison, Amazon ordered thirty hours of kids programming in that same two-year period (Westcott and Stuart 2015: 8), similarly embracing the value of co-viewing. In 2016, Amazon's head of kids' programming Tara Sorenson stated, "Philosophically, everything we do, from our preschool to our 6-to-11 content, has elements that we have embedded to create co-viewing opportunities for us" (Umstead 2016a: 7). While Sorenson referred to programming content, Amazon's release strategy too seemed geared toward generating involvement in children's television on the part of adult viewers. From 2013 to 2017, Amazon conducted "pilot seasons" in which users of its service could preview series in development and provide feedback to be used in deciding which series to greenlight. This opening of the development process to the public promised that the collective intelligence of Amazon users would take over for the "gut" instincts of executives in the gatekeeping process. "Watch the Shows, Call the Shots," Amazon promotions promised.

While Amazon put many of its in-development series through this process during that period, children's programs gained particular visibility and subjection to the scrutiny of pilot season participants. Of the first fourteen series in the initial 2013 pilot season, six targeted preschoolers or school-aged children. Three of those—*Annedroids*, *Creative Galaxy*, and *Tumble Leaf*—ultimately entered series production. Only two series not targeted at kids—the comedies *Alpha House* and *Betas*—survived the pilot process along with these children's series. The second pilot season in February 2014 followed a similar pattern: of ten pilots in contention, half clearly aimed toward kids, and two of those survived to receive a series order: *Gortimer Gibbon's Life on Normal Street* and *Wishenpoof!*. While the smaller-scale pilot season of August 2014 featured no children's series, the bumper crop of January 2015 reaffirmed Amazon's interest in kids' television. Six of the thirteen pilots catered to kids; four with animation and two with live action (Fisher 2015). The November 2015 pilot season included another six kids' series (Getzler 2015a). Thus by 2016 Amazon was "on pace" to premiere a new series for kids every four to six weeks (Umstead 2016a: 7). While many of these series targeted different demographics within children's programming (preschoolers versus elementary-age viewers, for example), kids in aggregate represented a significant taste and demographic focus for Amazon.

Yet the participatory framework of the pilot season situated that targeted appeal within a transgenerational framework, as it was the adult user (presumably a parent) hailed as the evaluator of these pilot programs for kids. Amazon marketing materials invited its customers and subscribers to watch these pilots on behalf of their kids to evaluate their appeal or suitability. Outside of the pilot season proper, Amazon Preview consumer research surveys even encouraged adult participants to watch similar pilot content with their children in order to report the reactions of younger viewers. Yet Amazon consistently constructed the evaluation of kids programming as a practice of co-viewing on the part of an adult participant. These invitations to participate in the process sometimes even flagged children's programming as an area in which some consumers might have special or heightened interest. In the summer 2016 pilot season, for example, the potential to have a say in kids' television programming provided a means of differentiated appeal in Amazon's customer outreach. In an email sent to an unknown cross section of its customer base, Amazon highlighted only the six kids' programming pilots involved in the voting cycle, constructing it as a special category separable from the other pilots on offer ("Want" 2016). By involving the user in that narrowed selection process, Amazon engaged their potential subscribers as co-viewers invested in kids' programming. These invitations to participate in children's television programming extended Amazon's strategic interest in co-viewing to the presumed consumer subjectivities of some of its adult consumers. For Amazon, adult co-viewing and co-evaluation of kids' television went hand in hand.

Beyond original programming, Amazon also secured the exclusive streaming distribution rights to a large block of children's programming broadcast in the United States by the Public Broadcasting System (PBS).

The 2016 deal made Amazon the streaming home for programs like *Daniel Tiger's Neighborhood*, *Wild Kratts*, *Dinosaur Train*, and *Nature Cat* (Pederson 2016)—a programming package that extended to Amazon partial claim to the PBS reputation for high-quality educational children's television. However, this arrangement with PBS paralleled even more significant attempts by competitor HBO to assimilate the public broadcaster's kids' programming to attract subscribers to its premium cable service as well as its growing HBO Now online streaming platform. In August 2015, HBO secured first-run distribution rights to the following five seasons of *Sesame Street* episodes, breaking a forty-five-year relationship of exclusivity between PBS and production company Sesame Workshop. For HBO chief executive Richard Plepler, this acquisition represented nothing less than access to "the most important preschool education program in the history of television" (Steinberg 2015). While PBS would eventually add these new episodes to its *Sesame Street* library after HBO's nine-month period of exclusivity, the series would no longer be produced with PBS programming strategies and priorities at the forefront. The exclusive terms of the deal also meant that Netflix and Amazon—with whom PBS had previously shared online access to *Sesame Street*—could no longer depend on the series to sweeten their programming libraries (Murphy 2015). Managing its own loss of identification with this children's television institution, PBS asserted its continued relevance in the field by highlighting all the kids' programs it did still offer: the decampment of *Sesame Street* did "not change the fundamental role PBS and stations play in the lives of families" (Steinberg 2015).

This jockeying for access to children's television programming suggested a genuine battle for streaming supremacy within this market. As Emily Steel (2015a) wrote in *The New York Times*, these streaming services were clearly "pouring resources" into efforts to serve younger viewers perceived to be moving to new digital platforms to find content to watch on a variety of digital devices. In 2015, *Kidscreen* circulated findings from the Nielsen study "Kids' Audience Behavior Across Platforms" that found that "traditional" television remained the dominant form of media engagement for all kids preschool to teenaged; yet what it meant to engage and watch television had changed for these children compared to previous generations. Most notably, kids' viewing had become increasingly "time-shifted," no longer adhering to the scheduled appointment viewing of linear television. Kids now watched when they wanted to watch, the study suggested, and by age eight their expanded, individualized interests led them to seek out content without parental guidance on phones, tablets, and other mobile devices under their own control (Getzler 2015b). Similarly—but pitched in the even grander terms of epochal changes—a 2015 MIPCOM market analysis by Tim Westcott and Anna Stuart posited "three ages of children's programming" culminating in the dominance of on-demand video services. Although the authors claimed that the industry still remained in a second age of children's programming defined by competition between the niche channels of the cable environment and the education-oriented public broadcasters, they predicted a "decline" for both these linear forms of television, precipitated by "the rollout of non-linear services like Netflix and Amazon" (2015: 4). Citing studies by UK regulator Ofcom, they believed that while traditional television sets currently remained the dominant viewing device, tablet ownership—having "almost doubled" over the previous year—pointed to a future in which kids engaged differently with the medium, no longer sharing television space with parents in the family room (5). In this technological and social context, it made sense for Netflix, Amazon, HBO, and others to compete specifically for the young viewers associated with the emerging television practices of the digital sphere.

Yet beyond just a battle to determine which platform could best adapt to the changing children's television market, the interest of subscription streaming services in kids' programming also extended from a relational aim to cultivate the widest subscription bases possible. As Tim Havens argues of Netflix, these services operate according to "ambitions of becoming the dominant provider of a broad range of film and video content for a wide subscriber base"; despite the difference between nonlinear portals and older broadcast television channels, Netflix shares the latter's "pursuit of a general entertainment audience, as opposed to the narrower niche orientation of cable channels" (2018: 329–30). In that light, kids have served as a disproportionate focus for streaming services not solely as a priority market niche but instead as a crucial building block in the construction of a wider subscription base. HBO, for one, "seeks subscriber growth" in the crowded streaming marketplace, and children proved to be an important part of expanding its existing subscriber base (drawn in part from its cable legacy) into something more broad-based (Steel 2015b). As Brian Steinberg (2015) argued in *Variety*, HBO targeted *Sesame Street* (while Amazon and Netflix sought to cannibalize other PBS programming) because "Kids' content is one of the biggest drivers of consumers picking up subscription-video-on-demand services." In this initial boom period for streaming services, the ability to sell subscriptions to consumers more broadly depended disproportionately on what the service was perceived to offer children specifically.

Imagine the parent faced with choosing between subscription services like HBO Now, Netflix, and Amazon Prime Video. Selfishly, that parent might most want to subscribe to HBO to watch *Game of Thrones* after the kids go to bed. However, that viewer may ultimately feel that money is better spent on Amazon if it seemed that library of mature dramatic programming was complemented with a better selection of animated and educational series for kids. When faced with a choice, adults might make subscription decisions based on which services offer better all-around combinations of general entertainment for all ages. Furthermore, as Joshua Brustein (2015) argues, the moment of consumer decision-making between competing streaming services recurs again and again in an economy where subscriptions can easily be suspended. Whereas canceling and restarting cable subscriptions might require numerous phone calls or appointments with cable technicians, online users can simply log in to start or suspend these streaming services at any time. For adult viewers particularly invested in *Game of Thrones*, then, there may be no reason to continue subscribing to HBO during the long wait between seasons or once the series ends; instead they might divert that money to Amazon for a month or two to access *The Man in the High Castle*. Loyal, persistent use of subscription services by kids, however, poses obstacles to such easy cancellations. Parents might find it harder to change their subscriptions if it means cutting off children from those television libraries (particularly when, as many programmers believe, children eagerly rewatch content they like). Parents subscribing to HBO, for example, might then find it harder to surrender the educational and entertainment value of *Sesame Street* just because *Game of Thrones* has concluded. In this way, industry analysts like Rich Greenfield saw kids' programming as the "glue" holding the emerging subscription economy together (Brustein 2015). Former Sprout president Sandy Wax concurred: "People tune into an HBO or a Netflix for the big tentpole events, but you also need an everyday reason to subscribe. If you're smart, then you're maintaining a really solid kids' library" (Umstead 2016a: 6). Or, as SNL Kagan analyst Seth Shafter most succinctly put it: "If my two-and-a-half-year-old was deprived of Curious George, my life would be a living hell" (Brustein 2015).

Clearly, children's television programming had evolved into something more than the kids-only niche that Nickelodeon branded in opposition to adult viewing patterns and tastes in the 1990s and early 2000s (Banet-Weiser 2007). Instead, in the streaming economy, kids' programming became an integral component in the packaging and selling of wider libraries for consumption by more than one type of viewer within an imagined consumer family. In this sense of co-viewing, parents and children became co-subscribers, even if they watched different content at different times on different devices. Within this model, moreover, the loyalty of younger audiences would furthermore be leveraged for years to come as viewers aged out of kids' programming and into the more mature fare available in the same streaming packages. As Mike Murphy (2015) wrote in *SiliconBeat*, "Offering an appealing lineup of children's shows not only gets parents to subscribe to the service, it wins the hearts and minds of the next generation of consumers." This investment in kids' programming by streaming services did not merely reconstitute a mass audience from the service of multiple niches—as in the case of television conglomerates who targeted different audiences across the array of different demographically defined cable channels they owned (Curtin 1996). The transgenerational strategy behind streaming instead supported co-viewing packages meant to construct relations across the boundaries of adult and child interests, imagining subscribers embedded in those family relations as longtime customers who would remain with the service across their own passage from childhood to adulthood.

Conclusion

In an age of streaming, co-viewing strategies play appeals to children and adults off one another, leveraging them to build something bigger across generational lines—whether that might be stronger appeals to advertisers, longer subscription maintenance, or greater levels of social engagement exploited in other ways. At the center of this strategy, transgenerational logics cultivate lifetime brand loyalty and nostalgia for long-running, franchised content, recognizing the consumer as a transforming subject that will be continually but dynamically embedded in relations between childhood and adulthood across which television can be shared. On cable, The Hub used this dynamic to engage adults in the programming their children watched, leveraging generation-long affective relationships with television, toys, games, and other legacy content. In online distribution, meanwhile, the sharing practices that constituted co-viewing for services like Amazon and HBO Now prompted adults to participate in the public evaluation of kids' television and in a process of making adult subscription decisions with the needs of younger family members in mind. Beyond recognizing children as a future generation of viewing consumers, co-viewing highlighted their position within the larger set of transgenerational family relationships that increasingly sat at the center of disrupted and evolving television industries.

Again, none of this means co-viewing was new or native to the post-network era. Sports television, for example, would likely reveal a longer history of co-viewing practices; parents have long shared their fandoms with children and made that identity a cultural inheritance transmitted through the everyday family routines of weekend television viewing. However, while this is a rich topic for future research, sports were rarely invoked in the emerging industry discourses on television co-viewing under examination in this chapter. This less overt interest in cultivating transgenerational viewing cultures for sports compared to kids' television—despite equal potential—likely stems from the specific pressures of the post-network, against which co-viewing offered a means of negotiating disruption of the narrowcasting logics that had surrounded children's television. Even if co-viewing in children's television evoked the broadcast ideals of family viewing, it did not represent a throwback so much as a negotiation of the complex and colliding demands that have transformed television since the broadcast context. By contrast, as Vicki Johnson (2009) argues, sports already served as an ideal form of post-network commodity, never losing their ability to command cross-demographic broadcast audiences even as they served narrowcast cable outlets too; at the same time, sports were long ago legitimized as part of a national culture already presumed to be shared across generational lines. Given this continuity and adaptability, the television industries may not have been as eager—or found it as necessary—to apply co-viewing strategies to sports in the same way as children's television. Of course, to the extent that sports marketers have recently expanded their efforts at explicit crossover appeals to women, further examination could problematize these claims and further reveal how, in the post-network era, co-viewing principles operate across gender in addition to age.

Meanwhile, although the sharing of television culture across generational lines does suggest a shift in the divisive logics of segment-making media, we should remain attuned to the limitations of the generational framework of family to that end. This strategy is *familiar* in more than one way, operating through everyday family relationships while building recognizable continuities of programming franchises, genres, and tastes across the gulf between old narrowcasting models and the new entertainment libraries of streaming. Co-viewing reproduces television into the future in continuity with the past. As deployed by the television industries in these ways, notions of family, generation, and reproduction trade in heteronormative assumptions about the construction of the future and ideal forms of relationships within them. The continued examination of co-viewing, therefore, must address its role in creating idealized, familiar subject positions for consumers to occupy over the course of their lives. Such exploration must confront the power accorded to parents and other transgenerational subjects as agents in the construction of co-viewing cultures. While kids' media may have previously considered parents as gatekeepers monitoring what children watch and doling out spending money, these transgenerational industries increasingly figure those adults as sharers, empowered as industry allies to enable the reproduction of culture rather than block the way. With that in mind, the next chapter considers media shared across generational lines with an eye to the way industries cultivate adults as key participants and gift givers in a process of cultural inheritance. At stake is not just the question of who inherits the transgenerational gift but also who might be granted the power to give it within these family relations.

CHAPTER 2

"Share Your Universe"

Generation, Gender, and the Marvel Dad

Until my oldest daughter was almost two years old, she and I shared weekly outings to the courthouse square in Denton, Texas, first visiting the local comic book store before getting ice cream cones a few doors down. While these excursions suggested reciprocity between us—she got a treat so I could get my comics—the reality was more complicated. What I really wanted was not just my own weekly comic fix but also an opportunity to share that experience. This store was, of course, no place to let a toddler roam free; beyond potential exposure to age-inappropriate content, she could accidentally damage valuable collectors' items. Yet as I held her tightly to my chest, I would point at our surroundings in a form of fatherly superhero pedagogy: "Look! There's Magneto! Over there—it's Batman!" By the time she was three, we had moved to Wisconsin and (ironically) no longer enjoyed the same proximity to an ice cream parlor on these trips; but by then, she remained just as interested in accompanying me, now wanting to acquire her own comics. Reaping what I had sown, I contended with child consumer desires much pricier than ice cream, and I therefore appreciated events like the annual Free Comic Book Day at our local store. In the next couple years, she and I would also attend fan conventions like Chicago Comics and Entertainment Expo and Wizard World Madison together. Slowly, however, my efforts to cultivate shared fandom came into conflict with her growing independence and rebellion against parental tastes. By that point, however, I had another toddler daughter, and while there was no ice cream shop next door, our two local comic book shops did offer kids free lollipops and cookies. So with a new sweet lure, the cycle of sharing continued.

Anyone can guess that I might soon face rebellion again. No less surprising—yet more importantly—this intense desire to share superhero comic fandom across generational lines as part of parenting presents a type of consumer subjectivity that media industries cultivate in order to reproduce patterns and practices of consumption into the future. To understand this transmission of consumer culture to the next generation, this chapter asks how and why media industries have developed efforts aimed at getting adult fans to act as the forward guard in sharing superhero comic fandom with children. As my own self-reflection suggests, the dominant framework for imagining such relationships is the dynamic shared between parent and child. In constructing transgenerational subject positions for adult consumers, media industries link roles of responsibility in the process of cultural reproduction to the authority of parental figures. To interrogate these subjectivities, we can therefore deconstruct their articulation of cultural and reproductive politics, while also keeping a sharp eye for the fissures in these dominant reproductive logics through which nonparental fans, too, might act as authorized agents within transgenerational consumer relationships. An examination of how and why the media industries figure transgenerational consumer subjectivity most commonly in terms of the authority and labor of parents reveals both the dominant frameworks governing the industrial reproduction of a cultural futurity and the terms against which other possibilities can be imagined.

In exploring the industrial phenomena mobilizing adult consumers as agents in the cultivation of child fandom, this chapter situates transgenerational strategies and practices in relation to wider concerns about economic convergence in a transmedia environment, the role of consumers in forms of promotional labor, and the construction of authority in and over the realm of culture. The chapter employs a case study approach that considers the many industry sectors that cultivate adult consumer subjects idealized for their ability to bring superhero comics to the next generation—looking specifically at a moment between 2000 and the present in which kids' flagging interest in superhero comics unfolded in tension with the increased presence of superheroes across many media. On the one hand, this analysis draws upon textual analysis to consider the ways in which publisher Marvel Comics built transgenerational appeals into comic products (like *All-New X-Men*, *Captain Marvel*, and *FF*) that adults might share with children. On the other, this chapter considers promotional campaigns by publishers and partners in the entertainment media that served to self-reflexively construct adult comic fans as agents of cultural reproduction. As such, the chapter draws from an archive of press releases, official statements, and promotional videos meant to cultivate these transgenerational consumer subjectivities. At the same time, published fan letters, blogs, and social media reveal the ways consumers reported engaging with these campaigns.

This research first makes it possible to situate transgenerational subjectivities in relationship to the position of comic book publishers in a transmedia economy. Marvel Comics, in particular, presents an apt case study. Despite being a part of a media conglomerate oriented toward younger consumers since acquisition by The Walt Disney Company in 2009, Marvel has had to confront the fact that kids' growing interest in its superhero brand across film, television, and gaming has not guaranteed an influx of new, young readers for its publishing division. On the contrary, intense child interest in superheroes via these other media businesses has called into question the future sustainability of an aging publishing market. Thus this chapter secondly examines the outreach efforts made by superhero comic industries in this context, from transgenerational appeals in Marvel's published product to wider industry promotional campaigns like Free Comic Book Day or Kids Days at comic conventions. Finally, the chapter zeroes in on a specific Marvel campaign called "Share Your Universe," which, starting in 2013, invited adult readers to play active roles in exposing children to the world of superhero publishing. The "Share Your Universe" campaign aimed to attract young readers to Marvel comic book products by enlisting adults to secure this new readership.

Yet not all adults were initiated into this promotional corps and the idealized fan subjectivities on offer by "Share Your Universe." In fact, as much as Marvel cultivated gender-inclusive forms of child consumption, it rarely did so without naturalizing the patriarchal authority of the Marvel Dad imagined to possess a legacy claim to superhero comics that might be passed down as cultural inheritance. Of central concern throughout the chapter, therefore, is the industrial construction of older comic book readers as the gendered agents of reproductive promotion that would share comic books with a new generation and thus ensure the continuation of the line. These efforts reveal how comic book publishers manage shifting media markets, tastes, and industrial priorities by relying upon the power of generation—and similarly dominant reproductive frameworks tied to heteronormative gender and sexuality—to imagine continuity of industrial structure and identity. Marvel's continued investment in its legacy publishing market has depended upon both a calculated transgenerational marketing strategy and the construction of gendered consumer identities that both facilitate cultural reproduction and enable privileged claims to authority over it.

Authority and Promotional Work in a Transmedia Age

Any study of contemporary comic book superheroes or publishers like Marvel or DC Comics demands attention to the dynamics of media convergence (Jenkins 2006) in which such products and industries are embedded. As subsidiaries of The Walt Disney Company and Warner Bros., respectively, Marvel and DC create and manage comic book characters figured as intellectual properties that support franchised extension across multiple media divisions. In that environment, comic books might be one of the smallest and least profitable businesses supported by superhero properties; characters like Iron Man for Marvel or Batman for DC generate far more revenue in terms of box office tickets, television ratings, and merchandise licensing than sales of printed periodicals. The three Marvel Cinematic Universe films released in 2017 (*Spider-Man: Homecoming*, *Guardians of the Galaxy 2*, and *Thor Ragnarok*) took in box office revenues of $1.04 billion in the United States alone ("Marvel Cinematic" 2018). By comparison, the entire comic book industry shipped only $522 million worth of product to North American comic retailers during the entire year, and Marvel's 38.3 percent share of the market amounted to $200 million ("2017 Comic" n.d.). Companies that trade in superhero brands must therefore be understood as fully integrated within a transmedia industrial landscape, where the work of producing comics operates in support of higher profile projects outside publishing that command far more conglomerate resources. Within Disney, Marvel Studios film projects become a greater point of strategic focus than Marvel's publishing division, as do relationships with Disney subsidiaries like broadcast television network ABC and cable network Disney XD.

While Marvel's character brands now serve the pursuit of "synergy" across the Disney conglomerate (Wasko 2001), the Marvel organization has not abandoned its longstanding targeted interests in the comic book market. Even as comic markets contract (and pale in comparative revenues to film, television, games, or licensing), the publishing division remains a crucial site of legacy and identity, as well as continued employment, for many managers and creators. At the heart of the "new" Marvel under Disney is therefore a contradiction and question about the persistence of the old. Recognizing these forces, much scholarship has explored Marvel's transformation in this transmediated context (Brookey 2010; D. Johnson 2007, 2008, 2009, 2012, 2013a; Yockey 2017). Beyond Marvel, much research on the comic book industry similarly focuses on transformations away from traditional print publishing and toward transmedia outlooks. Sam Ford and Henry Jenkins (2009), Kimberly Owczarski (2008), and James Gilmore and Matthias

Stork (2014) all consider what happens to comic books in an age of convergence, media multiplicity, and franchising. Nevertheless, there remains significant room to consider how such companies continue to function as superhero comic publishers while negotiating the changing and contradictory priorities, identities, and market emphases that constitute a business like "Marvel" as a subsidiary within Disney.

Of most relevance to this book, moreover, is how transmedia industry structures support and create capacity for transgenerational marketing. To be sure, Marvel's position within the Disney conglomerate requires negotiation of different business cultures and traditions while finding ways to overcome the obstacles involved in coordinating creative efforts across media with different storytelling conventions and production timelines (Elkington 2009). Yet these transmedia relations also require converging media industries to confront potential gulfs between their audiences—including perceived generational differences between comic readers, filmgoers, or game players. Put another way, as old and new media industries collide (Jenkins 2006), old and young audiences might collide too. The transmedia strategies of the culture industries, then, are fundamentally transgenerational strategies when attempts to synergize film, television, games, and comics confront the different perceived generational appeals possessed by different media. With the uneven industrial values ascribed to young versus old audiences, meanwhile, these differences create hierarchies of value and dominance within transmedia industries. Which of the many media markets implicated in transmedia strategy have growing, youthful audiences? Which have aging audiences—and thus may signal dying corporate divisions prone to obsolescence themselves? Just as transmedia strategies invite comparison of profit margins across different conglomerate divisions (Murray 2005: 428) they can also reveal differences and tensions tied to generational appeal. A publishing division like Marvel Comics must have a plan for growth into the future, and its participation in Disney's transmedia strategies offers both a transformative strategy for sustainability and a point of negative comparison to media markets enjoying greater attention from younger consumers. An examination of transmedia attuned to the transgenerational can reveal how colliding industries manage differences among businesses with unequal appeal to age-defined audiences.

In this context, media industries often rely upon their consumers as agents of promotion and transmission across these boundaries. Consumers play significant, participatory roles in the promotional culture that spreads marketing throughout the experiences of everyday life (Wernick 1991). Many media and cultural critics have focused on the "free labor" produced from the affectively engaged activities of media users, as articulated by Tiziana Terranova (2000) and expanded upon in relation to digital culture by numerous scholars, including Marc Andrejevic (2010), who zeroes in on the way in which a media platform like YouTube exploits "user-generated data" to sell to advertisers. David Hesmondhalgh (2010) has warned against reducing free labor to exploitation, however, looking to the difference between labor from which workers are truly alienated—deprived of autonomy in their productive actions—and labor that is freely and autonomously given. Taking that critique to heart, my own interest in the participation of consumers in transgenerational marketing recognizes both the productive utility of audiences to industries and the meaningful identities and affective registers articulated to such work in order to encourage it being freely given.[1] I extend these perspectives here by considering how adults' fan relationships to comic superheroes prove compatible with industry strategies that position that fan subjectivity as a *responsibility* to engage in the promotional labor of proselytizing to the next generation. Transgenerational work supporting the needs of industry, in this case, depends on the construction of affective consumer identities to figure that freely given work as a rewarding form of exchange between adults and children.

In this way, the responsibilities and pleasures of transgenerational labor become linked, where the appeal of sharing culture with others includes a sense of obligation to tradition, heritage, and legacy; at that intersection, the adult consumer engaged in free promotional labor bestows a valuable cultural gift to successive generations. Such an idea explicitly evokes free labor not as a simple form of industry exploitation but also as part of the gift economies that numerous scholars, including Suzanne Scott (2009), Tisha Turk (2014), and Henry Jenkins, Xiaochang Li, Ana Domb Krauskopf, and Joshua Green (2009), figure as central to the production and circulation of cultural works within fan communities. A focus on the transgenerational dynamics of gifting culture helps us to understand it in a unique way attuned to cultural inheritances bequeathed from one generation to the next. As Sarah Ahmed argues, the idea of an inheritance is explicitly political, bound up in the reproduction of existing social relations and orientations. Inheritances in this view are not only conservative forces that replicate existing power dynamics but also subjectivities and ways of living privileged through repetition (2006: 178). In this way, a transgenerational approach to the free participation of consumers in media industries reveals the politics of gifted labor in that it can support and extend from dominant orientations toward the reproduction of culture over time.

"With great power comes great responsibility," the young hero Peter

Parker has so often been told by his Uncle Ben in the many iterations of the Spider-Man story. If so, we might conversely consider how feelings of responsibility cultivated in consumer subjects by the transgenerational strategies of media industries also operate through power. To whom do media industries extend the power and authority to take on this responsibility? Although this chapter's focus is on the work of media consumers, rather than the professionals typically imagined as "authors," the notion of authorship may nevertheless be useful to think about how this kind of power is marshalled in the industrial cultivation of transgenerational labor. Michel Foucault (1975) understands authorship not in terms of flesh and blood persons but as discursive figures constructed to lay legal claim to and accrue value for cultural works. Or, as John Hartley puts it, authorship is a process of authorization, where the author is "never a simple individual, but *one who channels system-level or institutional authority into text*" (Hartley 2013: 25; emphasis in original). Rather than prompting recognition of fans as veritable authors, these models of authorship encourage us to consider how industries might authorize fans and other consumers to share in institutional power over cultural texts. Through what discursive processes and constructions of consumer subjectivities are fans empowered with the authority to participate in the process of gifting cultural inheritances? Such an approach can help to push conversations about authorship further away from real authors or even professionals to reflect more broadly on the production of cultural authority in, around, and by institutional forces. As we will see in the case of consumer participation in transgenerational promotion, authority is imbued in not just one generation as the perceived owner of a cultural inheritance but also in the gendered distinctions and reproductive divisions that mark some older consumers as the worthiest trustees for that next generation. To investigate these power dynamics, we can turn next to the case of Marvel Comics' publishing interests, considering their transformation and reorientation to the future amid the web of transmedia relationships in which they have been increasingly embedded.

Marvel Aged

While the market for superhero franchises has grown steadily over the past two decades—thanks to intertextual, promotional, and organizational relationships within film, television, gaming, and merchandising industries—the fortunes of the superhero comic publishing industry itself remain comparatively meager. According to market data offered by the website Comichron, the number of comics shipped at wholesale to North American comic book retailers has been in overall decline since the late 1990s. At the market peak of September 1996, specialty retailers ordered eleven million comic books from Diamond Comic Distributors, the exclusive distributor for the superhero titles sold by Marvel and DC. Sales soon dropped precipitously, however, hovering around seven million units per month in September 1998 and reaching a low point of under five million in March 2001 (Miller n.d., "Comics Sales to Comics Shops"). Comichron's numbers paint a rosier picture, however, in that overall dollar value of the market has steadily increased in this time. Although March 2001 would see a low point in retail dollars as well at under US$14 million, early 2013 retail sales of $25 million per month matched the prior peaks of 1996 and 1997. Moreover, looking beyond specialty comic book shops to include newsstands and bookstore sales of trade paperbacks, the 2013 estimated market of $780 million actually dwarfed the 1997 market of $300–$320 million (Miller n.d., "Comic Book Sales by Year"). Digital distribution added another estimated $90 million to that overall market total (up from $25 million and $70 million in 2011 and 2012, respectively).

Of course, inflation and increasing cover prices skew these increases. Market growth has not been the result of selling more comics so much as selling comics more often (recollected and in new digital formats) and at higher prices. While the 1991 debut of *X-Men* #1 sold a record eight million copies, the years since have seen far lower ceilings for individual titles. Between 1997 and 2017, the most retailer orders for a single issue came for *Amazing Spider-Man* volume 3 #1, at 532,586 copies in April 2014. More tellingly, outside of such highly promoted debut issues, top selling comics in any given month frequently sell less than one hundred thousand copies; in February 2011, the top selling comic of the month (DC's *Green Lantern* #62) sold only 71,517 copies (Miller n.d., "Comics Sales Records in the Diamond Exclusive Era"). Compare this to May 2001—the month with the lowest dollar volume ever—where each of the top ten selling comics still outsold this later low point (Miller n.d., "May 2001 Comic Book Sales to Comic Shops"). Comic book "hits" now reach far fewer readers than ever before, reflecting market fragmentation and niche marketing in the culture industries at large. However, the two major publishers have not lost their market share to new, competing distributors. From a market share around 25 percent in 1997, Marvel consistently captured 35–40 percent by the mid-2010s, as did its major competitor DC (Miller n.d., "Market Shares of Comics Sold to Comic Shops"). By contrast, television networks lost the bulk of the huge market share they enjoyed through the early 1980s to new cable channels and now services like Netflix.

Yet like the television business explored in chapter 1, the superhero comic industry has faced anxiety about continued relevance in a changing media landscape where savvy digital natives are perceived to be losing interest in older, analog media. Gloomy economic forecasts thus frequently took on the hue of generational conflict across different forms of media industry. The comparative success of superhero culture outside of comic book publishing called into relief not only declines in unit sales but perceived generational changes in its readership. A 2012 DC Comics report, for example, suggested that readers of its highly promoted "New 52" campaign were anything but "new," despite the stated aim of attracting first-time consumers. Nielsen market research suggested that only 5 percent of readers were completely new to buying comics, with 93% of readers supposedly being male and only 2% being under eighteen years old. On the website Comics Alliance, Laura Hudson (2012) suggested that these "troubling" findings represented "serious questions about DC's ability to expand their audience base, and the accessibility of their content to both women and younger readers." At stake in her analysis was the very future of the industry: this study "should worry anyone who cares about the future of superhero comics, and its ability to sustain an audience into the future." Lest we assume that DC faced these challenges alone, other industry reports confirmed "panic" about the increasing age of comics readers more generally (Hauman 2011).

Digital distribution held promise for reaching younger readers, and online comic applications like Comixology suggested some success in that regard. Comixology reported in 2013 that in addition to a "core customer" group of longtime male comic readers aged twenty-seven to thirty-six, a "new customer is emerging," one understood as female, "newer to comics," and aged seventeen to twenty-six (Kraft 2013). Moreover, digital distribution has made a wider range of comic genres more accessible (especially from independent publishers), and at the same time youth-oriented book publishers like Scholastic have transformed traditional book series like *The Baby-Sitters Club* into graphic novels (which then find distribution in school libraries). So while many children actually encounter an increasing number of avenues into comics readership, this greater variety of product and openness of access has done little to extend the market dominance that Marvel and DC enjoyed in the specialty retail periodical market or to guarantee a crop of new readers for superhero product.

Yet Marvel's transmedia success affirmed the persistent appeal of superheroes to children more generally. The most visible evidence was the runaway success of Marvel's films, as produced both by licensed studios and Marvel itself. According to figures compiled at Box Office Mojo, *X-Men* and *Spider-*

Man were, as of late 2018, the sixth- and ninth-highest grossing franchises in film history, at US$2.36 and $1.91 billion, respectively. Licensed by Marvel to outside film distributors like 20th Century Fox and Sony (in deals made before acquisition by Disney in 2009), these superhero properties sat just below Hollywood heavyweights like *Star Wars*, *Harry Potter*, and *Batman*, while above the likes of *Lord of the Rings*, *Pirates of the Caribbean*, and *Star Trek*. Yet Marvel has seen even greater success by self-producing its films under the Disney umbrella. The *Iron Man*, *Captain America*, *Thor*, and *Avengers* films comprising the "Marvel Cinematic Universe" were by 2018 the single highest grossing franchise in film history with a recorded domestic box office gross of $6.87 billion after tallying returns from *Black Panther*, *Avengers: Infinity War*, and *Ant-Man and the Wasp* ("Franchise Index—Series" 2018). Across these licensed and self-produced projects, Box Office Mojo ranked Marvel Studios as the single most successful production company in the history of Hollywood cinema. Its first fifty-three films (both licensed and self-produced) each averaged $231.6 million in domestic box office gross revenues, for a shared total of $12.28 billion, overshadowing second place Legendary Pictures' forty-nine films totaling $6.64 billion and $135.5 million average ("Franchise Index—Brands" 2018). Trade reports thus referred to Marvel as "the only live-action brand that matters to most audiences," and suggested that this clout gave Marvel CEO Isaac Permutter disproportionate influence within Disney conglomerate culture (Masters 2014b). Movie theater exit polling additionally confirmed that Marvel's signature tentpole, *The Avengers*, "played evenly across all demographics," inclusive of families with children. Analysts estimated the audience as a full 40 percent female ("surprisingly," to some) and 50 percent under the age of twenty-five, with 24 percent of the audience coming from family filmgoers (Pereira 2012).

Yet against these all-inclusive box office numbers, even greater evidence of a disconnect between transmedia success with children and aging comic readership emerged in smaller niche markets like television, video games, and toy merchandising. For Disney, the acquisition of Marvel followed at least in part from a desire to use these superhero properties to build greater appeals to young male television viewers. Having already succeeded in securing a young female viewership on The Disney Channel, the company could rely on Marvel-themed content to target boys on the new cable channel Disney XD (launched in 2009 just months before the purchase of Marvel) (Chávez 2018). Soon after, Marvel Television product became a staple for the channel. In 2013, Marvel's *Ultimate Spider-Man* became the top animated performer in the target demographics of boys two to eleven (197,000 viewers), boys six to eleven (138,000), and the gender-inclusive kids two to eleven (265,000) ("Avengers" 2013). The new *Avengers Assemble* series averaged 699,000 total viewers in 2014, making it the top-ranked animated series in the Disney XD lineup, with *Hulk and the Agents of S.M.A.S.H.* bringing in another 480,000 viewers (Hutchins 2014). Of course, many of those viewers included adult fans—but even discounting those viewers, *Assemble* remained the top-ranked animated series in the boys six to fourteen demographic, as well as second highest in the boys two to eleven demographic (Kondolojy 2014). In the boys six to eleven television niche targeted by Disney XD, therefore, Marvel superheroes proved a consistent draw for children, quite in contrast to the publishing market.

While Marvel's successes in video games have been less dramatic, they also evince a disconnect with the flat children's market for superhero comics. In 2013, the most visible Marvel game title was the cobranded *LEGO Marvel Super Heroes* released across all major consoles and several mobile and PC gaming platforms. Although the actual consumer base would surely have been a mix of children and adult fans, the game's content rating of E-10 ("for everyone" over ten years old) by the Entertainment Software Rating Board suggests that designers and marketers perceived the appeal as far younger than that of M (mature) and A (adult) games that otherwise dominate software sales.[2] This suggests that Marvel's superheroes actually offered a more powerful draw for kids in a video game market geared toward older consumers than it did in a comic book market that similarly skewed older. By 2014, Marvel also played a new role in the ongoing marketing and production of another game franchise called *Disney Infinity*. An action adventure sandbox experience, the game mixed characters from across the Disney house of brands (including *Fantasia*'s Sorcerer Mickey, *Toy Story*'s Buzz Lightyear, *Frozen*'s Elsa, and many more) while supporting future purchases beyond the software itself: players could add new characters to this "toys-to-life" game by purchasing separately packaged plastic figures. While these add-ons included Disney princesses, the default characters packaged with the core 2013 game (*Pirates of the Caribbean*'s Captain Jack Sparrow, *Monsters Inc.*'s Sulley, and *The Incredibles*' Mr. Incredible) echoed the targeted outreach to boys and masculinized play themes similarly driving Disney XD. With the 2014 sequel figured as *Disney Infinity 2.0: Marvel Super Heroes*, the E-10 title's continued franchise development embraced the Marvel characters dominating blockbuster film and niche boys' television. Until its cancellation in 2015, the Disney Interactive division focused "all of its efforts" on the *Disney Infinity* platform, framing Marvel's ongoing film and television appeal as a way to "[keep] things fresh" in the E-10 video game market (Gaudiosi 2014).

In their emphasis on material playthings, both these video games hinted at Marvel's parallel significance to children in toy merchandising. Beyond the Disney conglomerate, Marvel licenses its properties to several third-party toy manufacturers who find consistent success connecting superhero product with children. Hasbro, for example, has produced action figure lines based on Marvel characters. Though some of these products appealed to adult collectors, lines like Marvel Legends offering super-articulated action figures in the US$15–$22 price range often failed to find sufficient support from retailers ("Toy Fair" 2014). By contrast, more basic toy lines aimed at young boys continued to perform quite well for Hasbro. Trade journal *Kidscreen* credited Marvel product (alongside brands like *Transformers*) as driving a 32 percent year-to-year increase in second quarter 2014 revenue for Hasbro's "boys category" in the US market (Fisher 2014a). In addition to cobranding with Marvel in the game market, The LEGO Group has licensed the right to produce physical construction toys from Marvel and DC superhero properties since 2012. At the 2014 London Toy Fair, LEGO representatives named Super Heroes as an "evergreen" line, suggesting that the company's attempts to connect toy product with children would depend on characters borrowed from these comic publishers for some time to come ("London" 2014).

Across film, television, games, and toys, Marvel properties have appealed to children more reliably than in the legacy market of comic book publishing. Yet the impact of this difference on publishers' strategies is unclear. In 2014, Marvel Comics editor-in-chief Alex Alonso insisted that transmedia considerations did not shape publishing decision-making: "whether we own the media rights to a character informs so little of what we do in editorial. Our job—my job—is to tell stories that sell comics. And we want all our comics to sell. . . . It's important that we maintain and grow the popularity of characters that are already popular, and that we elevate characters we want to make popular—like Guardians of the Galaxy, Ant-Man, Inhumans and Doctor Strange" (Ching 2014). Although Alonso coincidentally aimed to make popular the characters that had just happened to have feature films forthcoming at the time, he positioned the work and culture of publishing as separate from other media markets. Yet to "sell comics," publishers necessarily confronted the aging market for comic book readers, the lack of young readers waiting in the wings, and the potential frustration of seeing other divisions within Marvel connect more effectively with that new generation.

As a result, Marvel—like the comic publishing industry at large—has developed strategies to manage the generational tensions underlying superheroes' transmedia success story. Increasingly, transmediated comic book publishers have taken steps since to try to proactively regenerate younger readership—both within the content they produce and through the promotion of it. Throughout, these strategies have not just depended on more specific appeals to children but also on concerted attempts to enlist older readers as the builders of these transgenerational bridges.

Building Bridges and Enlisting Consumers

One obvious response to these conditions has been to produce new comic book product that takes its cues from the transmedia economy in which superhero characters already find greater traction with children. Both Marvel and DC have developed lines of "all-ages" comics envisioned as appropriate for younger readers. From 2004 to 2010, for example, DC Comics unified under its "Johnny DC" imprint comics aimed at younger readers—in many cases adapting narratives and visual styles from animated superhero television series produced by Warner Bros. Animation. For Johnny DC writer Sholly Fisch, this product aimed to reclaim a cohort of underserved readers. While he believed that adult readerships had certainly helped win superhero comics greater legitimacy, Fisch argued that the industry now needed a corrective outreach effort: "in the '80s and '90s, everyone was so busy trying to prove that comics aren't for kids that they forgot that what they should have been proving is that comics aren't only for kids" (O'Donnell 2009). In that interim, "no one was really publishing comics for kids. And, as a result, we lost an entire generation of comics' fans." When asked what audience he imagined writing for in a title like *Batman: The Brave and the Bold*, however, Fisch clarified that his "all ages" approach aims "to appeal to both kids and adult fans who like their superheroics with a touch of fun" (Mozzocco 2010). Fisch's strategy for reclaiming a lost generation did not, therefore, operate solely in terms of kid appeal; instead it cultivated a readership overlap that bridged age categories.

This bridge-building strategy extended well beyond the "all-ages" market. Similar efforts could be seen in the comic titles anchoring publishers' adult-skewing, mainline titles. For example, in 2012, Marvel experimented with introducing younger versions of established adult characters and pairing adult heroes with more child sidekicks. By that point, a franchise like *X-Men* required readers to have a basic awareness of decades of serial development as its mutant heroes had transformed from students at the Xavier School in the 1960s into adult revolutionaries with their own nation-state as well as, often, their own children. New readers were thus significantly disadvantaged. The launch of *All-New X-Men* late that year, however, offered a reset to those more youthful origins. For plot reasons too complicated to describe here, the five original student X-Men from 1963 time travel to the present day and become permanent residents, allowing storylines to increasingly focus on younger iterations of Cyclops, Jean Grey, Ice-Man, Beast, and Angel rather than their aging adult counterparts. As these younger X-Men adjust to their new timeframe, teen Ice-Man even reveals himself as gay in a new, seemingly more millennial take on the character. By 2014, the younger Cyclops anchored a series outside the team book, with *Jean Grey* and *Ice-Man* solos following in 2017. The *Cyclops* narrative very much positions its hero as a sixteen-year-old, eager to make sense of his relationship with his father, the cool, mustachioed space pirate Corsair. The book focuses on that father-son relationship, as Scott asks what kind of man he wants to become (like his father, his adult self, or something else). Meanwhile, Corsair's dialogue reflects on how he does not "know how to *be* [Cyclops'] father." Rather than some sudden swerve on Marvel's part toward younger readers, books like *All-New X-Men* and *Cyclops* more carefully tried to balance existing appeals to older consumers with new points of entry and identification for younger readers. Even as Cyclops aged down, figures like Corsair remained as point of focus for adult characterizations and concerns. Notably, advertisements in series like *Cyclops* echoed this transgenerational appeal, pitching *Amazing Spider-Man 2* shirts sold at Kohl's as both "Project BOYS Dept." and "Project MENS Dept."

The relaunch of *Captain Marvel* in 2014 similarly reframed Marvel's superhero narratives in a transgenerational way. In issue #1, readers are introduced to Kit, a young girl who aspires to be a superhero like Carol Danvers, who had recently adopted the Captain Marvel moniker (replacing her previous nom de guerre, Ms. Marvel). As Kit's mentor, Carol shares the world of superheroism with her, offering a potential metaphor for fans sharing the genre with children in their own lives. Notably, the series envisions female-driven transgenerational relationships in complement to the focus on father-son relationships at the heart of *Cyclops*. As Kit lives with Carol in her secret base within the Statue of Liberty's crown, she also plays a key role in how new readers are introduced to the established Captain Marvel character. The first issue presents Carol Danvers's backstory as a one-page *Captain Marvel* comic ostensibly written by Kit herself. New readers thus meet the hero through Kit. Even as Kit is left behind on Earth in issue #7 while Carol goes on a space mission, the adult hero acquires a new youthful sidekick in Tic, a teenage alien stowaway (whose name is a backwards phonetic mirror of "Kit").

Reader letters selected by the editors for publication in the pages of *Captain Marvel* reinforced the centrality of these adult-child relationships to the narrative—and in particular, the idea that readers might, like Carol, share their love of superheroes with young girls. "As a new dad," one fan wrote, "I finally found a comic I can proudly show to my little girl as she grows up (wouldn't really have done that with Ms. Marvel)." This contrast he drew to Ms. Marvel likely referred to the more sexually objectifying costume accompanying previous iterations of the character. In reply, editor Sana Amanat wrote, "So glad you have a book you can read with your daughter proudly. She's got a wise dad with good taste if I do say so myself." The letter column activated transgenerational narrative relationships in the reading of *Captain Marvel* but also flattered readers for the role that they might play in reproducing consumer relationships with Marvel product—though in this case, Marvel notably highlighted the potential for a dad to share with his daughter, rather than the adult woman represented narratively by Carol Danvers.

The relaunch of *FF* (volume 2) in late 2012 also evinced this emphasis on transgenerational relations through a specific focus on teaching and parenting. The series followed the Future Foundation, a think tank comprised of young superhero geniuses mentored by Ant-Man Scott Lang while the Fantastic Four travel off-planet. While the greatest number of characters in the cast are kids like Alex Power, Leech, and the Moloids (Tong, Turg, Mik, and Korr), the narrative perspective remains parental, with stories focused on Lang's efforts to guide these students, cope with the previous loss of his own daughter, and protect children from the horrors of the adult world. Issue #7, for example, opens with Lang's admission that he fears for the children all of the time. That rumination on parenting and family continues in a confrontation with villain The Wizard, who challenges the legitimacy of the diverse family over which Lang frets. "All of you pale before our heteronormative cisgendered classification of family!" The Wizard exclaims, to which Lang responds, "Who gave YOU the right to decide what is and isn't a family?" Anything but subtle, the narrative nevertheless conveys the theme that the Future Foundation represents family no matter how unusual its structure or different its members from one another. The focus on family does not necessarily indicate that Marvel envisioned an all-ages appeal for the book. While almost every advertisement in issue #6 featured a child-centric or child-friendly product (including toys and boys swimwear), the narrative itself—while a compelling and thoughtful story about Tong coming out as transgender—might have been difficult for Marvel to pitch as a story for children given potential backlash from conservative readers. Instead it carried a T+-rating, carving out more of a middle ground between child and adult appeals. In the incredibly self-reflexive issue #10, moreover, Lang actually meets fictionalized versions of writer Matt Fraction, artist Mike Allred, and editor Tom Breevoort. Fraction is portrayed as using adult language (censored in the dialogue balloons), to which Lang asks Breevort, "You let THIS guy write an all-ages comic book? Eesh." This dialogue, as written by Fraction, suggests that he, at least, might have considered his book to have broad age appeal (despite its T+ rating and lack of official "all-ages" standing). Later in the issue, however, dialogue from Lang seems to cast some doubt on the strength of that appeal: "Sure, sure, kids love reading comics about complex family interdynamics," Lang notes sarcastically.

Interestingly, if the *FF* narrative clearly constructed a thematic reflection on family, its letter columns offered a consistent rumination on the longevity of the *Fantastic Four* franchise and its family themes as a means of bridging the gaps between childhood and adult fandom. The first issue featured a letter from a Vancouver reader who believed recent *Fantastic Four* stories had allowed him to recapture his childhood and feel as he had back in 1968 when he first started reading comics. In issue #5, a letter from a fan of "almost five decades" complimented a scene of parental affection from another recent *Fantastic Four* title, writing, "Sue checking on everyone before retiring and comforting Franklin's fears would have been lost on me years ago before I became a father." The letter writer characterized his fandom as something that transformed in intersection with child-rearing experiences. In issue #7, Matt Fraction used the letter column to share fanart of Turg created by his own son, framing his own authorial fandom as a transgenerational one. Anxiety about these generational relationships, meanwhile, underpinned another published letter from issue #3 concerned that Marvel's priorities lay with younger readers and not the tastes of established fans: "I hesitated to tell you I'm an older reader as it seems you don't really want us around. It's ok to seek more readers, and new, younger readers. Just please don't shut us older folks out; we've been there for decades." All these letters—all from men—certainly revealed to Marvel editorial the existence of fan subjectivity oriented toward these transgenerational concerns; but the decision to print pleas like these also provided editorial the opportunity to respond to readers and reaffirm its own interest in that older demographic sending letters. Tom Breevort responded, "I would have to disagree with your sentiment that we don't value our long-time, loyal readers—we love you guys the most, who've been with us through thick and thin!" Throughout these letter columns, Marvel hailed readers of its family-themed superhero narrative as a valuable audience of older fans whose reading practices were informed at once by their childhoods, passage into adulthood, and now relationships with their own children. Marvel's attempts at building transgenerational narratives dovetailed with cultivation of transgenerational consumer subjectivities in which the feelings of fandom could be meaningfully felt across the transformation from childhood to adulthood.

Once constructed, such subjectivities could support explicit promotional campaigns meant to turn these affective experiences and transgenerational fan identities into more concrete consumer actions. Marvel's attempts to direct these subjectivities at this particular moment in its publishing history occurred within a wider industrial context in which promotional strategies sought to enlist older comics readers as literacy ambassadors for the next generation. Since 2002, retailers, distributors, and publishers have cooperated in support of the annual Free Comic Book Day (FCBD) aimed at exposing new readers to comic books, typically timed with the May release of a blockbuster superhero film to maximize potential awareness. This industry-wide promotional campaign positioned comics as a literacy gateway meant to draw "non-readers" in greater numbers through comics' entertainment appeal. In fact, FCBD has also coincided since 2009 in the United States and 2011 in Canada with the Children's Book Week campaign established in 1919 by the American Book Sellers' Association, American Library Association, and Boy Scouts of America to encourage middlebrow consumption of "good" children's literature ("About" n.d.; Nichol 1922). While Children's Book Week occurred in November for its first nine decades, the scheduling change corresponded with the campaign's increased attention to comics as a legitimate literary genre. Although separately organized, the national Children's Book Council has directly promoted FCBD as part of its Book Week ("Celebrate" 2015) and emphasized that link in promotions by local libraries and other organizations ("Free" 2015; Earls 2015). Adults have long figured as key participants in this transmission of literacy to the next generation, with attendant resources like the Children's Choices booklist envisioned as a guide for "parents, grandparents, and caregivers" who bear responsibility for shaping the cultural lives of children ("Children's" 2009). These efforts enable publishers, librarians, and booksellers to manage literacy as a consumer relationship shared between adults and children.

One of the primary aims of FCBD as an industry event, however, was to use the lure of free product to drive greater customer traffic to brick-and-mortar comic book stores. As such, retailers have invested capital in the event: in the United States, the comics available for free to consumers must still be purchased at wholesale from Diamond Comic Distributors (Driscoll 2014). As their exclusive distributor, Diamond has enlisted major US publishers Marvel and DC as "Gold Level" sponsors who provide superhero product for retailers to order and stock in conjunction with the event. FCBD superhero titles have sometimes reprinted popular issues or provided backstory for new readers; at other times, they have offered wholly original stories meant as promotional prologues for publishers' next big titles or events—and thereby encourage the FCBD patron to return again as a paying reader. Diamond has also worked with smaller "Silver Level" publishers to make FCBD promotions available; many of these smaller publishers actually prove far more active in producing promotional material aimed at kids than Marvel and DC (for whom FCBD offers equal chance at pitching more mature titles to new adult readers). Nevertheless, Marvel and DC's "all ages" and animation tie-ins have offered perennial sources of FCBD promotion, too. Retailers decide at their own risk, however, which titles to order, and they reserve the right to limit the number of free titles each customer receives. As a result, individual retailers have determined how much outreach to offer to younger and newer readers. Some shops have organized contests and activities to bring children into the store, while some have declined to participate entirely. Indeed, as suggested by the media website CNET, the aims of FCBD extended beyond cultivating new readership to encourage lapsed adult readers to return to the fold as well (Trenholm 2015).

Nevertheless, the marketing of the event placed greater emphasis on attracting newer, younger readers to the industry. In summer 2014, the main hub of the official FCBD site featured images of the most recent event from shops around the United States, thanking consumers for their participation. Of fifteen photos immediately visible, at least ten featured images of children—boys, girls, and even babies—dressed in superhero costumes and proudly displaying their comic book hauls ("Free" 2014). As a visual representation of organizers' priorities and preferred perceptions of the event, these images suggested that its success could be measured by the number of children it reached. At the same time, images of children with their parents—or rather, more exclusively, their fathers—conveyed that FCBD organizers figured the event as an opportunity for transgenerational marketing in which fathers would introduce a new generation to the medium and the space of the comic shop. This interpretation of the event as a form of child outreach carried forward into popular reports on FCBD as well. In 2015, *Time* carried a "promotional video" that highlighted the event's mission of building kids' interest in comics (Berenson 2015). With parents and shop owners speaking to the pleasures of sharing comics with kids, the video ruminated on the recurring theme of children's literacy, but it trained its focus specifically on the dynamics of fandom and especially their potential to be shared within the relations of family.

Therefore, while FCBD promotions emphasized outreach to children over adults, they did not entirely ignore that older audience either; instead older readers—as parents—emerged as the agents of comic fandom's transmission to the next generation. Within FCBD, adult comic reading mapped onto the transgenerational relations of parenting and child-rearing. This theme resonates in the intersection of parenting blogs and fan sites in which FCBD has been discussed. At one blog called *Unleash the Fanboy*, writer Jay Dietcher seized upon FCBD as an occasion to extol the positive impact of comic books on children's vocabulary, moral sense of good versus evil, and creative interests in writing and drawing. He also nominated Barack Obama and Nobel Prize winner Bishop Desmond Tutu as role models who read comics in their youth, presenting comics as fundamentally good for kids. From that value emerged an appeal to good, responsible parents who would "make sure to bring you [sic] kids to Free Comic Book Day" (Dietcher 2013). Although Dietcher's author biography explicitly mentioned his nonreproductive status (at a point in his life before his fiancée "makes him have kids"), he nonetheless wrote with an understanding of FCBD as a ritual of parenting and child-rearing. At the blog *GeekMom*, Lisa Tate similarly offered a FCBD "plan of action" that framed the event as a "gateway" for parents to help guide children to greater knowledge, creativity, and cultural awareness. More than just a chance at child enrichment, however, Tate saw comic books as a platform for connection across generational lines, where families found greater closeness in sharing "something special together" and adults could recognize that they too are still kids on the inside; "next thing you know," she wrote, "the generation gap is gone" (Tate 2014). Tate also explicitly figured mothers as key participants in these transgenerational relationships, insisting in the title of her post that "Every Mom Should Take Advantage of Free Comic Book Day." Although her emphasis on educational enrichment followed gendered caretaking scripts associated with motherhood, her imperative envisioned adult female participation in ways ignored by official FCBD promotions that preferred to envision the father as transgenerational sharer.

This imagination of the adult consumer as sharer extended to promotion of conventions and other rituals surrounding comic book fandom as well. Like the comic book publishing and retail industry it works to promote, the convention circuit has often failed to provide welcoming appeals to kids and families. So-called mommy bloggers at *Mommy Poppins*, a blog for parents and caregivers, warned readers of the less "kid-friendly" dimensions of the New York Comic-Con, zeroing in on the sexy and scary costumes adult attendees frequently wear; at the same time, however, parents expressed additional concern about the event's function as a platform to sell products, wary of the potential for tense standoffs with impressionable and demanding kids (Snook 2011). Scorn for parents who bring their children to conventions revealed additional boundaries between adulthood and childhood at such events. Citing fire codes, San Diego Comic-Con implemented a stroller ban in programming rooms in 2012, for example. For Amy Graff (2012) at the *Mommy Files* blog, the stroller regulation discouraged the parental practice of sharing convention experiences with young children who might disrupt the enjoyment sought by other adults. While Graff's sympathies appeared to lie with the "geeky parents" impacted by this rule, she also responded to commentary in publications like *Jezebel* and *Vanity Fair* that expressed both distaste for adult performances of cosplay in these sites and passed judgment on parents who would bring their children into that world. These criticisms of "spectacle" and "costumed mayhem" implied that attendees had failed at being adults—childish in their middle-aged dress-up play and foolish in their parenting decisions. Indeed the fact that conventions like San Diego Comic-Con offered paid childcare services from organizations like Kiddie Corps spoke to assumed age boundaries surrounding the event. While mom or dad might ogle sexy Harley Quinn cosplayers, their kids could do typical preschool and day camp activities like drawing, story time, and group games. The childcare organizers' command to "Bring the Kids!" to San Diego was thus not a full invitation to share Comic-Con with them so much as an assurance that adult forms of fandom need not be lost even to parents who had to bring kids along for the trip ("Bring" 2015).

In response to these barriers, a Kids Comic Con has sought to offer a separate event tailored exclusively to kids. Founded by juvenile fiction author Alex Simmons in 2007, Kids Comic Con presented opportunities for younger readers to learn more about how to create comics, to attend panels in which professionals discuss their work, and to share the pleasures of the medium within a larger community—comparable to major events like San Diego Comic-Con or New York Comic-Con, if only at a much smaller scale with free admission, less industry participation, and fewer crowds. Simmons described the event as an "age appropriate comic book convention for children, families, and educators" (Simmons 2011).

Yet the major conventions against which Simmons juxtaposed his event have made their own efforts to improve the potential for transgenerational appeal and make the pleasures of attending the event a more sharable, family affair. Undoubtedly, child presence at conventions continues to be driven in part by parents interested in sharing their fandom with their children; but organizers have taken specific steps to encourage this practice. Convention organizers have differentiated kids as a separate class of attendees, most prominently in terms of ticket prices, but also by providing targeted programming for children. At San Diego Comic-Con, children twelve and under received attendee badges for free with paid adult admission. Yet organizers also carved out a class of attendees called "juniors" aged thirteen to seventeen who paid for their badges at a reduced rate compared to adults ("Child" 2014). These age differentiations suggest an industrial imagination in which older children become semi-independent consumers in their teenage years, with a convention experience no longer directly linked to a paid parental companion. Other major conventions like the New York Comic-Con did not offer the same blanket free admission to children but instead designated reduced ticket fares—often with a specific day of programming designated as "Kids Day." While any child older than six had to pay the regular adult price during the first three days in October 2015, for example, kids between six- and twelve-years-old could gain admission on the final day of programming on Sunday for only US$5 (again, with purchase of an adult ticket required). Other conventions like San Diego Comic-Con, New York Comic-Con, Wizard World, and Chicago Comics and Entertainment Expo hosted their own Kids Days, suggesting a concerted attempt to look beyond adult attendees. Yet speaking to the persistent unease over the prospect of inviting children into the convention space, as well as any associated liability issues, organizers often recommended adult escorts for kids under a certain age. For example, the 2015 New York Comic-Con "recommends" that "all children under 18 attend with an adult" and required adult supervision for all children under thirteen ("Tickets" 2015). Although kids thirteen and up were imagined as somewhat more independent consumers, such recommendations operated in dialogue with concerns about content appropriateness on parenting blogs to frame the convention-going experience as one best shared with children by attendant adults.

As such, convention Kids Days reflected the industrial management of the tensions between an adult-oriented market emphasis and the growth- and future-oriented imperative to engage children. A *Publisher's Weekly* feature on New York Comic-Con's first Kids Day in 2008 described the event as part of "a big outreach effort to kids," highlighting the participation of several different publishers as well as major media companies like Disney and PBS. If "Comic Con is playland for adults . . . ," show manager Lance Fensterman promised, Kids Day "will be playland for kids" (Hudson 2008: 25). Included in over sixty planned events were games, contests, workshops, and a "101" panel for parents who wanted to learn more about what the comics industry had to offer their children. In 2013, San Diego Comic-Con offered a "Kids" filter on its online programming guide, helping attendees navigate the wider array of programming and narrow the scope to their all-ages offerings ("Comic-Con" 2013). Wizard World Philadelphia took special care in 2012 to identify the "kid friendly" programming available on its Sunday Kids Day and provide a framework to safely navigate children through the unruly space of the convention floor. Child attendees would receive a "Passport" that would guide them from one space of approved interaction to the next—a scavenger hunt that would ideally keep kids away from the kind of convention experiences that would attract parent complaints ("'Kids Day' Activities" 2012). In Chicago in August 2015, Wizard World added to this passport strategy a "Kid-Friendly" button that panelists and vendors could wear as a seal of approval for activities and sessions throughout the convention center that could be shared by families ("Kids Rule" 2015).

Beyond designating kid-friendly programming, these organizational efforts have also emphasized the roles adult attendees can play in sharing fan experiences with children. Kids Day programming has often included sessions on being a "Geek Mom" or "Geek Dad" that dispense advice on how to raise the next generation of fans. Producers of the *Geek My Kids* podcast, for example, became recurring participants in the transgenerational outreach of the convention circuit. Most episodes of *Geek My Kids* centered on interactions between father Chris and some combination of his three children as they discussed the narrative of a media text. However, the podcast became a framework to support fan celebrity personalities who then made their own appearances on convention panels. In one episode produced live from a *Geek My Kids* panel at Indianapolis Comic-Con, adult personalities Lilith and Kelly discussed their favorite memories as media fans and their process of becoming "geeks," positioning comics as a means of relationship building with their fathers. Both women discussed their working-class backgrounds in which comics provided a much needed means of connection with distant, overworked fathers. Throughout the episode, they called upon convention attendees to share their own stories and advice on how to best inhabit the role of geeky parent. Like many other parenting discourses, *Geek My Kids* podcasts and convention panels produced a dialogue about what it meant to be a good parent; yet they did so by framing parental responsibility in terms of transmission of media fandom. Interestingly, a 2015 panel at Indy Pop Con called "Help! My Kid is A Geek!" flipped this script by promising to support parents who did not understand their children's media interests ("Help" 2015). The parents imagined by this programming would have been dragged to the convention by their children, in opposition to all these other efforts to mobilize parents as geek instigators.

This discourse of geek child-rearing and fan identity sharing has permeated popular reflections on convention events. Publications like *Time Out* offered "Five Tips for Attending NYC's Comic-Con with Kids," normalizing the idea that the convention could be made an accessible space for families and children (Lambert 2014). Even skeptical mommy-bloggers figured conventions as a potential source of parent-child bonding. Offering a list of panels and experiences that served the needs of parents and children alike, writer Raven Snook (2011) suggested on *Mommy Poppins* that a convention properly navigated, filtered, and curated could be "worth every penny." In similar advice on "Making the Most of a Comic Con's Kids' Day," Shaun Manning (2013) acknowledged how difficult it could be for adult and child alike to equally enjoy such an event. Yet he noted how much the professional community at the event supported these attempts at sharing fandom, praising author Jill Thompson for accommodating parent and child alike when his daughter threw a tantrum. Meanwhile, at the *GeekDad* blog, writer Will James chronicled his own experience trying to share the 2015 Emerald City Comic-Con with his son. He highlighted the inherent difficulties of balancing his fan interests with his child's, reporting that his attempt to sit in on panel programming, for example, only worked because some "ladies" in attendance helped to entertain his bored son. By contrast, however, James described participation in cosplay as a more engaging form of father-son bonding—from their own coordinated *Legend of Zelda* costumes to marveling together at other attendees' costumes, including other father-son duos (James 2015). James's reliance on female attendees to accommodate this sharing hints at the gender privilege behind his fatherly role as cultural teacher and fandom initiator (but not quite full caregiver). Other bloggers like Jasper Gonzales (2013) of *Nerd Locker* similarly emphasized the potential for conventions to explicitly support relationships between fathers and their children. In his report on Amazing Las Vegas Comic-Con, he synonymized Kids Day and Father's Day. Although the parallel *GeekMom* blog offered its own analyses of Kids Days as something to be shared between parents and children (Reeve 2008, 2013), rarely if ever were such events so specifically framed as Mother's Days.

Across the narrative strategies used by comic publishers, the outreach efforts of industrial promoters, and the engagement of fans with the consumer subjectivities on offer, these transgenerational promotion strategies have sought to broaden the appeal of comics and superheroes beyond older, established audiences in order to build bridges to a younger readership. Those efforts have not supplanted or replaced interest in older readers, but instead have cultivated pleasures turning on fan relationships shared between adults and children in which superhero comics can be bequeathed from one generation to the next. Although this strategy could be seen within the pages of superhero comics produced by Marvel, industry-wide efforts like Free

Comic Book Day and convention Kids Days revealed the wider mobilization of adult fans as industry agents who might share consumer practices with children. Mapped onto parental roles and child-rearing practices, the consumer subjectivity of the adult sharer rendered fandom as a transgenerational inheritance—but in that articulation, fatherhood frequently accrued privilege as the source of this cultural productivity. As Marvel increasingly sought to consolidate this strategy, therefore, the transgenerational power of the father's authority over superhero comics was only further reinforced.

Make Theirs Marvel

Within this industry interest in devising and harnessing transgenerational subjectivities as part of child outreach efforts, Marvel launched a dedicated promotional campaign in 2013—aiming to deploy transgenerational relationships in tandem with the transmedia relationships in which its superhero properties were embedded. Announced via publicity releases and a conference call to the entertainment press on July 9, the new "Share Your Universe" (SYU) campaign promised to more effectively leverage Marvel's success in children's cable television as an asset for the publishing division. This would be accomplished through a feat of transgenerational promotion in which Marvel's existing adult readers would usher young television viewers into the publishing market. The announcement on Marvel's website described SYU as "a landmark new initiative encouraging fans to share their favorite Super Heroes with the next generation who will make theirs Marvel. . . . [T]here's never been a better time for parents—or anyone with young fans in their lives—to pass on the timeless lessons of power, responsibility and heroism to a new generation" ("Marvel" 2013). The strategy thus explicitly designated fans as stewards of an inheritance with the responsibility to bequeath superhero comic reading practices to the next generation. Moreover, this legacy would be passed down through the transmedia relationships in which Marvel's superhero properties circulated. As understood by industry journalists, the campaign was "designed as a bridge between the animated programming available on Disney XD and all-ages comics. At heart, it serves as a way for parents and older readers to share their love of Marvel Comics and their characters with younger generations through modern platforms" (Montgomery 2013). While this bridge could support two-way traffic, Marvel's strategy appeared most interested in traffic from animated cable television in the direction of comics. As another journalist reported, "this program is meant to turn fans of that material back to the comics from which all those ideas spring" (Phegley 2013). In a show of solidarity and interest in the legacy of the Marvel organization, Vice President of Television Animation Jeff Loeb agreed: "[w]e want everyone to realize that it all starts with publishing. It all starts with comic books" (Montgomery 2013). While the growth of Marvel's television division certainly outpaced that of comic publishing, the new campaign publicly recentered comics within that overall transmedia strategy.

In this reframing, Marvel acknowledged the challenges in connecting children with comics. As publisher and president of the Print, Animation, and Digital Divisions, Dan Buckley explained to the press that "sometimes it's hard for us to refer a younger kid to content in the Marvel Universe easily, because our comics have grown up" (Ching 2013). Marvel recognized barriers to entry for children, given its longstanding market focus on adult readers. Claiming knowledge about children's tastes and reading strategies from focus group testing, moreover, Buckley told the press that the campaign would need to negotiate the challenge children face in parsing multiple interpretations of a single superhero across different comic titles, films, and television series. When character models do not match, Buckley reported, children ask "which Spider-Man is the real one?" (Montgomery 2013). The SYU campaign, therefore, managed that perceived challenge by coordinating appeals across media, using greater visual consistency in character designs to dissolve barriers to transmedia and transgenerational consumption of its comic books. This feat was far easier said than done, however; some analysts doubted the feasibility of building such bridges, wondering whether a "house style" unifying different character interpretations across comic and television projects would produce excessive homogenization (Montgomery 2013). A skeptical *Hollywood Reporter* also questioned the viability of the campaign: "Sure, the entire world has become overrun by superhero culture . . . but that doesn't mean that it's been easy to get kids into reading about their favorite fictional heroes on a regular basis" (McMillan 2013). Acknowledging that Marvel hoped to get "new readers into the habit of supporting what used to be the company's core product," this analysis predicted a need for new kinds of product more suitable for six- to ten-year-olds, "clearly marked and marketed as such to make it easier for parents to know what their kids are reading." Yet the trade journal concluded on a less than confident note: "The question is, will any of this make the kids any more eager to actually read the comics . . . ?" (McMillan 2013). Playing into assumptions about the hostility of contemporary children to reading and perceptions of comics as a fading industry, *Hollywood Reporter* predicted an uphill battle for the SYU strategy.

With its work cut out for it, the new campaign encouraged opportunities for cross-promotion and most crucially hailed the adult comic book fan as an integral participant in the project of recruiting children to superhero readership. At launch in July, SYU was supported with free print samplers distributed to comic book shops that existing customers could acquire and pass on to other, younger readers (fig. 2.1). This sample contained three short all-ages comic book narratives, interspersed with advertisements for three different Marvel television series airing on Disney XD. In that material, the ever-popular Spider-Man provided a vital linkage between the television and comic book worlds as well as those of adulthood and childhood. In one of these short comic stories, Spider-Man asks a little girl for help, literally inviting her into the superhero world on the page. Meanwhile, advertisements highlighted Marvel publishing products linked to the animated television series. One ad in the sampler encouraged readers to purchase digest versions of comic book titles based on the *Ultimate Spider-Man* cartoon, while the back cover offered one final reminder of the relationship between that television series and Marvel comic books. A similar *Iron Man* story included in the sampler, meanwhile, ends with a cliffhanger, directing interested readers to a trade paperback collection in which the story is completed. These comic adaptations of the *Ultimate Spider-Man* and *Avengers Assemble* television universes explicitly encouraged the consumer to move stories from the TV "to your hands" through reading. Advertisements for comics adapted from the *Avengers Assemble* television series also highlighted the inclusion of smaller backup stories featuring LEGO minifigure versions of these superhero characters. The linkages between television and comics constructed here built as well upon relationships to merchandising, in which television series adapted from comic book characters were licensed to toy manufacturers like LEGO (where such toy product could bear trade dress specifically matched to the logo, style, and branding of the *Avengers Assemble* television series, not just the Marvel name more generally). In this case, Marvel invited fans to try comic book adaptations of licensed toys based on television series based on comics. While that appeal to familiar playthings targeted younger readers, the same *Avengers Assemble* advertisement hailed presumably adult collectors, too, by promising exclusive variant covers for these comic book adaptations. The SYU sampler thus bridged multiple media markets through distinct but interrelated appeals to the tastes and reading practices of different generations.

Beyond this initial sampler, the SYU logo also started to appear across a large number of Marvel comic book releases, signaling the print product as part of this incitement to participate in transgenerational inheritances. Like

Figure 2.1. The free "Share Your Universe" sampler comic available in print and digital forms imagined multiple points of connection between comics and television with which to leverage the interests of younger readers.

many of Marvel's ubiquitous rebranding and marketing initiatives—from "Marvel Now!" to "Join the R'Evolution"—the SYU logo was imprinted on individual comic covers, joining the Marvel brand, series and character logos, and author names as part of the standard trade dress on these periodical publications. While the sampler emphasized the all-ages comic book adaptations of television series geared toward a younger readership, this wider SYU branding could be more subtly included on even more mature comic book series—if only to remind adult readers of the potential linkages between their mature content and the wider transgenerational campaign.

For example, *Uncanny Avengers* had served as a T-rated flagship for the Marvel catalog for almost a year prior to the start of the SYU campaign, uniting its *Avengers* and *X-Men* franchises in a story written by breakout star Rick Remember and drawn by fan favorite artist John Cassady. This series offered a decidedly mature appeal; the first issue ended with the evil Red Skull lobotomizing the corpse of hero Professor X. Like *Captain Marvel* and *FF*, this series' letter columns modeled fan participation in transgenerational relations. In issue #1, a fan wrote, "I've been a Marvel fan since I figured out how to read, and I will continue forever more. Some folks pass their love of baseball or politics on to their kids, I'll be passing down my love of the Marvel universe!" Another letter on this topic in issue #2 suggested that the mature content of the series worked to thwart these gifting practices, however. "I have two sons, 5 and 3," it read. "And I would love them to grow up with comics in their life, the way I did. But not with this kind of heroes [sic], not with this kind of sadism." Similarly, another letter in issue #3 shares, "Some of the best memories in my life are lying on the living room floor thumbing through comics with my Dad. . . . I would love to continue that tradition with fresh new work, but I don't feel comfortable sitting down and reading with my kids out of modern Marvel comics." While the pages of *Uncanny Avengers* thus positioned adult fans within a gift economy of inheritance (much like *Captain Marvel* and *FF*), they confounded that participation as much as offering support for it. By issue #10, however, the appearance of the new SYU trade dress on the cover (released two weeks into the campaign) repositioned *Uncanny Avengers* within this inheritance economy. On the one hand, as a motto, the "Share Your Universe" logo communicated a more explicit imperative to cultivate and accommodate the transgenerational subjectivities already in play. On the other hand, the shared trade dress that connected the mature *Uncanny Avengers* to other less problematic and all-ages Marvel content could remind readers of other resources through which their transgenerational pleasures could be better explored.

However, this linkage depended significantly on prior reader knowledge about SYU. The SYU imprint stood alone on the cover, seemingly a self-explanatory imperative. Although another SYU-branded advertisement for the animated series *Hulk and the Agents of S.M.A.S.H.* did appear within *Uncanny Avengers* #10 and other titles, nothing within these publications themselves actually explained what SYU was. The cover branding hailed only those readers already familiar enough with Marvel's promotional campaigns to recognize what "Share Your Universe" meant, understand their responsibility to think across the wider variety of titles upon which this imperative appeared, and pass on their love of superhero comics to younger readers. SYU thus worked by flagging to existing, very much in-the-know readers their potential participation in a campaign that operated across numerous titles, products, and—crucially—media platforms.

Outside of comics themselves, the Marvel mobile application similarly offered digital giveaways of all-ages comics to reach readers without access to or interest in brick-and-mortar comic shop patronage. A new Marvel Kids website branded with the SYU imprint drew linkages between these different platforms in Marvel's superhero empire. This site featured four clearly labeled menus for "shows," "games," "comics," and "activities," inviting users to toggle between these different modes of engagement with Marvel properties. While children were offered simple puzzles, mazes, coloring tasks, and other interactive experiences in which to engage, other content on the site explicitly hailed adults as important participants in a transgenerational interactivity with comics. "Marvel is YOUR Universe. Now, make it THEIRS," a dialogue box commanded. "This is the place to get the latest information on family-friendly Marvel comics, movies and TV series to help you share your passion for Marvel characters and stories with the next generation of fans" ("Share Your Universe" 2014). The SYU logo and key art drove home this bridging function, featuring on the left side a line-up of superheroes drawn in comic book styles evocative of the 1980s, and on the right-side mirror renderings of the same superheroes in the contemporary style of Disney XD animation (fig. 2.2). Outside of kid-specific web spaces, "Share Your Universe" also became a categorizing tag in the online comics catalogs on Marvel.com, identifying almost twenty different first-issue offerings that would give younger readers pleasurable entry into Marvel publications ("Share Your Universe!" n.d.). This tag thus offered a guideline to inform and encourage adult readers' digital purchases on behalf of children.

With this much energy focused on bringing children to comics from television, the campaign also worked to encourage that valuable viewing, promoting Marvel television series on Disney XD. For the first week of the campaign, Xbox Live and Windows 8 users could access free episodes on-

Figure 2.2. Key art on the "Share Your Universe" Facebook page put the visual styles familiar to a previous generation of comic book readers in dialogue with more modern renderings from the Disney XD animated television series. (Screen capture.)

line. These attempts at cross-promotion migrated to the campaign's Facebook page, where from July to November users could get regular updates, suggestions, and strategies for bridging the divide between television and comics, childhood and adulthood ("Share Your Universe" 2013). This Facebook page proved to be the most dynamic component of the campaign, continually reminding visitors of upcoming episodes on Disney XD, encouraging viewers to "check in" with GetGlue to earn virtual reward stickers, and prompting fans to transform cable television viewing into comic reading experiences. In the first week of the campaign, for example, the Facebook feed inquired "[h]ow often do you visit your local comic book store with your kids?," effectively asking adult fans to declare their dedication to transgenerational transmission and perhaps feel guilty for not pursuing that responsibility with more frequency and zeal.

Exhortations commanding fans to take up this evangelist role did not always meet with unqualified acceptance; indeed reactions on Facebook were sometimes hostile. In response to the plea to "Take a family trip to your local comic book store and pick up the latest issue of Marvel Universe Ultimate Spider-Man (2012) #17, out tomorrow!," one commenter refused: "No, I won't. This show is SHIT." Adult fandom and the mission of child outreach thus did not always prove compatible. Against requests that fans play a role in promoting *Avengers Assemble*, one fan contrasted the newer television series to previous ones perceived to better meet his adult interests and tastes. He complained, "I waited my whole life for a show as awesome as Avengers EMH [Earth's Mightiest Heroes] n you cancel it for this lazy uninspired . . . 'show'!? This is worse than that baby show The Super Hero Squad Show." In this age-based taste hierarchy, awesomeness is juxtaposed to youth and infancy, disinclining the fan with distinguished taste to willingly participate in Marvel's promotional efforts. When Marvel invited its Facebook fans to explain "How did you introduce your kids to Spidey?" that same fan referenced Disney XD's ongoing *Ultimate Spider-Man* series to say "Don't watch that garbage!" and suggested kids try the 1994 Fox Kids *Spider-Man* animated series instead. This response affirmed alternative fan investment in the cultivation of transgenerational taste formations but did not endorse the strategies pushed by the SYU campaign. Many others highlighted the economic challenges of sharing comic books with children, as the "outrageous" price of individual comic books made the cost of a "family" trip to the comic store quite prohibitive. To these Facebook users, superhero comics fit better with the disposable incomes of adult hobbyists than larger family groups for which Disney XD television provided a more cost-effective entertainment option.

Beyond comic shops, web spaces, and television tie-ins, the SYU campaign also piggybacked on transgenerational promotions at comic book conventions. At the July 2013 San Diego Comic-Con, for example, Marvel held an SYU costume contest, calling attention to and rewarding child participation, then making reports on the event a part of the Facebook newsfeed. At New York Comic-Con in October, Marvel held a contest to "Be the Face of Share Your Universe," framed as a search for the perfect transgenerational evangelist: "Are you the ultimate Marvel fan? Do you share the Marvel Universe with your friends and family? And do you want to bring the world of Marvel to the next generation?" ("NYCC" 2013). While the campaign focused on child outreach, the face of that campaign was to be the adult who could best help Marvel reach that younger audience. Video entries recorded in a special booth at the convention could "include children with parental permission," but the rules explicitly called for a winner over the age of eighteen envisioned as fan spokesperson for Marvel in future promotional videos.

Altogether, these efforts demonstrate not just cross-promotional aims but also the desire to establish adult fans as participants in the corporate promotion of transgenerational relationships surrounding superhero-themed transmedia culture. Moreover, as idealized in industrial discourse, these generational relationships took shape in relation to invocations of family that often—but not always—hinged on gendered assumptions about comic reading as a masculinized experience to be passed down from the authority of father figures. First and most generally, Marvel consistently framed the "share" of this campaign as a family experience. In the invitations to participate made on Facebook, invocations of family repeated: "will you and your family be attending NYCC Kids at New York Comic-Con on Sunday?"; "Celebrate Halloween early with your family by checking out this special episode on October 5!"; "Where would your family like to go on vacation: Asgard, Stark Tower, or somewhere else?"; "Help Captain America defeat the Red Skull with your family in this online game!"; "Hawkeye is super skilled in archery, but what does the young Marvelite in your family have a super skill in?"; "Take a family trip to your local comic book store and pick up the latest issue of Marvel Universe Ultimate Spider-Man (2012) #17, out tomorrow!" ("Share Your Universe" 2013). Diminutive mentions of the "youngest Marvelites" sometimes offered a less limited imagination of this transgenerational relationship, where "you and your little Thor fans" could allow for a broader range of adult relationships with children (including nieces, nephews, students, and more). But more frequently, Marvel framed SYU as a consumer relationship occurring within a nuclear family unit.

Within that family narrative, Marvel concretely pitched the transgenerational sharing of comic books as a gender-inclusive activity; yet frequent slippages in industry and promotional discourse privileged the role of an idealized father. To Marvel's credit, it overtly presented "Share Your Universe" as a way of explicitly inviting young girls into comic reading culture. Managed statements about the campaign's goals deployed gender-inclusive language that imagined girls within the next generation of Marvel fans: as publisher and president Dan Buckley sold it, "Every Marvel fan has a unique story for how these heroes, their stories and the experience of entering the Marvel Universe helped shape their childhood—and we want to make it easy to continue that tradition with your kids, nieces, nephews, and loved ones" ("Marvel" 2013). Shrewd Marvel representatives also identified as the campaign's inspiration the four-year-old girl Mia Grace who had gained notoriety on YouTube and *Jimmy Kimmel Live* in spring 2013 for her vast knowledge of Marvel trivia (Phegley 2013; Ching 2013). In doing so, Marvel deflected accusations that it sought to extend a comic book boys' club to a new generation, recognizing that its future rested in the hope of a broader, more inclusive appeal. In the execution of the campaign, Marvel also took advantage of opportunities to highlight the participation of young girls in this new generation. From the San Diego Comic-Con costume contest, for example, the SYU Facebook page shared a photo of a young girl participant captioned: "What do you think of this little Captain America?" ("Share Your Universe" 2013). Other group photos of convention cosplayers similarly highlighted girl participants. The SYU campaign thus imagined its transgenerational family relationships as ones that crossed gender lines.

Nevertheless, this promotional discourse also contradictorily privileged the role fathers could play in building this bridge to the next generation. Unsurprising due to the disproportionate number of men working in management positions at Marvel, representatives speaking at the initial press announcement framed the initiative specifically around father-son relationships when invoking their personal histories and identities to sell the concept. Despite Buckley's strategic imagination of a gender inclusive future, other executives' personal narratives reframed this transgenerational dynamic as one dependent on a father in the nostalgic past. Chief creative officer Joe Quesada explained in the press conference that "[f]or me, it gets down to the core of what it was that got me into the Marvel Universe at first. It brings back memories of my dad buying me my first comics. It was just that sharing experience where one person leads to another leads to another" (Ching 2013). Quesada leaves open the possibility that this "one person" behind the sharing need not be a father, but the notion of the Marvel fan passing on a comic book inheritance becomes tangible through repeated fatherly imagery. Marvel Television vice president Jeff Loeb reinforced that articulation by imagining "Share Your Universe" as a masculinized generational link: ". . . the interpersonal stuff of whether you're a father or a son and wanting to talk about this stuff is amazing" (Phegley 2013).

This tendency to frame the adult fan responsible for Marvel's generational transfer explicitly as a father continued throughout the campaign's execution. In addition to sharing Marvel's promotional messages about television airdates and comic book availability, for example, the Facebook feed linked to episode reviews that came "straight from a Marvel Dad" ("Share Your Universe" 2013). To be clear, Marvel did not imagine the adult "sharer" in exclusive terms of fatherhood, and more often than not succeeded in framing "Your Universe" as something to be shared with both boys and girls in the imagined family. However, in laying out a number of different idealized fan subject positions throughout the campaign—the family, the Youngest Marvelites, and the Marvel Dad—the potential for a Marvel Mom remained significantly underexplored. The idea of a mother passing on "her universe" to her sons and daughters rarely if ever surfaced explicitly within SYU, suggesting that while the inheritors of the Marvel Universe might be of any gender, that inheritance would be the gift of a father. This failure to articulate a Marvel Mom extended in large part from the limited corporate vision driving promotional sites like the SYU Facebook page, but it also unfolded in users' practical engagement with it: among all the news updates by Marvel and comments from fans alike, in only one instance did a self-identified mother mention her attempts to share Marvel with her child (in this case, through her own "love" of the *Ultimate Spider-Man* animated series) ("Share Your Universe" 2013).

Despite this emphasis on the father, a few exceptions did push against this imagination of patriarchal authority over the superhero inheritance. In issue #10 of *FF*—only the second issue of the series to carry the SYU trade dress and the first to carry any internal advertisements related to the campaign—the letter column included a compelling note from a female reader who had recently borrowed some of her mother's *Fantastic Four* comics, finding them fascinating. Most of her letter focused on the parental themes in the *Fantastic Four* narrative, praising Sue Storm's mothering and, by contrast, taking Reed Richards to task as a father (claiming that villains like Namor or Doctor Doom would actually be better parents). In an issue carrying the "Share Your Universe" branding, her comments represented an important recognition of the possibility that comic reading might extend from a mother's interests. At the same time, her dig at father characters stood in contrast to the lionization of fathers and their gift of comic book reading as presented throughout the rest of Marvel's campaign.

In addition, two behind-the-scenes videos available on Marvel.com a year prior to SYU had previously articulated the possibility of the Marvel Mom; yet they marginalized and erased that figure as well. In one-minute videos posted to the Marvel website (and its AR, or "augmented reality," app), viewers gained glimpses into relationships between editorial personnel and their mothers. The on-screen title of the second video, "Marvel Moms, Flash Card Game," even provided a terminology for considering this maternal counterpart to the Marvel Dad. As the video starts, X-Men assistant editor Jennifer Margaret Smith introduces herself then points to the woman sitting next to her to explain: "and this is my mom!" The mother-daughter pair proceed to play a Password-style flashcard game, where Smith cannot see the images of various *X-Men* characters, and her mother must, without using names, offer descriptions to help her guess them. The Marvel Mom's use of contextual (rather than just visual) hints—like the synonym "Intrigue" to help her daughter guess the character Mystique, or "many lives" for the frequently resurrected Jean Grey—suggest that she has not just mother-daughter rapport but also some fan knowledge of her own. No future videos took up the Marvel Mom name, however. A preceding Marvel Mom video, however, did not afford its mother character with the same insider subjectivity. In it, editorial staff member Daniel Ketchum asks his mother to predict the contents of a comic based only on its cover, and their banter focuses on her lack of familiarity with superheroes. This video thus stood in opposition to its follow-up, in that Ketchum's mother appears unable to share in the superhero comic culture in which her son is invested. The lack of additional Marvel Mom content beyond these first two videos—even once the SYU campaign made these kinds of subjectivities a promotional priority a year later—underscores Marvel's failure to explore these possibilities.

A more significant exception to this imagination of sharer-as-father came in the announcement of the winner of the New York Comic-Con "Be the Face of Share Your Universe" contest. More than six months after the convention, a May 2014 blog post on the Marvel website declared Constance Katsafanas, a thirty-one-year-old neurology student and Marvel fan for twenty-five of those years, as the ideal embodiment of the SYU principle. As Katsafanas described her lifelong relationship with Marvel: "I didn't like to read. So my grandmother, in her infinite wisdom, when I was six years old, bought me an X-Men comic book from one of those spinner racks in the gas station. That was it. I was completely hooked" (Stevens 2014). Contrasting SYU's tendency to figure transgenerational inheritances as paternal gifts, Katsafanas located the origins of her fandom in the cultural intervention of a grandmother, rather than a father, uncle, or even another beneficent individual of indeterminate gender. Yet as the new face of the campaign, Katasfanas also contradicted its single-minded focus on sharing the Marvel universe within the reproductive context of nuclear families. Katsafanas's experiences as a Marvel sharer operated in relation to her friendships rather than her biological relations: "[My] friends have young children—which is bizarre, that I'm at the point of my life where my friends have kids—and I get to share [comics] with them," Marvel quoted her. This statement disarticulated Katsafanas from the family world of reproduction and child-rearing to which Marvel had otherwise hitched its campaign. The emphasis on her professional life in residency further differentiated her from the parental role—she played more the role of a parent's cool friend. When Marvel quotes her as saying "my husband says that I am like a little kid whenever I talk to him about this," Katsafanas can also be imagined to be more in touch with the tastes and sensibilities of the young Marvelite than the adult parent position so frequently emphasized elsewhere in the campaign.

Marvel's selection of Katsafanas was both surprising and refreshing, in that it worked to disarticulate the SYU campaign from normative ideas about transgenerational inheritance via masculine authority over Marvel and traditional notions of family reproduction. While her invocation of a grandmother's influence mitigated Marvel's greater failure to imagine maternal figures as equally responsible for gifting superhero culture to the next generation, it may be somewhat more radical to imagine those transgenerational relationships outside of reproductive familial relationships altogether (perhaps revealing new ways for Marvel's persistent invocation of "family" to be interpreted). It is with much irony, then, that her selection as the face of the campaign happened after the campaign downshifted. Although SYU trade dress and advertisements continued to appear sporadically in printed comics at least into 2017, the "Share Your Universe" Facebook feed ceased its regular updates in November 2013, and no further announcements or SYU-related news stories on Marvel.com followed the reveal of Katsafanas. In the campaign's initial announcement, publisher Dan Buckley claimed that the "success" of "Share Your Universe" would be measured by "the general response we get on the Internet, Facebook likes, people engaging with us in general, how they actively respond to this activity at the various cons that we go to with this initiative" (Ching 2013). Having retreated from spaces like Facebook, and not announcing the results of a convention contest until some sixth months later, Marvel's overall pursuit of the strategy met with failure by its own standards of measurement. At best, Katsafanas represented a strategic rethinking of the initiative a year into launch according to a different set of principles. Yet while her appointment as SYU ambassador meant "the opportunity" to record six promotional videos featured on Marvel.com ("NYCC" 2013), there was no guarantee that any strategy would remain to support those videos (if and when they were ever made public).

These contradictions and apparent failures offer several important insights. First, in trying to concretize a transgenerational transmedia marketing strategy, Marvel identified a core audience of adult fans and worked through the campaign to provide a set of generational and familial identities for those fans to inhabit. As Buckley argues, the SYU initiative was meant "to do something that was very unique and took advantage of the very unique network of fans we have through social media and through comic shops." In privileging familial relationships, reproduction, and fatherhood, while belatedly allowing for the possibility of young female professionals as ideal transgenerational spokespeople, the campaign also evinced Marvel's efforts to ascribe industrial authority to segments of its audience. This power, moreover, centered on the company's struggle to bridge not just adults and children but also the futures of its different corporate divisions. The drift toward valorization of fatherly relationships amid a clear strategic commitment to exploring a wider range of possible transgenerational engagement with superheroes reflected the company's overall dilemma of trying to hold on to the old amid the pursuit of the new. On the one hand, SYU represented recognition that building a new generation of comic readers meant expanding appeals beyond boys and men. On the other, the contradictions of the campaign suggested resistances to such shifts. Greater gender inclusivity may be the way forward for comic books, but with a cable television outlet like Disney XD focused almost exclusively on boys and figured as a key promotional partner, the potential for change was limited. When asked if SYU would be used to justify greater promotion of female characters and outreach to female fans, Cort Land, vice president of Animation Development and Production, replied with an anecdote about how the appeal of "strong female leads" like Black Widow and She-Hulk to boys would indeed enable that kind of outreach in the future (Phegley 2013; Ching 2013). Here the practicality of gender inclusiveness in comics followed its relative compatibility with a market focus on boys in television. In that context, the imagination of Marvel Comics as a consumer inheritance depended on the intersection of privileged generational and gendered subjectivities.

Conclusion

Although the "Share Your Universe" campaign dwindled, the imperative remained. Marvel will likely continue to pursue some set of strategies for both constructing a new generation of comic book readers and imagining transgenerational roles for audiences to play in helping to realize that corporate goal. Indeed these efforts support the larger imperative of transgenerational promotion shared with Free Comic Book Day and convention Kids Days that enlists adults as agents in aging industries' promotional outreach to new generations of consumers. In that ongoing process, speculation will continue to abound about how to sustain print-based legacies and audience loyalties as companies like Marvel continue forward into new media sectors as part of their embeddedness in corporate transmedia relationships. This chapter has therefore put the question of transmedia in relation to transgenerational strategy, focusing on how Marvel has imagined its ideal core audience while laying out productive identities for them to adopt in service to the next generation. In the Marvel family, the Young Marvelite, the Marvel Dad, and only later the female professional outside of patriarchal relationships, the SYU campaign gave Marvel a way to construct transmedia audiences in transgenerational terms—a project of cultural reproduction imbricated by gender and sexuality. Although this analysis of transgenerational transmedia marketing has revealed the relations of political economy between different

Marvel divisions invested in markets of unequal value, it has also yielded valuable perspective into the meaningful audience subject positions constructed by media industries as a means of participating in the transmission and inheritance of popular culture.

In the end, this was a story about ownership of and authority over the Marvel Universe. The command "Share Your Universe" depends on understanding who has claim on it, and thereby who can be empowered to share it. Within Marvel itself, the initiative grew from industrial tensions and anxieties over where the center of that superhero universe might rest—within emergent markets like film, television, and new media, or in the legacy market of print? As the campaign reached out to potential consumer agents of promotion, the construction of ideal Marvel families, fathers, and friends invoked claims about who might have power—and with it, great responsibility—over that world to pass it on through time. Returning to my own participation in these economies, as the father eager to bring my daughters with me to the comic book shop and thereby share my love of superheroes, I must recognize my own privilege and complicity. On the one hand, my identity as fan and father supported a form of consumer subjectivity in which I happily and freely participated in the industrial reproduction of superhero comic economies over time. Parents like me have incorporated into the subjectivities and practice of child-rearing a reproduction of the markets on which media industries depend. On the other hand, the forces encouraging consumers like me to do so work on the privileges of fatherhood and the sense of cultural authority that comes with it. While there are indeed just as many mothers—and aunts, teachers, friends—eager to share their love of superhero comics with kids, the fathers engaged in this work do so with a greater authorization constructed in and through the organizations of campaigns like Free Comic Book Day, Kids Days, and Share Your Universe. This participation in a patriarchal brand of transgenerational inheritances does not make the identities or pleasures of sharing superheroes any less real. It also, I would hope, does not make a father's desire to share fandom inherently problematic. Yet reassessing my older daughter's eventual resistance of the inheritance I tried to pass down, it may be profitable to see instead of heartbreak the potential for these transgenerational lines of patriarchal authority to be disrupted.

CHAPTER 3

Junior Executives

Producing Adult Professionalism in Children's Media Industries

While media industries cultivate a certain kind of adult consumer to pass fandom down to subsequent generations, they also rely upon specific forms of adult professionalism—and the identity work that accompanies it—to produce media for children. Not just anyone is ideally suited to the work of crossing boundaries between adulthood and childhood. In a 2011 interview with former *Sesame Street* performer Kevin Clash meant to promote the documentary *Being Elmo: A Puppeteer's Journey*, ABC News' Julie Chen offered a barrage of questions that acknowledged Clash's professionalism as a children's entertainer but positioned him as oddly outside normal adulthood because of that professional proximity to childhood. Chen insisted that there had to be a distance between Clash and the childishness of his Elmo character, asserting that otherwise "people would think you're too weird!" Her voiceover narration framed his talent as something that emerged from a childhood "obsession" with puppets. When Chen returned onscreen, she emphasized Clash's alterity by describing his professional accomplishments as "not bad for a kid who plays with dolls." Throughout, Chen positioned Clash's adult and professional identities as an extension of his childhood, ultimately asking the leading question, "Are you a big kid at heart?" Clash accepted this professionalized childishness when he affirmed, "Yeah, I have a Peter Pan syndrome." This line of questioning about transgression of boundaries between adulthood and childhood of course took on more troubling overtones a year later when Clash was implicated in an underage sex scandal, which made his professional identity not just unique but explicitly problematic.

More than twenty years earlier, Fred Rogers, creator of *Mr. Rogers' Neighborhood*, similarly occupied this awkward gap between adult and child identities during a promotional appearance on *The Tonight Show*. Guest host Joan Rivers struggled to make sense of Rogers beyond the terms of some arrested childhood and did not engage with him as a typical guest. Although Rogers rather soberly explained his expertise and career trajectory, Rivers repeatedly lost her composure and interrupted him to remark to her audience, "It's so funny, he's talking to me, and I just feel like he's eight years old." Rogers did not act particularly childish during the interview, yet Rivers's barb landed with her audience by virtue of his professional proximity to childhood. She frames his professionalism in the realm of children's media as an embodiment of childhood itself, but also as something amusingly incongruent with her own late-night conversation space. While separated by several decades, these interviews with Rogers and Clash both link the identities of professionals working in children's media to the audiences they serve. Working in the world of kids' media, these men appeared kids themselves, out of place in the more adult industry sectors of television in which interviewers like Chen and Rivers operated, and occupying narrower professional subject positions clearly defined by their transgenerational industry work. Despite the patronization that came with this identity, both Clash and Rogers also seemed willing to accept the role of the man-child as one from which to build an understanding of their professional practice.

Looking at the way the professional identities of children's media professionals are constructed as well as the rituals, practices, and communities through which such workers navigate those constructions, this chapter focuses on the transgenerational identity work of adults who participate professionally (or aspire to participate) in the industries that produce popular culture for kids. These professional identities reveal how status and expertise in the production and marketing of culture for children are constructed, claimed, and contested in negotiation of adult proximity to childhood. Looking beyond the individual notoriety of entertainers like Clash and Rogers, however, I consider the children's media industries in terms of a wider "production culture," thinking about identities, meanings, and values of media work as they circulate and constitute communities of practitioners (Caldwell 2008; Mayer, Banks, and Caldwell 2009; Mayer 2011). Triangulating textual analysis of media representations of these industry sectors with participant observation fieldwork in the spaces in which professionals interact with one another, this chapter examines exactly how and why media producers navigate the transgenerational identities that articulate their very adult pursuit of professional success to the voices and experiences of childhood—both as positioned by others and in subject positions professionals claim for themselves. On the one hand, it seems quite logical for kids' media producers to claim transgenerational affinity with the audience they serve; yet on the other, not everyone in these production communities has the same opportunity to generate professional authority and status from such claims to affinity. Depending on hierarchies of labor authority as well as privileges based in gender and reproductive status, producers within this industrial production culture find themselves able to perform this identity work of "pediocularity" (Cook 2004: 3) in different, unequal ways. This chapter therefore investigates the navigation of professional childhood affinity as produced within media representations and as performed within the "ritual" space of industry events (Havens 2006: 71–72; Caldwell 2008: 69), arguing that the production culture of kids' media centers as much on the transgenerational production of adult status and identity in relation to kids as the making of product for kids.

As a starting point, this chapter turns to television narratives that, like the interviews conducted by Chen and Rivers, provide an ideological framework for understanding the professionals who would devote their creative energies to making cultural product for kids (as an audience to which they themselves do not belong). The reality competition series *The Toy Box*, distributed by the US broadcast network ABC in 2017, provides an instructive case study. In this two season series, aspiring toymakers competed for a chance to have their product concepts made by industry leader Mattel and sold at Toys "R" Us stores. The twist on similar competition formats, however, was that their inventions faced judgment not only by adult professionals but also (and later in the series, exclusively) by a panel of kid judges who served as the ultimate industry experts and gatekeepers. In the reversal of roles between children and adults, *The Toy Box* imagined the industry culture of toy work as one produced in the management and transgression of boundaries between adulthood and childhood (generating network television programming with co-viewing potential in the process). Considering the cross-promotional function of the series for ABC, Mattel, and (the now defunct) Toys "R" Us as well as the transgenerational identities through which the series forged those partnerships—where adult creators identify with children while children act as executives—this analysis reveals the representation of transgenerational work across these boundaries.

To examine how professionals inhabit these roles outside the representational framework of television narratives, the chapter secondly examines the Kidscreen Summit as a space of production culture and professional labor identities, considering how it produces knowledge about kids while remaining a realm of adult professionalism largely exclusive of direct participation by kids. Organized by the eponymous *Kidscreen* trade journal, the annual

Kidscreen Summit attracts professionals in children's animation, merchandising, games, and more from around the globe, providing a ritual space for networking, celebration, exchange of ideas, and continuing competition within a shared community. Around this trade event circulate and crystallize a set of knowledges and beliefs about children and at the same time strategies about how to negotiate the industrial challenges of the "post-network era" (Lotz 2014) in which old strategies of television distribution (and, by extension, toy merchandising heavily reliant on television) face disruption from new digital platforms. Although children do not participate in this professional world in the ways that the fantasy of *The Toy Box* might suggest, kids nevertheless become important topics of discussions and even props in industry struggles over audience knowledge, where the adult who can incorporate the identities, experiences, and voices of childhood into their own performances of professionalism gains not just authority but also capital with which to potentially shape or disrupt "industry lore" (Havens 2006: 123; Havens 2007) circulating at the event.[1] Long-held beliefs about the "naturalness" of gendered marketing, for example, gain their power in this ritual space from the affinities that adult professionals are able to claim with their child consumers.

This chapter thus pays special attention to the moments in these industry rituals in which professionals claimed for themselves the knowledges and identities of childhood—and just as importantly, the forces that prevented them from doing so. Some attendees claimed to be "big kids" in an arrested (but professionalized) state of development—owning the roles ascribed to Fred Rogers, Kevin Clash, and many of the adult participants in the reality competition world of *The Toy Box*. Meanwhile, others strategically positioned themselves in more indirect relation to childhood in roles clearly defined as parental, teacherly, or otherwise authoritative over children. Examining who could and could not claim to speak professionally for and as children—and why—this chapter shows how kids' media producers carefully position their own gendered identities and reproductive potential to lay claim to professional authority over and knowledge in this cultural economy. Across the representational and ritual dynamics of these industry cultures, childhood becomes a complex and contested terrain for the production of adult professionalism and identity in transgenerational media industries.

Industry Cultures and the Power of Kid Surrogates

This interest in the narratives and communities in which professionals operate in the culture industries builds significantly on a recent strand of research often described as "production studies" (Mayer, Banks, and Caldwell 2009; Mayer 2011). Distinct from studies of media industry attuned to the top-down economic power of corporate institutions, this work has embraced a cultural studies perspective to direct greater attention to the everyday, on-the-ground relations of power in which media workers engage in their work and negotiate in meaningful ways the conditions of labor in which that work unfolds. As Mayer, Banks, and Caldwell write, production studies focus on "how media producers make culture, and, in the process, make themselves into particular kinds of workers in modern, mediated societies. . . . They shape and refashion their identities in the process of making their careers in industries undergoing political transitions and economic reorganizations" (2009: 2). My interest here in the transgenerational subject positions inhabited by adult professionals in children's media industries is thus significantly indebted to this research program, particularly in the attempt to explore how toy inventors and animation programmers alike produce themselves as valuable participants in that industry through their affinity with the audience. Production studies offer significant methodological inspiration as well. Attuned to the stories, communities, meanings, and identities that circulate around production work, John Caldwell recommends studying "deep texts and rituals" that assign shared meanings, values, and identities to certain kinds of work, work categories, and communities of workers (2009: 202),[2] much as Tim Havens (2007) and Denise Bielby and C. Lee Harrington (2008) have looked to industry trade shows as ritualized points of access to the worlds of media industry work cultures.

Yet in considering the Kidscreen Summit as what Havens calls a "high holiday" where industry culture is performed, displayed, and enacted, I also seek to develop a somewhat more expansive view of deep texts than has been commonplace in production studies. Caldwell distinguishes among three different kinds of deep texts: embedded artifacts that circulate only among professionals, the semi-embedded artifacts intended for professional audiences that circulate among different labor communities, and the publicly disclosed artifacts that represent industry cultures to the outside world. No one type of deep text provides a more "authentic" or unvarnished window into production cultures—instead all three contribute to industry realities that "are always constructed" and thus require an interpretative approach (2009: 201). While access to embedded production texts continues to represent a coup for researchers,[3] Caldwell's formulation of deep texts offers an invitation to approach publicly disclosed narratives and representations of industry worlds as an equally significant and viable means of analyzing production cultures. Publicly disclosed representations of industry cultures—including television programs—offer crucial points of entry into those worlds within and against which professional subjectivities might be imagined and constructed from the outside by consumers and aspirants alike.[4]

My specific interest in the transgenerational subject positions occupied by media professionals also builds upon a specific strand of production research that has situated producers' understandings of their professional practices and identities in relation to the consumer cultures served by that work. In these studies, professional subject positions cohere in relation to the ability to perform and conjure knowledge of the audience (Ganti 2012; Gitlin 2000; Punathambekar 2013). The most relevant work in this literature comes from Stephen Zafirau, who rejects generalized conceptions of Hollywood professionals as "either opposite their audiences or thoroughly a part of their audiences," to instead theorize such producers as drawing from their own everyday private lives to generate knowledge about an externalized audience, occupying "a kind of liminal space (or gray area) between these statuses as 'removed producers' and 'audience members'" in doing so (2009: 192). Crucially, Zafirau attends to producers' relationships with their own children, who emerge as an everyday means of accessing emerging audience tastes outside the industry proper. Beyond its nod to the construction of audience knowledge across generational lines, Zafirau's perspective informs this chapter in its emphasis on boundary crossings and liminal spaces, where the transgenerational identities of adult professionals emerge in everyday relationship to those of child consumers to which they may be proximate yet never peer.

Building on this specific model of production studies that put questions of audience at the fore, this chapter conceptualizes the child consumer both as "other" to the industry producer (excluded from the adult world of media professionals) and as a powerful point of reference and identification around which industry communities and forms of knowledge cohere. Conceiving of industry cultures transgenerationally means attending not just to the oppositions between adult producers and child consumer cultures but also to the crossed boundaries of identity, knowledge, and experience between them. In doing so, we can reach deeper understanding of the complex relationships between the professional subjectivities always under construction in production cultures, the consumer cultures that they serve, and the perceptions of the audience external to industry communities. The analysis of kids' media sectors in this chapter therefore considers how producers generate industry lore about children as a consumer group, while using that lore to construct their own professional identities and claims to expertise in a work world constituted around the idea of childhood.

Through this approach, this chapter builds upon research into the specific production communities that produce media culture for children, extending discussions about the power of adult professionals to shape childhood to an examination of the power of childhood identities in that adult work. In his study of industry lore, Havens (2007) examines how ideologies of and about childhood circulate in the space of the MIP Jr. trade show, a kid-focused event spun out of the annual MIPCOM international television sales conference in Cannes. Similarly, David Buckingham foregrounds this power of adult professionals to "define the interests of children and to speak for them" (2000: 204).[5] To this understanding of the power of adults in the media industries over childhood, however, this chapter adds more explicit consideration of the value, identity, and meaning of childhood within these professional communities. While children themselves may be structurally excluded from these production worlds, they remain discursively and ideologically omnipresent within the identity work of adult professionals in that industrial space. Numerous scholars have examined the unique boundaries of children's media production cultures: both J. Alison Bryant (2007) and Dafna Lemish (2010) identify the children's television community as a distinct sector with its own industrial culture built from unique, prosocial commitment to serving the "cognitive, emotional, and development" needs of children (Bryant 2007: 1). In this sense, the audience makes the children's television community imaginable as a cohesive, distinct industry community—one constituted through the meanings and values of childhood as well as struggles over taste and agency in which children are implicated. As much as adult professionals have power over childhood in their role as surrogates for consumers materially excluded from direct industry participation, the values, meanings, and identities of that adult work also appear to extend from the construction of childhood as an audience with special needs requiring specialized professional knowledge.

Through an exploration of this tension, I identify children's consumer cultures as the transgenerational expression of adult professionals' identity work, taking inspiration from the dynamics of "pediocularity" that Daniel Cook ascribes to children's consumer cultures within the capitalist economies of the early twentieth century. As industrializing fashion industries positioned themselves as surrogates for the "special needs" of children, they constructed new consumer subjects based on idealized ways of seeing and positions of experiencing the world; these idealized perspectives transformed "from seeing the world as a mother would to the beginnings of seeing the world through children's eyes" (Cook 2004: 3, 23–26). This pediocular way of seeing enabled the construction of children as consumer subjects independent of parents who may have previously made consumer choices on their behalf. Although Cook tends to focus on pediocularity as a means of generating idealizing forms of consumer subjectivity, I argue that we might productively use it to think about professional subjectivities within industrial work cultures as well, as adults adopt pediocular ways of seeing in their everyday work cultures. Put another way, the power to see through the eyes of a child plays a defining role in the construction of children's media production communities—where pediocular professional subjectivity becomes a meaningful and valuable position to occupy within children's media industries.

At the same time, I recognize that the power of pediocularity is not equally accessible to all within these professional communities, insisting that this process of identity- and community-building overlays institutional structures that produce media workers as gendered, raced, and sexed labor subjects. As demonstrated in the work of Miranda Banks (2009), Erin Hill (2016), Vicki Mayer (2011), and Leslie Salzinger (2003), feminist production studies uncover the ways in which bodies are imagined or empowered to do different kinds of work within media industries, analyzing the instances in which labor and gendered subjectivities intertwine.[6] Such an outlook reveals how the ability of transgenerational professional subjects to claim to see through the eyes of a child depends on their differences as sexed and gendered subjects with different positions of industrial status. As a potential means of claiming authority, knowledge, and prestige in children's media production communities, the identity work of pediocularity operates not only in the boundaries between adulthood and childhood but also within a set of power relations that produces gendered, sexed, raced, and classed workers in unequal ways. Citing the unique contributions of Julie D'Acci (1994, 1997) to media industry research, Banks also highlights the value of feminist textual analysis to production studies, based in its potential to situate media texts within specific social and political contexts, and thereby "better define the industrial struggles" faced by creators (2009: 88). With that in mind, exploration of the transgenerational pediocular subjectivities constructed in television texts like *The Toy Box* provides a useful context for examining how unequally empowered professionals negotiate their position in relation to such constructions in the space of deep industry rituals like the Kidscreen Summit.

"Welcome to the Toy Box"

"Kids!" exclaims Marguerite Spagnuolo, as aspiring toy inventor from Staten Island. "My favorite people!" In the hopes of seeing her toy concept—the

Grandmas2Share doll—acquired and manufactured by industry giant Mattel, Spagnuolo is one of thirty-five contestants appearing on the first season of reality series *The Toy Box* in 2017. Having just entered the eponymous space of the "Toy Box," she finds herself confronted by a panel of children who will ask questions about, play with, and ultimately evaluate the merits of her prototype. The pleasure she performs in meeting these children in the Toy Box set, however, contrasts with her reported reactions in crosscut interview footage: "these kids are holding the key to my success," she narrates. Contestant Rick Aguila shares this assessment in a separate episode. "The tables have flipped here," the inventor of the Party Cannon notes, explaining that as a middle school teacher he typically holds the power to assess the ideas of children. Yet here in the television world of *The Toy Box*, children evaluate the creative efforts of adults and serve as gatekeepers for the culture industries. The pleasures of the series thus turn on the conceit of inverting typical power relationships between children and adults while imagining the knowledge, expertise, and evaluative perspectives of children as productive and even crucial components of real industry decision-making processes.

This pediocular representation of industry processes makes *The Toy Box* a rich site of analysis not just for the growing commercial partnerships between toy and television businesses but also for the construction of transgenerational professional subjectivities that bridge the gaps between the young and the old, the amateur and the professional. In seeking to create crosspromotional value across television and toy industries before its cancellation after two seasons, *The Toy Box* emphasized how that economic project depend on professional boundary crossing between adulthood and childhood. Within that boundary work, claims to authority in and over cultural production turned significantly on the perspectives of children and—crucially—the ability of professionals to adopt those perspectives. In this sense, *The Toy Box* was ultimately a show about the ways in which power in these children's culture industries could be perceived to extend from the management of the boundaries between adults and kids as well as the production of pediocularity at that intersection. At the same time, the series echoed the priorities and preoccupations of the transgenerational media industries explored in previous chapters: on the one hand, its role as a means of attracting family audiences for ABC through this intersection of adult and child subjectivities reflected the co-viewing strategies of chapter 1; on the other, the function of the series as cross-promotion for television and toy businesses links transgenerational strategies and transmedia practices as explored in chapter 2 (and as revisted in chapter 5). In the case of *The Toy Box*, these dynamics produced a transgenerational articulation of adulthood, childhood, and creative labor. While the series presented children as industry workers, adults performed identities that established connections to childhood framed as appropriate to the habitus of creators aspiring to this industry space. Ultimately, *The Toy Box* represented children's culture industries as a space of production defined by confrontation and negotiation of the unequal power relations between adults and kids, producing professional subject positions from transgenerational creative work that could cross those boundaries.

The "aspirational" themes of *The Toy Box* situated the series as part of the ABC network's overall investment in the reality competition genre, and in doing so encouraged viewers to read the narrative as a story about breaking in to a creative industry. Although capturing smaller audiences, *The Toy Box* evoked the same dependable format as ABC programs like *The Bachelor* (2002–), *The Bachelorette* (2003–), *Dancing with the Stars* (2005–), and its reboot of *American Idol* (2018–): participants competed with one another for validation in a competitive neoliberal market that encouraged individuals to become "entrepreneurs of the self" (du Gay 1996: 72, 182; Ouellette and Hay 2008: 103). *The Toy Box* bore closest resemblance to ABC's *Shark Tank* (2009–), in that each aspiring inventor presented an entrepreneurial concept to a panel of business experts. In the first season, competitors subjected their inventions to the judgment not only of kids who held dominion over the Toy Box segments but also adult professionals who evaluated prototypes and served as the preliminary layer of expert gatekeeping in the first half of each episode. These adult experts included creative director for Pixar toys Jen Tan, candy bar creator Dylan Lauren, and professional toy reviewer Jim Silver. For the second season, ABC eliminated this adult layer of review to focus solely on the evaluations of child judges (Stanhope 2017b; "Toy Box: Season 2" 2017). On the series' Facebook page, ABC framed this change as one of handing more power over to children: "Who run [sic] #TheToyBox? KIDS! We're having a lot more fun for Season 2" ("The Toy Box" 2017). This effort to place more focus on kid judges supported the network's wider interest in child-focused reality series, as ABC simultaneously developed a "kid-centered" spin-off of *Dancing with the Stars* (Stanhope 2017a).

The selection of actor Eric Stonestreet—best known for his concurrent role as Cameron on ABC's *Modern Family* (2010–)—as the host of *The Toy Box* further aligned the series' to the network and strengthened the potential for co-viewing pleasures. In speaking lines like "Welcome to the Toy Box!," Stonestreet orients both viewers and contestants to this industry world. Despite the kid-centric nature of *The Toy Box*, Stonestreet frequently flirts and engages in double entendres with adult contestants, inviting comparisons to the flamboyant character he plays on his sitcom. He asks one inventor if she is "double fisting" as she carries her display models, and another if he has small race car prototypes in his pocket or is just "happy to see me." At the same time, Stonestreet remarked in the press how his prior clown training (a talent that informs the "Fizbo" alter-ego of his *Modern Family* character) suited him for engaging the kid judges on *The Toy Box* (Lynch 2017). As a celebrity host, Stonestreet struck a position of transgenerational appeal, shifting between the pediocular and a more mature lewdness.

Yet while the series offered a valuable degree of industrial intertextuality for the ABC network, it was more significant for building strategic partnerships between that television platform and the toy industry. While ABC served as domestic broadcast distributor for the series (with smaller firm Elcctus managing international distribution), *The Toy Box* was the first major television project produced by Mattel Creations, the content arm of the US-based toy manufacturer (in partnership with Hudsun Media, which handled practical production) (Stanhope 2017a). In promising contestants (and viewers) that Mattel would actually put winning toy concepts into production, the series provided the company both an extended marketing opportunity and a means of acquiring new toy concepts and creative talent. On the one hand, *The Toy Box* effectively served as a "program-length commercial"—or perhaps more accurately, a season-length commercial—building up to the announcement and release of a new Mattel toy.[7] On the other hand, the reality competition format of *The Toy Box* afforded Mattel significant research and development labor. Although the winning contestant was promised US$100,000 in exchange for providing Mattel the rights to their toy concept, the Submissions Agreement that casting firm MysticArt Pictures required all aspiring *Toy Box* contestants to sign explained that any concept featured on the television program became Mattel's property to exploit. "By participating in the Program," the contract held, "You grant and agree to grant to Mattel and the Toy Box Entities a perpetual, royalty-free, gratis non-exclusive license to use the Submission in and in connection with the development, production, exhibition, advertising, publicity, promotion marketing, commercial tie-ins, and other exploitation of the Program and/or related to the Program . . ." ("Toy Box 2017" 2017). The nonexclusive nature of this agreement did allow a nonwinning program participant to subsequently market their creation independently (or sell it to another toy manufacturer willing to work without exclusivity). However, Mattel retained perpetual license. This transmedia relationship thus figured the aspiring reality television contestant as an exploitable source of creative labor for the toy industry.

This cross-promotional partnership between television and toy industries extended to the retail sphere as well. Just as the series promised the winning contestant a manufacturing agreement with Mattel at season's end, it also promised that the winning toy would be immediately available at the major US retailer Toys "R" Us (prior, of course, to the chain's 2018 bankruptcy, after which the entire promotional project of the series collapsed). In the first season finale on May 19, 2017, the series' panel of judges selected Ryan Stewart's Artsplash (a device for creating three-dimensional liquid art) as the winning toy; by store opening the next day, shoppers could find Artsplash stocked exclusively at their local Toys "R" Us.[8] In the gap between production of the series and its distribution on ABC, Mattel manufactured the toy product and distributed it to its retail partner. These retail dimensions made the reality competition series a source of marketing and promotion not just for Mattel's product but for Toys "R" Us as well. Subscribers to the marketing email lists at ToysRUs.com, for example, received weekly reminders to watch the television series in anticipation of the experience of buying the winning toy in stores after the season finale. In fact, these emails encouraged readers to reserve the winning toy in advance in order "to be part of this moment in toy history!" Other weekly emails from ToysRUs.com encouraged customers to enter a contest to win a trip to Los Angeles to meet the winning contestant and receive a tour of Mattel headquarters. Throughout, retail space served as a means of inviting consumers into a fantasy about labor that bridged the toy and television industries, with Toys "R" Us providing both the weekly reminder to watch the series and exclusive access to a product generated in the industry world represented through reality competition.

Considered as a television series alone, *The Toy Box* seems fairly insignificant by comparison. Industry reports suggested it was "quietly renewed" for its second season in 2017, without any fanfare or special attention. Nielsen ratings reported a draw of only 2.4 million viewers total for the first season finale—a respectable but unremarkable performance (Hipes 2017). Nevertheless, the industrial significance of the series ultimately rests beyond its status as a television series in its attempts to forge development and marketing partnerships across the commercial worlds of television and toys. At launch, industry analysts did not ask whether *The Toy Box* would simply serve the network television business, but instead questioned, "Can the show energize 2 different industries?" (Lynch 2017). The May 19 press release that announced Artsplash as the winning concept thus explicitly highlighted this result as the culmination of the partnership between Mattel, Toys "R" Us, and ABC ("Artsplash" 2017). Yet the significance of *The Toy Box* goes beyond the season-long making and marketing of new toy product via television; the series' reality competition format also rendered the labor of the toy industry meaningfully visible. Through television, the work adults do to make toys for children became culturally legible—and with it, the work of creating, negotiating, and transgressing boundaries of adulthood and childhood, amateurism and professionalism. While *The Toy Box* turned on the strategic crossing of industry boundaries, its reality competition also thrived on the crossing of these identity boundaries.

The ongoing development and refinement of *The Toy Box* format suggested that producers and marketers saw the spectacle of giving precocious children power over adults' professional fortunes to be the primary narrative appeal. Promotional updates on the series' Facebook page, for example, consistently focused on the panel of kids judges to emphasize how "These kids are in the driver's seat when it comes to their toys" and how "Kids are taking control of their toys." Matched to this emphasis on the control the series afforded child judges over toys was a focus on the power kids held over adults working in that creative space. "If you want to see children crush the dreams of adults . . . ," one update read, "#TheToyBox is new at Friday 8/7c on ABC" ("The Toy Box" Facebook 2017). The power that the series promised to give to its child participants was thus an industrial power over adults, determining who would and would not be allowed to move from the sphere of reality television competition to participate in creative and professional work relations with Mattel. In this way, the series positioned children as cultural gatekeepers with the power to determine which adults might cross from amateurism into creative industry professionalism. With that power, kids became the arbiters of adults' professional dreams—a pediocular theme that recurred throughout the first season. Positioning the child judges as key participants in the toy industry, while also arbitrating the worthiness—or lack thereof—of adult contestants to be professional creators in that kid-centric space, this television series rendered the creative work of toy making as a transgenerational enterprise, where the aspirational narratives of achieving professional success undermined adulthood and childhood as stable, discrete categories.

The Toy Box used the power of television to afford new visibility to the toy manufacturing industry, offering representations that made that business meaningful to viewers in new ways. Marketing analyst Jason Lynch noted in 2017 that some toy professionals envisioned the series as an opportunity to bring greater notoriety to the industry: "Toy experts applaud the new spotlight the show will put on the toy industry, which operates largely anonymously." The series centered the Mattel brand in that industry spotlight, presenting it as an object of desire for contestants who sought to win a contract with the company, while asserting the company's legacy and authority in the marketplace. However, beyond this corporate focus, the series shone its spotlight on ground-level creative labor, telling stories about aspiring toy designers, their perspectives, and their potential agency within that industry. One consultant interviewed by Lynch compared the toy industry negatively to other creative industries at the level of authorship: unlike literature or songwriting, "very rarely do you know the names of people who invented some of the most important games and toys we have." The reality competition of *The Toy Box* promised to correct that absence, where now "you're going to care about the person who created the product" (Lynch 2017). While *The Toy Box* positioned toy designers as potential authors, its simultaneous emphasis on the work of product evaluation and gatekeeping invited recognition of managerial labor as a crucial and compelling point of identification too.

The series framed the creative labor of the toy industry not only in terms of adult designers but also in terms of a pediocular arbitration and legitimation of that creative work. While the toy industry of course relies upon children as market research subjects and toy testers—as will be discussed in chapter 5—*The Toy Box* both represented this kid feedback as a novelty and repositioned children in the evaluative role of executive authority. To be clear: *The Toy Box* did not reveal the toy industry as it actually functioned but instead reframed that industry within the aspirational narratives of a reality competition series; as such, it performed the the cultural work of positioning of children as central participants in the labor relations of a creative industry. Following news of the series' development, *Variety* noted, "What better way to test a product's worth than by having the end user be the arbiters?" (Schwindt 2016). Similarly, Mattel's chief content officer Catherine Balsam-Schwaber claimed that being "able to see our business from a kid's perspective is a great opportunity" (Lynch 2017). What *The Toy Box* added to basic market research—through its fantastical emphasis on the literal power of kid evaluators over adult participants—was a meaningful, pediocular framework for reading the industry as one in tune with and governed by the perspectives of children.

Indeed the child judges embodied something more than typical market research subjects, as all were aspiring child actors (with prior professional credits) who in this instance played the role of everyday children playing professionals. Within this framework, the child judges overtly embodied the executive and managerial forces driving the industry. While each judge benefited from the adorable cuteness of childhood, reality television conventions positioned them as titans of industry inhabiting markedly adult modes of professionalism and status. In the episode that introduced each judge in the first season, Aalyrah is shown in line at a coffee shop alongside busy businesspeople, presumed peers from whom she is only differentiated by her choice of hot chocolate instead of a latte. The same episode shows judge Sophia Grace stepping out of a limousine, right behind a woman framed from the waist down in glamorous high heels and skirt; this almost sexualized juxtaposition lends the child adult power and status by association. The dialogue used to establish each judge's character similarly establishes them as forces of industry power and professionalism. A third judge, Toby, shares that he wants "to give constructive criticism when I crush someone's dream," while Sophia Grace claims to be "the serious judge. Like, I don't mess around." The series thus presents its child judges not as end users but as tough professionals with a knowledge and expertise that puts them at the top of the industry hierarchy (despite, of course, the lack of child executives in any creative industry in the real world).

Most exemplary of this pediocular narrative strategy is seven-year-old judge Noah, who is consistently costumed in ties and blazers to affect an adult executive habitus (fig. 3.1). In the introductory episode, he is shown in a barber's chair, asking for only "a little off the top." His precociousness extends to a claim of expertise in the field, where "I know toys like the back of my hand, just like I know where I got this scar: treadmill accident." Like all of the judges, Noah was previously a child actor, with prior appearances on *The Ellen DeGeneres Show* (2003–). Here he performs a role defined by markers of adulthood and professionalism, inviting us to imagine him squeezing some exercise into a busy work schedule. His precocity extends to popular culture references too adult for his age, including his quote from *Scarface* while testing a projectile parachute toy in a later episode: "say hello to my little friend!" When Eric Stonestreet remarks "that's a highly inappropriate movie for children!," the transgression of childhood boundaries nevertheless reinforces Noah's belonging in the adult space of the toy industry. Notably, of the four original judges, Noah was the only one contracted to return in the second season, suggesting that his brand of executive performativity fit best with the ongoing vision for the series.

At the same time, Noah's performance can be read as a parody of this adult executive habitus. His frequent combination of nonsensical remarks, strong claims to expertise, and combative attitude highlight the possibility that those in positions of industry authority may lack the knowledge they claim in arbitrating (often cruelly) the creative labor of others. Noah translates his experience building forts out of pillows and blankets, for example, to a claim that he had a prior career as an architect. In response to a line of multicultural dolls with specialized hair brushes, Noah remarks, "that will be really good for kids that live in the world of disco!" and refuses to pronounce

Figure 3.1. On *The Toy Box*, kid judge Noah offers a parodic embodiment of adult executive habitus, emphasized by his costuming, props, and gestures. (Screen capture.)

the doll's non-Western name, Niya, correctly ("Potato, Potato" he offers when corrected). In a later episode, he fashions a crude implement out of the prototype for construction toy TubeLox and asks his fellow judges, "who needs a back massage?," to which a justifiably creeped out Sophia Grace responds, "um, not me." While embodying a pediocular executive power, Noah also allows executive authority to be read in relation to childishness and hints at the white, male privilege behind his make-believe performances of industry power. Whether such a critical parody of industry hierarchies was intended, *The Toy Box* deployed Noah and the other judges to refigure the industrial roles played by children, elevating kids' perspectives to the adult, executive level rather than that of the end user. In this way, childhood was articulated to adult professionalism.

Meanwhile the performances of program contestants blurred categories of age and generation in other ways, defining their status as aspiring creative industry professionals in relation to the nostalgic ideologies of childhood dreams, parental identities defined in relation to childhood, and the transgression of adult boundaries. Showrunner Susan House credited the series' ability to frame adults' professional creative ambitions in relation to childhood aims as a means of providing broad co-viewing appeal across generational lines: "It's celebrating invention, creativity, childhood and nostalgia," she explained, "and everyone can relate to that" (Lynch 2017). More subtly, however, the series related successful creative invention to creators' greater subjective proximity to childhood. By far the most common narrative framework imposed on contestants during the course of the first season was one that positioned their work as a culmination of childhood desires. Party Cannon inventor Rick Aguila, in the first episode, describes his aim of working with Mattel as something that would "fulfill a childhood dream." So too does contestant Padmini Sriman stress that "signing a deal with Mattel would be a dream come true." This recurring theme extended to the conclusion of the first season, with the press release framing Ryan Stewart's victory as a function of childhood desires come to fruition: "Ever since I was young, inventing was my dream and I created Artsplash to give kids a new way to create their own masterpieces. . . . To be able see something [sic] I created on-shelf at Toys "R" Us is a childhood dream come true" ("Artsplash" 2017). Significantly, the transmedia industry partnerships driven by the series accrued meaning through the destabilization of distinctions between professionally validated adult creativity and childhood imagination.

At the same time, inventors on the series personalize their creative labor by situating it within the bounds of family and child-rearing. Frequently, toymakers present themselves as parents; in the first aired episode, all five featured contestants situate their creative labor as an extension of relationships with their kids. Rick Aguila describes his Party Cannon as both a means to "provide a better quality of life" for his family and a desire to make them proud of him. The package for Greg Spigel, inventor of the Snap N Roll car, shows him with his family—his "ultimate priority"—and stresses how, after marrying his childhood sweetheart, he now wants to share "the American Dream of inventing" with that family. Rachel and Steve McMurtney, designers of TubeLox, similarly share their story of adopting two children after having difficulty conceiving, crediting those sons as "the driving motivation for what we do." Attempts to establish professional credibility through proximity to children manifest once more when Rachel offers that their home state, Utah, has the most children per capita in the United States. Interestingly, this connection between creative labor and child-rearing frequently involves both the possibilities of risk to children and collaboration with them. The producers and editors of the series foreground stories about pulling kids out of school, investing money otherwise earmarked for college savings, and losing valuable time with children to the inventing process. At the same time, contestant Troy Orsburne notes in his episode that his appearance is a "big moment" for his family because the concept is one "I came up with with my children." As presented in the series, such an inventor-child dynamic could indeed often compensate for other missing markers of creative professionalism. In the fourth episode, Larry and Steven Huetteman present their concept for Chromotag without any polish or style, embodying amateur ordinariness in their plain white tees and khakis. Yet the presentation of the Huettemans as a father-son team throughout the episode helps to justify the selection of Chromotag at the end of the episode over competing concepts that equally excited the judges. United as father and son, the Huettemans occupy a transgenerational habitus that other contestants (like their opponent, the fresh-out-of-college inventor of Parashoot) do not.

Within this transgenerational crossing of boundaries, some contestants perform an explicitly pediocular childishness of their own. After receiving feedback from the industry mentors, one toymaker in the first episode remarks, "that was so much fun." Later on, when meeting the kid judges in the Toy Box, another behaves exuberantly, describing herself as "so excited." And when his AryaBall ultimately wins the approval of the judges to return in the finale and be considered for the grand prize, Babak Forutanpour gushes that "you guys have given me the best birthday present!" These aspiring professionals frequently surrender adult composure and decorum, allowing a childlike enthusiasm and energy to bubble to the surface in contrast to the industrial authority of the judges. Many other contestants willfully adopt the playfulness of children when demonstrating their prototypes, as when the inventors of the Piñata Backpack wear the product themselves, and in doing so present themselves as potential users of the toy. While Melissa Rivera, inventor of the LightBox Terrier, does not claim parental identity or any other connections to children or child-rearing, her success in the fourth-aired episode results from her "cool" factor and her ability to impress the judges with her seemingly more authentic proximity to youthful hipness. Admiring Rivera's spiky hair and orange pants, Sophia Grace asks her, "are you really as cool as you look on the outside?"

Notably, the series also disciplines participants who do not occupy this transgenerational way of being. In the fourth episode, a Sacramento inventor describes himself as a genius, but one who works without any participation and appreciation from his children. "I just do this for myself," he explains. The industry mentors quickly dismiss his Walking Dinosaur before it can face the kid judges, citing the inventor's inability to talk about manufacturing costs and his undeveloped business plan. Exposure of his technical amateurism follows his failure to work across the boundaries of adulthood and childhood. Similarly, Michelle Gorman, inventor of the Butterfly Book, fails because of her seeming inability to inhabit an appropriate habitus. The episode presents her as suspect from the start; as she walks on to the set, she seems to flirt with Eric Stonestreet, who responds with discomfort (despite his own flirtatiousness in other instances). Her interaction with the industry mentors is more explosive; she blows up at them for offering constructive criticism: "I can't fight anymore! I don't have any fight in me. I'm a fifty-year-old mother! I don't need any—I don't need this!" While her dialogue emphasizes her parental status, she comes across as a "bad," out-of-control mom. She insists that her Butterfly Book is something "some super cute mom" will want for her baby, but the emphasis placed on her tirade suggests that she is not that super cute mom or otherwise a good surrogate for parent consumers and their children. She too is quickly dismissed, unable to operate in the overlapping space of childhood and adulthood to which the series articulates toy industry professionalism. Outside that transgenerational space of creativity constructed at the convergence of reality television and toy manufacturing cultures, she remains an amateur.

In the end, *The Toy Box* was a reality series that turned on the troubling of boundaries. On the one hand, the industry strategies driving the series generated partnerships across television distribution, toy manufacturing, and retail marketing. The series carved out a cross-promotional relationship between ABC, Mattel, and Toys "R" Us in which television content could be merchandised as new product hyped through a season-long build-up. On the other hand, in rendering the creative labor behind that product more meaningful and visible, *The Toy Box* told a story about a professional world in which power derived from the ability to destabilize notions of adulthood and childhood and then work in that intersection. While kid judges on the series performed, and even critiqued, an executive managerial agency that inverted typical power relationships between adulthood and childhood, the presentation of contestants often ascribed creative authority and acumen within a pediocular relationship to the dreams, identities, and relationships of childhood and child-rearing. *The Toy Box* established a transmedia marketing strategy between industries and then rendered creative labor relations meaningful by articulating professional status and authority to the transgenerational. Of course, this was all reality television and no indication of how the toy industry actually worked. Yet as a reality competition television series, *The Toy Box* marketed not only products but also perceptions of industrial value and authority. By triangulating this representation of pediocular industry cultures with the off-screen trade rituals in which professionals navigate their autonomy and authority, this chapter next examines how the production of transgenerational professional subjects depends upon, intersects, and reinforces the power relations of gender and sexuality within those industry cultures.

Behind the Scenes at Kidscreen

While the narrative pleasures of *The Toy Box* rest significantly in the voices of children, that population remains almost entirely absent from the ritual spaces of semi-embedded trade events like the Kidscreen Summit. Given the specialness and difference ascribed to kids' media industries, and the role of the audience in defining that separate community space, one might expect the trade ritual of Kidscreen to ooze with the trappings of childhood. As I let my imagination run wild prior to arriving at the 2014 event, I considered whether I might encounter hundreds of adult professionals indulging in the pleasures of childhood experience and media culture. I imagined that a space defined by service to childhood would be ruled by an ethos of fun and even perhaps opposition to the business cultures of traditional entertainment industries. Yet any such expectations proved more of a kind with the popular fantasy offered by *The Toy Box*. Instead of a pajama party, my arrival at the Hilton conference center in New York City revealed a scene typical to any trade (media or otherwise). As I surveyed the exhibition space, I saw a sea of neutrally dressed business people, pairing jeans with sport coats, checked shirts, and sweaters. While the room may have been adorned with large posters promoting various studios' animated television offerings, and our lanyards all featured the image of Peppa Pig, the people themselves seemed virtually indistinguishable from academic conference attendees. These were media workers doing everything they could to present themselves as adult professionals. As part of my registration fee, I was entitled to attend one Master Class, and this too was a fairly straightforward and conservative instruction on how to build brands through proper market fit and systematic attention to "brand codes" that enable the process of brand discovery, strategy, execution, and success. Very little resisted the decorum of adult professionalism and corporatism.

Most of the energy in this space seemed devoted to the process of pitching potential ideas for kids' television and toy concepts, with the geography of the space designed to organize interactions among buyers and sellers. While I was generally free to roam around the event space, I soon encountered more carefully guarded areas of exclusivity, where major program buyers occupied reserved tables to hear pitches and aspiring program creators who opted to participate in the summit's "speed pitching" program shared their ideas behind curtains. While these pitches ran in the background, expert speakers in meeting rooms also led panels and workshops designed to help those making the pitches to better reach their goals. Usually, these expert speakers were executives in a position to buy or otherwise speak with authority about what program distributors wanted. For example, a series of sessions called "30 Minutes with . . ." allowed executives from Nickelodeon, PBS, and other major kids' programming outlets to offer their wish lists to the eager ears of prospective sellers. These conversations allowed executives to relay information and communicate their beliefs while keeping lines of hierarchy, authority, and distance between buyer and supplier intact. These sessions also modeled ideal relationships between buyers and suppliers, with Adina Pitt, Cartoon Network vice president for content development and production, suggesting that, for the program creator, the network "should be your therapist." Undoubtedly, these panels crystallized and circulated industry lore about how hierarchical production communities could best operate. At the entrance to the exhibitor's room, and presumably on many attendees' smart phones, a flat-screen television displaying the #kss14 Twitter feed showed that commonsense lore forming in real time, as attendees recirculated comments from recognized experts throughout the conference. Perhaps making the seriousness of this affair most clear was the presence of what Caldwell (2013) calls para-industry—shadow economies designed to support the needs of workers struggling to succeed in competitive labor markets. While conference admission itself cost the typical attendee almost US$2,000, I met several attendees who, as clients of SellYourTVConceptNow.com, had paid an additional $5,000 to gain the mentorship of experienced producers and on-site support in pitching ideas to buyers. This was serious business, with very real stakes to the participants.

As childhood figured into this space, therefore, it was primarily as a discursive object of knowledge over which members of the community claimed to have varying levels of expertise. During several days at the conference, I heard countless claims about children made by professionals enabled to speak authoritatively by their place in the official program. Much of this dialogue centered on contested notions of what kids' want from programming amid ongoing social and technological shifts. For example, Pitt claimed that kids want "wish fulfillment" and the ability to laugh with identifiable, aspirational characters. Meanwhile, Lauren DeVillier, vice president of digital media for Disney, claimed that immersion and interaction with characters was key to engaging kids. James Stephenson, senior vice president of content development at Nickelodeon, countered that kids want characters with whom they feel they can hang out. Claims about children also contrasted their needs and desires to that of adults: Nickelodeon content president Russell Hicks held that kids were embodied consumers who move differently than adults, unable to resist grooving to the music of animated series like *Breadwinners* and willing to explore in more uninhibited ways when exposed to VR technology. Much of the knowledge claims made about children further distinguished "post-millennials" as an emerging generational market category. In a session called "Meet the Post-Millennials," Jane Gould and Erin Miller of Nickelodeon Consumer Insights characterized this generation as a cohort of "nice," over-protected rule followers, whose exposure to "Velcro" parenting styles made them fluent in "grown-up" but also emotionally inhibited and immature. Yet, as social media "savants," this new generation used media technology in more sophisticated ways, abandoning traditional television for Netflix, consuming content at a record rate, and more focused on brands than on differences between media platforms.

Particularly significant in this expert discourse on childhood were claims made about gender roles—both for children and their parents. Daphne Lemish (2010) has studied in detail the beliefs and dispositions toward gender and sexuality in the children's media industries, and here, too, conservative gender binaries common to corporate children's media remained strongly in play. Representing Disney, Lauren DeVillier argued that the way to reach kids most effectively was actually by using social media to talk to their mothers. A Sprout executive echoed this claim, suggesting that while his programming appealed 100 percent to kids, he knew it really served parents as an "ally" before bedtime. Tracy Paige Johnson of Yummiloo also identified as a parental "ally," while Nickelodeon's Gould and Miller identified the contemporary mom as the "CEO of the house" whom kids' television services ignored at their peril. Thus parents, and often mothers more specifically, loomed as the real target of the kids' media industry marketing apparatus due to their gendered caregiving roles. Meanwhile the expertise of official program presenters reinforced the idea of essential gender differences between girls and boys. At a mentor meeting on the subject of toy television licensing deals, one executive promised that four-year-olds have no interest in gender-neutral play patterns, having already had to pick "are you a boy or a girl?" Elsewhere, Cartoon Network's Pitt baldly claimed that girls simply don't have as much interest in watching cartoons. Dreamworks head of television Marjorie Cohn stated these differences as a universal, unchangeable binary between "farts and friendship," with girls loving princesses and boys preferring action.

Together these examples reveal Kidscreen as a space dominated by performances of expertise about childhood: performances that underwrote the authority of buyers who had the power to decide what projects would and would not survive. More broadly, however, this litany of claims about children, the ways they consume media, and changes in those dynamics also produced a collective sense of knowledge about an audience excluded by age from this industry community. Pronouncements about children affirmed that industry leaders indeed possessed the perspective necessary to develop new strategies and manage the challenges of a digitized post-network era in which elusive kids became harder to attract to traditional television and toy products. In fact, a keynote speech by noted anthropologist Grant McCracken worked less to disseminate academic expertise to industry and more to affirm the existing everyday knowledges of producers.[9] McCracken characterized media scholars as dour Frankfurt School critics who had been proven "wrong." Instead, "you're experts," McCracken told his audience, affirming their status as knowers of children and their relationship to media culture. Despite or perhaps because of this flattery, McCracken's claims later became points for industry leaders to offer their own expert perspectives by contrast. Taking issue with McCracken's idea that television "got better" through greater narrative complexity, Nick Jr.'s Kay Wilson Stalling took a moment in her "30 Minutes with . . ." session immediately following the keynote to counter that people pitching concepts should actually beware of things "too sophisticated" for the kid audience. Pitt and Marjorie Cohn of Dreamworks too positioned themselves against this notion of complexity, claiming expertise and experience that trumped those of an academic keynote speaker. Thus, in the space of the summit, the notion of a new, changing generation of kid consumers provided a powerful framework for generating industry lore about the economic shifts of the post-network era while also affirming the expertise and status of those in positions of leadership. This dynamic located expertise more in some professional subject positions and perspectives than others, however—in buyers, not sellers; practitioners, not academic researchers.

Yet this professional authority and expertise about children also proved contested as other participants sought their own status and capital in this trade ritual space. For example, during a workshop on pitching television concepts to toy manufacturers who might help fund production, Jennifer Bennett, the Fisher Price licensing acquisitions executive leading the session, found the room over capacity. Without solicitation, one eager participant volunteered to solve the leader/learner ratio problem by stepping in to share Bennett's "mentorship" role, transforming herself from panel attendee into a coleading expert. Both of them, however, established expertise by circulating similar industry lore about gender binaries. Participants seeking to succeed in both the television and toy industries were advised to push against gender stereotypes "at your own peril," with the suggestion that only a nonprofit without commercial obligation would have the liberty to fight against static gender experiences and expressions. Both seemed to agree that if you give a boy a stick, he would fight with it, whereas a girl would turn it into a doll. Professional expertise and mentor status cohered here in upholding and speaking through industry lore.

Yet the Kidscreen Summit was also a place in which industry lore could be challenged and competing forms of expert knowledge constructed. To disrupt established lines of ideological power, professionals had to demonstrate greater understanding and proximity to childhood than those who upheld the lore. In one particularly interesting moment, that claim to greater knowledge of childhood unfolded through the mobilization and management of children themselves within the ritual space. After everything I had heard at the Fisher Price session on the first day of the summit, I was truly dreading the presentation on "Boys vs. Girls: Really Understanding the Gender Divide" by Sarah Chumsky and Stacey Matthias of the Insight Strategy Group, fearing more binary-driven industry lore. Instead the session mounted a surprising challenge to that received knowledge, positioning its strategy consultants as endowed with pediocular knowledge beyond that of network and toy executives. Chumsky and Matthias countered that culture, not biology, pressures kids to adopt strict gender roles; rather than being natural phenomena, the gender binaries undergirding industry logic were "our fault," referring to the marketing efforts of the culture industries themselves. The discourses about gender circulating elsewhere at the summit made these claims anything but uncontroversial. The presence of Chumsky and Matthias on the official program granted their competing knowledge some official sanction—yet as strategists who would most typically work as third-party consultants in support of client projects, their expertise may seem more advisory than grounded in the experience and decision-making power of a Nickelodeon or Disney executive. To put more power behind their counterclaims about the audience, Chumsky and Matthias marched about a half-dozen kids onstage to share their feelings about gender and the media.

Each child brought with them some object of meaning to them, such as a LEGO creation or a *Frozen* Elsa figure with which they could talk about their media experiences, the pressures to conform to gender, and often their own resistance to that conformity. Chumsky and Matthias asked each child about their chosen objects to highlight common threads and interests shared among boys and girls. While the children onstage were particularly passionate, this was clearly a constructed conversation, in that the kids had been prepped or even coached beforehand, with the moderators prompting them to restate what was said "when we were talking before." However, it matters less that these concepts may or may not have emerged independently from the children themselves and more that they were deployed by the consultants through the managed voices of kids. Of all the supposed professional experts in the room, Chumsky and Matthias were the only ones whose knowledge about children was directly, immediately authorized by the reported experiences of actual, embodied children. Otherwise absent from the adult-only community of professionals, children helped—even as props—to extend authority and legitimacy to ideas that pushed hard against industry lore. These consultants mobilized the very audience materially excluded but discursively omnipresent in this work world, defying industry lore by demonstrating closer proximity to this audience and their way of seeing.

Given the advantages of such proximity to the audience, one might still anticipate the Kidscreen space to have been more significantly marked by explicitly pediocular performances of affinity to childhood identities, with many professionals laying claim to the same Peter Pan syndrome that Julie Chen once saw in Kevin Clash. However, in my three days at Kidscreen, I only viewed such professional performances of and direct identification with "kidness" on a handful occasions. Yet each revealed potentially different modes of access with which participants in these industry rituals could claim proximity to childhood.

The most obvious instance of an adult participant at Kidscreen claiming kid identity came in the form of a children's entertainer who hoped to attract attention (and a production deal) by attending the event in his character's brightly colored and rather childish-looking costume. Just as significant as the entertainer's flamboyant performance itself were attempts by others within the larger industrial community to discipline it. Cartoon Network executive Adina Pitt singled him out in her session for failing to abide by community norms. Pitt implored potential producers to keep "sell sheets" and complex calling cards to themselves and, pointing out the garish attire worn by this individual, profiled him as someone who would probably engage in such a gauche approach. "Don't," she commanded. As it turned out, this individual did indeed have a detailed portfolio of his creative accomplishments and satisfied parent testimonials to share, a copy of which he was happy to give to me—rather than saving it for industry executives—once the document had been marked as outside the norms of pitch etiquette. This individual was by no means the only person to come prepared with swag and other self-promotional gimmicks; but his outlandish and childish appearance relative to other participants crossed a line that subjected these practices to greater disciplinary sanction. In fully embracing a pediocular identity, this industry aspirant saw his status as an adult professional questioned and subjected to community evaluation. His childlike identity as an aspiring professional opened him to being disciplined like a child. Disappointed, he shared with me that he would have expected a kids' media conference to be less "corporate"—but being a part of this corporate work ritual meant maintaining some distance from childhood even as expertise might be claimed through it. Going "full kid" was not a strategy by which aspiring community members might establish professional identity and expertise to get a foot in the door.

For others, however, performative embrace of professional pediocularity proved more successful. At a small group mentorship lunch, I met a programming executive from one of the major US children's cable channels who described himself with the summation: "I am a nine-year-old." Like the brightly costumed individual discussed previously, this executive exceeded the boundaries of the staid, professional dress dominating this industry space. Both his earring stud and his glasses were emblazoned with recognizable kids' media brands, and he seemed eager to show his lunch group the 1980s children's animation wallpaper on his cell phone. That cell phone's protective case also literally turned the business communication device into a plaything upon which LEGO blocks could be attached. Yet these accoutrements accessorized a smart blazer and jeans combo, integrating his distinctive style within an executive-identified middle ground in contrast to a bright character costume. Furthermore, unlike the fully costumed aspirant, this executive already sat in a position of power and authority that granted him more uncontested access to this pediocular subjectivity. Throughout the lunch, the executive emphasized his "geek" identity through personal fan investment in the 1980s and 1990s toy properties that broadcast and cable outlets sought to bring back to television as part of the transgenerational programming strategies discussed in chapter 1. "No one would make a better *He-Man* [series] than me," he promised. Identifying nostalgically as both fan and child, he positioned himself as part of the audience unrepresented in this ritual industry space in order to claim superlative expertise about that audience. Denying his adulthood, he built his professional identity out of an alternative allegiance to childhood.

Whether securing status and capital within the community or not, these pediocular performances of professionalism closely embodied much of the lore circulating at the summit. During a lunch break, one award-winning BBC producer explained to me that to be successful in the business, one had to either have kids or have another way to get to know kids in order to get a sense for an audience absent in the adult and industrial world. At a panel on "Cultivating Creative Communities," Nina Hahn, senior vice president of international production and development for Nickelodeon, equally stressed the need to "think like a nine-year-old." Marc Goodchild, a technology development executive and consultant, similarly opined in his talk that beyond having good stories to tell, producers must be obsessed with understanding what is happening in the heads of seven-year-olds. Curtis Lelash, vice president of comedy animation at Cartoon Network, emphasized that the greatest challenge in hearing pitches came in finding people who actually want to write for the six- to eleven-year-old audience, connecting with them without under/over estimating them. His panel on "Comedy: The Kings of Kids TV" even ended with all the panelists sharing jokes supposedly written by "real" kids; much like Chumsky and Matthias's panel on gender, these producers proved their expertise as kids' comedy writers by channeling the voices of that audience. In this context, the cable executive's claim to a nine-year-old identity appears fairly strategic, playing directly into industry lore about the need to connect with and represent the external audience and its tastes. However, that affinity may also have served as compensation for another form of lived identity and executive expertise he lacked. While he described himself as a nine-year-old, he described his colleagues by contrast as *parents* of nine-year-olds. Lacking the same access to children in his own everyday life—a factor Zafirau (2009) reveals as empowering executives' claims to knowledge about changing audiences and generational shifts—this executive very likely required an identity other than parenthood to grant him credibility and access to childhood.

More commonly, then, parental identity enabled both access to the audience and a professionalized authority over it during this trade ritual. Larry Seidman of Dimension Branding Group did not just position himself as a parent but also figured the entire business of branding children's media as a parenting process. In his Master Class, he articulated a theory of "brand parenting" and argued that successful brand managers must act as parents for the media properties under their care. Brands are "much like children," Seidman explained, in the way that they are "sponges for content, images, and feelings." Within this framework, brand managers must act as parents to "embrace uniqueness, provide solid foundation, be protective, be responsive, be consistent, and accept risk" for their brand children. Even the basic act of devising a name for one's brand takes on the significant parental parallels of naming a new baby. Brand managers should develop a "parenting style" that is not "too indulgent" or "neglectful," but instead establishes "boundaries" while accepting "the realities of your brand" in order to "love them for who they are" (Seidman 2014).

I do not wish to suggest, however, that parental identity granted producers inherently greater advantage in constructing professional identities in kids' media production, particularly as a relatively larger number of women work in children's programming, and these parental identities thus manifested as professional subjectivities through the complex and ambivalent gendered figure of the mom. It does not appear coincidental that the producers who sought to adopt overtly childish pediocular professional identities appeared to be men; given the sexism that persists in corporate spaces, many professional women might fear not being taken seriously were they to act as childish (and indeed this is no surefire tactic for men either, given the potential invitation to being disciplined as a child). Despite the relatively larger number of women in powerful decision-making capacities in this industry sector, pediocularity appeared in the ritual space of Kidscreen to be the privilege of an already authorized professional man-child.

However, the figure of the industry mom carved out another kind of transgenerational professional subjectivity by which women could claim industry authority through association with childhood and children. Joan Lambur, a production executive for Breakthrough Entertainment, positioned herself in her panel discussion not as a child, and not as a mother of children, but as a mother to those beneath her in the industry hierarchy. Describing the protective stance she takes toward the "vulnerable" creative practitioners that she works with, she claimed "I'm almost like their mom." She also used that metaphor of being "very motherly, really" to establish her place at the top of the production hierarchy, explaining that it was her role to step in and intervene in the work of her dependent creative personnel "if I see them behaving." Similar identities beyond motherhood enabled female professionals in the kids' media space to adopt the role of the industrial caregiver. As part of "The Big Pitch"—a ritualized pitching competition at the end of the summit in which two producers vied to win the approval of a panel of expert judges—one team of hopefuls shared a video presentation in which the producer's spoken claims to experience as a performer and "freelance mentor" is humorously decoded as "babysitter" by onscreen text chyrons. Echoing the competition format through which reality programs like *The Toy Box* construct industry authority, the Big Pitch centered competition over pediocular identity within trade show ritual. Here a connection to children and caregiver authority over them underwrote creative identity. Beyond the mom or babysitter figure, Adina Pitt similarly played with the identity of teacher to effect authority over both children and those attending her panel. "I used to be a teacher," she explained, implying expert knowledge of children before extending that authority to command the event participants: "I'm giving *you* homework."

Whether mother, teacher, or babysitter, women in this space constructed professional identities by staking out proximity to children, but in positions of authority over them that affirmed potential for industrial power too. They spoke not as children but as *managers of kids* who might make good managers of kids' media industries. Few if any men I encountered made the same kinds of claims about their roles as fathers, suggesting a somewhat less pressing need to establish authority (or, at least, a need that manifested differently). Some men did seem more comfortable taking on identities of childhood more directly, with mixed results discussed above. As much as these dynamics reveal male and executive privilege in this industry space—where a male cable executive can speak directly as a child, while female consultants must get real children to voice their claims—it is not as simple a question as what positions men can adopt in relation to kids that women cannot. Heteronormative reproductive ideals articulated to parenthood gave some adult professionals a sturdier platform with which to legitimize their claims to knowledge of childhood, whereas other kids' media producers—men, women, or trans, who might be single, queer, or otherwise outside of the realm of child-rearing—may have needed to do extra work to position themselves and their expertise within this ritual space.

Ultimately, the 2014 Kidscreen Summit was an industry ritual that negotiated the contradictions between the imagined, idealized world of childhood and the professional, industrialized world of the kids' media business, with participants trying to build professional identities and expertise in the space between. The awards ceremony held on the final full day of the event revealed those tensions, with comedian Sean Cullen gently mocking the contradictions between the consumer and producer identities in play. "How could you not have a good time?" he joked of the event. "It's for the kids! It's for the screen! It's for the money!" Cullen became dark and aggressive in opposition to the sweet earnestness with which he otherwise cast the world of children's television, telling one audience member, "you have a fresh face . . . that I want to destroy." Similarly, after making a joke about the award nomination committee having been killed, he admitted that the joke "was kind of gruesome for children's TV. . . . If anyone shows any fun in their heart, they will be killed. That's children's television. . . . Trying to make it fun. And a little creepy. That's what Kidscreen is all about." Despite the jumbled delivery, the point seemed clear: as a spectator from the outside of the community, Cullen adopted a more "adult" countenance to reinforce by opposition a child-identified sense of community. In this way, the Kidscreen Awards show recognized not only what was valued in the community but also the disjunctures between that community and other arenas of professional entertainment work. This ceremony was therefore a microcosm of the Kidscreen Summit itself—a space of construction and contestation for the identities of industrial professionals and their proximity to an imagined audience of kids outside of that work world.

Conclusion

In part, this fieldwork confirms the somewhat obvious—that media producers, regardless of the specific consumer market they serve, have a vested interest in constructing professional identities based in knowledge of their audiences. However, what remains unique and significant here is the specific tension between adulthood and childhood in this professional identity work, both as represented in popular television texts like *The Toy Box* and as experienced in semi-embedded trade rituals like the Kidscreen Summit. The negotiation and embrace of identities related to childhood (and parenthood) in these spaces helps us to see the meanings and values that shape this industry culture, the performances in which professionals engage, and the way knowledge is constructed in that work world. In other words, the ideas, meanings, and values of childhood have power over culture industries as well as the labor of adult professionals working within them. Furthermore, beyond the discourses of childhood circulating in industry rituals or performances of identity in relation to childhood, this analysis of how producers strike pediocular poses opens up a space to consider the material role of actual children in industry cultures—as will be explored later in chapter 5. Childhood is a powerful discourse within industry, but as Chumsky and Matthias's panel on gender norms suggested, or the antics of the kid judges on *The Toy Box* fantasized, the voices of real children can play powerful roles in producing adult professionalism in the media industries despite their outsider positions. As I have written elsewhere, attention to the "author-function" through which cultural works accrue value through author figures (Foucault 1975) might be productively combined with increased consideration of an "audience function" (Johnson 2013b) in which the value and meaning of industrial work is also discursively constructed by reference to an audience. Through such dynamics as well as the pediocular orientation of media workers toward childhood, cases like *The Toy Box* and the Kidscreen Summit help us conceptualize the links between kids and professional work cultures, despite commonsense assumptions about and labor structures built upon their mutual exclusivity.

Ultimately, this chapter reveals transgenerational media industries as work cultures dependent upon the management of boundaries between intersecting axes of identity across age, gender, and sexuality. Throughout the deep trade stories and rituals that manifest in *The Toy Box* and the Kidscreen Summit alike, professional identities and relations of power cohere in ways that communicate established lore and privileged ways of being professional to aspirants, affirm the power of legitimated industry leaders, and suggest means by which upstarts might disrupt that power. In these industry narratives and rituals, professional subject positions that grant access to and knowledge of children external to the production community accrue significance and value. The children's media production community is defined by that which is outside it generationally and professionally, validating the pediocular producer who can operate across those boundaries. Yet access to this pediocularity proves contested and unequal in these industry narratives and rituals, revealing the power of gender, reproductive status, and other labor divisions to arbitrate these transgenerational subjectivities. While some pediocular privilege appears reserved for man-children already secure in their positions within this industry community, many women struggling with this state of affairs have cultivated other professional subjectivities (like the industry moms, babysitters, and teachers at Kidscreen), found tactical opportunities to deploy the voices of children (like the consultants who disrupted existing lore about gender binaries), and unfortunately still find themselves excluded on that basis (the "bad" mom aspirant eliminated from *The Toy Box*). These transgenerational professional subjectivities certainly prove integral to children's media industries—yet they may be equally relevant for the other industry sectors in which generation, reproductive status, and age intersect in the professional subjectivities of industry workers.

The Toy Box and the Kidscreen Summit represent only two case studies from which these transgenerational professional subjectivities can be examined—and future research could deepen our understanding of how adult producers manage their careers in relation to the identities and ideologies of childhood. Although chapter 2 focused on the comic book convention as a site of transgenerational market outreach in which parents play as consumer evangelists, there too professionals participated in these transgenerational outreach campaigns. In introducing its 2015 Kids Day programming, for example, the Wizard World Philadelphia convention explicitly highlighted some of its industry professional guests, like Chewbacca actor Peter Mayhew and former child star Melissa Joan Hart, by endorsing them in the program as "kid friendly." As the event organizers acknowledged, "we like to think every Wizard World celebrity loves kids, but . . ." ("'Kids Day'" 2015)—with the emphasis on "but" acknowledging that not all professionals in the convention space would welcome that association. This promotional copy invoked transgenerational professional identifications as a marker of distinction and belonging for only specific communities of production. For those professionals who were engaged in this transgenerational space, however, Kids Day campaigns represented an opportunity to claim leadership by challenging industry lore. As articulated on her blog and in her CNET contributor profile, author and former Lucasfilm employee Bonnie Burton explicitly tied her licensed work with franchises like *Star Wars* as part of a feminist project concerned with the politics of girlhood, where participation in Kids Day programming like the "How to Draw Star Wars Kids" panel at Las Vegas Comic-Con, for example, could shape the future of fandom (Burton n.d.; Burton 2013). Similarly, Alex Simmons, organizer of the independent Kids Comic Con, positioned his event as part of his work as both a juvenile fiction author and an arts and education consultant engaged in the activist project of disrupting the politics of race and gender in the comics business (Simmons 2011).[10] Through further investigation of cases like these, the transgenerational construction of professional subjectivities could be more clearly ascertained as part of a struggle over boundaries of all kinds within the hierarchical production communities of the media industries.

For now, however, the next chapters complicate the role of audiences within the power relations of industry cultures by moving from a focus on consumers as an imaginative focus in production communities to an exploration of consumers as material participants. If this chapter has focused on the discursive and ritual function of the child audience within professional communities serving them, the next turns the tables by directing attention to the ritualized participation of adult consumers in the everyday spaces where children's media is created. Chapter 5, in turn, considers the material labor of children, figuring them not as the external other against which adult professional subjectivity is produced but instead as active creative participants in digital media production economies. This move to consider adult consumers of kids' product and children alike as transgenerational workers further reveals the productive effect of boundary crossings with industry cultures.

CHAPTER 4

"I've Got a Golden Ticket!"

Adult Fans of LEGO in the Child-Centric Factory

In the 1971 family film *Willy Wonka and the Chocolate Factory* (based on the book *Charlie and the Chocolate Factory* by Roald Dahl), young Charlie Bucket gains the rare opportunity to visit the famed candy manufacturing plant where his beloved Wonka Bars are made. With his family only able to afford one Wonka Bar each year on his birthday, Charlie's discovery of a Golden Ticket that will admit him and his adult chaperone, Grandpa Joe, to a once-in-a-lifetime tour of the factory represents a fantasy about class, childhood, and labor. In navigating the mysterious work world of candy magnate Willy Wonka and the Oompa Loompas in his employ, Charlie experiences consumer plenty and imagines feeding his out-of-work family with the lifetime supply of chocolate promised to him; but to secure that prize, he must follow Wonka's rules for protecting trade secrets and corporate interests over his selfish consumer wants. When Charlie returns an Everlasting Gobstopper sample rather than keeping it to sell to a competitor, the once standoffish Wonka embraces Charlie as the ideal labor subject of his candy empire. "So shines a good deed in a weary world," Wonka tells a befuddled Charlie. "I had to test you, Charlie, and you passed the test," he clarifies, revealing his intent to put his ideal child consumer in charge of the factory. "Who can I trust to run the factory when I leave and take care of the Oompa Loompas for me? Not a grown up. A grown up would want to do everything his own way, not mine. That's why I decided a long time ago that I had to find a child. A very honest, loving child to whom I could tell my most precious candy making secrets." In this conclusion, Charlie's idealized childhood identity permits him to transcend his initial consumer role (or, really, the poverty preventing him from consuming) to find new agency and professionalized economic mobility within Wonka's production world.

Since launching its annual Inside Tour in 2005, The LEGO Group has offered consumers similar opportunities to fantasize about industry labor and participate in the factory world of toy production. Like Charlie's visit to the Chocolate Factory, this three-day consumer tour of LEGO corporate facilities in Billund, Denmark, ascribes heightened value to the meanings and ideals of childhood. As the world's largest producer of toys (Smith 2014), The LEGO Group places a premium—in both the external branding of its interlocking construction bricks and the internal management of corporate culture—on its dedication to the needs of children and its duty to "continuously inspire and develop the builders of tomorrow" (LEGO Group 2013: 8). At the center of this corporate identity is an avowed commitment to the value that play holds for children. "Play changes the world," corporate reports promise. Through play, the company figures children "as the builders of tomorrow and our primary stakeholders. To us, all investment in children is investment in the future" (18). Like Willy Wonka, LEGO locates its corporate future in the values of creativity, childhood, and play; yet *unlike* the fantasy of the Wonka factory, children are not the idealized participants of the LEGO Inside Tour. Although each tour group varies and The LEGO Group caters to the needs of a diverse group of participants, children under seven years old are not eligible to attend, and the resulting tour groups can be dominated by AFOLs, or adult fans of LEGO. This dynamic makes the Inside Tour not just a means of inviting outsiders to participate in corporate values and industry production cultures but also an experience where the meanings of childhood, adulthood, and their transgenerational relations come under significant negotiation. By allowing tourists to cross boundaries between amateur consumption and professional production worlds, the LEGO Inside Tour reorients adult transgression of age-defined marketing categories toward the child-centric brand values preferred by the company, recasting it as a form of productive labor attuned to those corporate childhood ideals.

This chapter examines the Inside Tour as a matrix of interaction between the social identities of childhood and adulthood as well as the industrial relations of producer and consumer, arguing that the experience serves as a ritual interface between industry and audience that transmits a corporate production culture to adult consumers. In the process, adult toy consumers transform from a surplus audience into transgenerationally professionalized subjects engaged in production practice on behalf of children. Through this argument, the chapter bridges the concerns of the previous two, focusing both on the "pediocular" production worlds of chapter 3 and the adult consumers invited to participate in transgenerational industry promotions and market outreach from chapter 2. Here, however, culture industries invite adult consumers of children's playthings to imagine themselves as participants in those professional work worlds. In doing so, the chapter extends this book's concern for troubled boundaries beyond the axis of childhood and adulthood in order to consider the management of transgenerational relations between adult cultures of production and consumption. Inside Tour participants enter the production factory as outsiders in at least two respects: first, as outside the workaday world of labor in their role as consumers and second, in their adulthood, as outside the child-centric target market imagined by the company's branding campaigns. Yet from this outsider tourist position, participants have been invited to imagine themselves inside corporate production cultures, reinscribing their consumer transgression of age categories within productive industry relations.

I situate my analysis of The LEGO Group and the tourist experience of labor it offers as part of a larger investigation into the culture industries (Curtin and Streeter 2001; Horkheimer and Adorno 1944/2012; Miege 1987; Rodriguez-Ferrándiz 2013), particularly insofar as this institution's power over the production of play accords it significant relevance to any consideration of how narratives, identities, communities, ways of life, and other cultural forms, practices, and technology take shape under the aegis of capital. More specifically, however, I consider The LEGO Group as part of the media industries, operating in dialogue with the comic book and television industries already explored in this book. LEGO cannot be separated from major Hollywood players like Time Warner and Disney (and their attendant comic book divisions, DC and Marvel); the company has relied on media licenses like *Batman* and *Avengers* to market successive waves of brick playsets while also partnering with those same media conglomerates to bring original properties like *The LEGO Movie* (Warner Bros., 2014), *The LEGO Movie 2* (Warner Bros., 2019), and *The LEGO Batman Movie* (2017) to theaters as well as *LEGO Ninjago: Masters of Spinjitsu* (Cartoon Network, 2011–) to television. LEGO has also become fully embedded in the digital sphere of online and console video games, with its brand anchoring recent gaming experiences like *LEGO Minifigures Online* (2014–16), *LEGO: Marvel Super Heroes* (2014), and the toys-to-life game *LEGO Dimensions* (2015–17). LEGO has also been repeatedly identified as an industrial site of "mediatization" whereby consumer products increasingly transform into media experiences (Hjarvard 2004, Johnson 2014b, Karmark 2009, Lauwaert 2008). As a result, I do not hesitate to consider the culture industry of plastic playthings from a media studies framework.

This makes perspectives and insights from critical media industry studies (Havens, Lotz, and Tinic 2009) and production studies (Caldwell 2008; Mayer, Banks, and Caldwell 2009; Mayer 2011) equally useful for conceptualizing the "corporate cultures" (Negus 1999) of LEGO. Despite differences between LEGO's plastic product and traditional audiovisual media, moreover, its corporate work cultures are equally constructed in and through media. In her innovative study of moving-image media in corporate work cultures, Kit Hughes identifies the "media affects" that support positions of subjectivity within corporate organizations (2015: 43). So whether we agree on LEGO's status as a media company or not, its transgenerational work culture depends on such affects insofar as corporate values and identities are produced through mediated texts and experiences.

In considering the intersections of tourism and industry, this chapter develops insights into the roles that consumers might play within such affective corporate relations. Caldwell acknowledges that deep texts and rituals include "publicly disclosed" artifacts and performances that communicate the meanings, values, and identities of an industry culture across different communities (2009: 202). In this sense, I argue that touristic engagement with spaces of professional work offers a productive axis along which to consider industry cultures in terms of intergroup relationships with amateurs from the outside. As a ritualized performance of corporate culture that puts professional communities in dialogue with consumer communities, work settings in collision with tourism, and adult expertise in tension with service to branded childhood ideals, the LEGO Inside Tour presents a unique opportunity to think through these possibilities. Drawing from ethnographic fieldwork conducted as a participant in May 2014, I consider the Inside Tour as a site of collision between cultures of consumption and production as well as childhood and adulthood, all intersecting through shared interest in the manufacture of play and play-oriented corporate values. In addition to the formal presentations, impromptu conversations, participatory activities, and navigation of mediated workplace environments built into the tour, I also draw upon corporate disclosures, press releases, employee newsletters, and other media texts produced by LEGO to triangulate that consumer experience within a managed construction of corporate identities and values shared across different communities.[1] From analysis of these producer-consumer interactions, I reveal how the corporate management of adult consumer participation within professional production environments resonates to build a community of stakeholders united by these shared transgenerational identities, affinities, and values. In the process, adult consumers invested in playthings marketed to children transform from a "surplus" audience (Jenkins, Ford, and Green 2013: 129) into participants in a preferred corporate brand culture.

That transgenerational brand culture is also explicitly transnational. LEGO produces and distributes its product throughout the world, maintaining offices and facilities for product development, manufacturing, marketing, or customer service across twenty-eight different nations as of 2018 ("Locations" n.d.). While its headquarters may be located in Denmark, LEGO ultimately contends with different regulations for children's playthings and expectations for support of children's needs in each of these different cultural contexts. Against this challenge, LEGO cultivates a business ethic based on corporate responsibility to children—one that smooths over and simplifies various regulatory requirements across the whole of its global network. Similarly, despite the linguistic and cultural diversity of the locations in which LEGO operates, English has emerged as a common language for both conducting business internally and organizing events like the Inside Tour pitched at a global fandom. All parts of the Inside Tour are conducted in English, and participants are expected to be comfortable with that presumed lingua franca of global consumer culture. Permanent signage in the factory spaces featured on the tour carries the English language as well, suggesting that this standardization does not merely cater to the needs of global visitors but instead represents the globalized corporate culture in which the Danish company operates. So while the examination of LEGO in this chapter offers a more globally expansive view than previous chapters focused on US-centered television and comic industries, it also figures the transnationalism of this transgenerational industry formation as one in which local corporate cultures unfold in relation to one another and the inequalities of global cultural privilege in which they are situated.

From this perspective, I first situate the Inside Tour experience as part of a larger culture of "media industry tourism," exploring how the presence of consumers within industrial spaces supports a process of affective and subjective transformation that can be deployed in the management of corporate brands. Second, I draw from publicly disclosed artifacts like the corporate *Responsibility Report* to examine how The LEGO Group foregrounds childhood play in the articulation of its core brand values and identities, often in opposition to its adult consumer appeals. Finally, the construction of these affinities can be read against the Inside Tour itself, examining how and why the company invites consumers to take part in a staged corporate ritual.

Reflecting on the experience of the tour, and the way it positions tourists as both consumers of LEGO product and temporary participants in its professional culture, the analysis examines how the event invites outsiders to orient themselves to the inside world of labor, role-play as workers in that realm, imagine themselves as future LEGO employees, and act as stewards of its child-centric corporate brand. Ultimately, as a reflexive industry ritual designed to put professional producers in dialogue with amateur consumers, the Inside Tour mediates and manages the boundaries of a transgenerational corporate culture, transforming the tourist from an age-based market outlier to an aspiring but privileged participant in a pediocular culture of production.

Managing Brands through Media Industry Tourism

Any examination of the pediocular production experiences tailored for adult consumers within this industrial context must confront the power of the LEGO brand as a set of meanings, values, and identities around which the company has organized its cultures of consumption and production both. While Catherine Johnson (2012) and others highlight the power of brands in shaping the circulation and meanings of cultural products, Sarah Banet-Weiser has emphasized branding as a means of cultivating self-identity, where participatory brand logics structure "the way we understand who we are, how we see ourselves in the world, what stories we tell ourselves about ourselves" (2012: 6). Although Banet-Weiser focuses on consumer identities, the ubiquity of branding makes it a powerful force of identification in industry production cultures too. Indeed if corporate cultures cohere as "mythical" environments in which the work of making product is experienced and understood, as Keith Negus argues of the recording industry (1999: 65, 69), brands may act as fundamental forces in the production and experience of those corporate myths. As such, the brand cultivated by a company like LEGO provides a lever between production and consumption where a shared set of meanings, values, and identities can be established between both.

In this way, corporate brands can be considered broadly as a force of management, communicating shared frameworks against which the play and work worlds of LEGO might both be understood. The brand does not just structure the environments and experiences of professionals within corporate cultures but also enables industry to manage amateur consumer practices by incorporating them within those branded corporate cultures. Fan studies have frequently highlighted this linkage between brands, consumers, and management. Whether described as the disciplinary containment of "fanagement" (Hills 2012: 425) or the incorporation of consumer agency within the structures of "brandom" (Guschwan 2012), brand management can refigure fan consumption as a source of productive input. In the case of a toy like LEGO, brand management might also transform play culture into work culture, translating the perspectives and subjectivities of consumers into those of brand stakeholders. Notably, fan experiences like the Inside Tour sit alongside a host of other initiatives aimed at managing the LEGO brand in relationship to its adult fan community. As one company representative wrote to me, LEGO prefers not to describe its relationship to AFOLs in managerial terms, opting instead to describe the relationship as an attempt "to engage with the fan community and have a great dialogue with them." Unsurprisingly, corporations prefer to publicly discuss customer service relationships in terms of engagement rather than the more suspicious sounding practices of management. Internally, however, the LEGO Community Engagement Department has hired employees called community managers, who can serve as members of a specific AFOL Relations and Program Team (Tran 2016). This department has also supported the LEGO Ambassador Network aimed at supporting that engaging dialogue between the company and its adult fans ("LEGO Ambassador" n.d.). For a global company like LEGO, therefore, engagement with fan communities (even if not always conceptualized as fan management) supports brand management, with its adult consumers proving to be a particular point of focus despite (or perhaps because of) a brand and market focused on children.

Within this branded fan management, experiences like the Inside Tour remain somewhat unique as a point of contact between consumers and the world of production, through which the adult fan can encounter the professional. Like Matt Hills (2012), Suzanne Scott (2019) considers the potential for fans to go "pro" and insinuate themselves within the world of industry, comparing the desire to professionalize against the industry management structures that extend privilege unequally to fans based on factors of gender and race. From that perspective, the management of media brands and fans turns in part on identifying consumers to whom the status of professionalization and privileges of incorporation into branded work cultures will be extended. However, while Scott reveals symmetry between target demographics privileged by industry and the professionalization of fans, the generational differences at the heart of the brand relationships in this chapter point to a different dynamic. Although children may be a privileged market for play culture, their historical status as a special, protected, "extracommercium" class outside of industrial labor relations (Cook 2004: 8) limits their capacity for professionalization. Transgenerational media industries, in this sense, create the capacity for audiences otherwise understood to be surplus—what Scott (2013, 2019) describes as outside this privileged market focus—to be professionalized and thus repositioned within brand management strategies. For child-centric companies, adult fans represent a surplus audience to be managed (or "engaged") and thereby transformed, their consumption harnessed and made more productive as a form of fandom compatible with branded corporate cultures.

While this transformation could be accomplished in many ways, tourism has emerged as one mechanism through which brand management and engagement can allow fans access to professionalized realms. Media theorists like Nick Couldry have long recognized the power of place in media consumption, revealing the practices of pilgrimage that emerge from the identification and interaction of "non-media people" with studios and other locations in which media institutions are embedded (2000: 3–4). In this model, non-media people can play a crucial role in producing, challenging, and denaturalizing the power of media institutions. Contrary to fan studies focused on the symbolic journey of textual engagement, Aden (1999), Brooker (2007), Couldry (2007), Hills (2002), Mills (2008), and others have revealed how the material practices of cult audiences who embark on "pilgrimages" to production locales reshape media power and redefine institutional spaces in affective ways. From this vantage point, the fan tourism supported by the Inside Tour could be considered to offer its participants power and potential transformative agency within the industrial factory space. Moreover, much of the research on "media tourism" (Reijnders 2011) and "film-induced tourism" (Beeton 2005) recognizes visits to filming locations, production studios, theme parks, and more as an arena of significant economic potential, in which journeys to the places of media power can be organized and commodified by tourism industries. Research on media tourism as a form of economic development often seeks to understand tourists' desires, the impact of tourist activities on local economies, and overall the unique forms of tourism all this might support (Carl, Kindon, and Smith 2007; Roesch 2009).

Within this dialogue about fan pilgrimage and media tourism, I aim here to call greater attention to the specific dynamics of *media industry tourism* whereby structured, place-based encounters between consumers and media institutions in corporate contexts produce media power in myriad ways. Much of the existing research focuses on the tourist's entry into imagined narrative spaces rather than the professionalized spaces of corporate production cultures. Nevertheless, there remains significant room to move beyond this emphasis, as indicated by research in which Abby Waysdorf and Stijn Reijnders consider the "technical imagination" of *Game of Thrones* tourists whose pilgrimages revolve around not just inhabitation of fictional narrative space but also the act of envisioning themselves to be "part of the team that put it all together" (2017: 187). In this way, tourists seek participation in professional as well as "fictive" contexts. Media tourism, in this light, can provide access to the industrialized arenas of cultural production, where the tourist participates in institutional cultures through that crossing of professional and amateur boundaries. Specific attention to media industry tourism reveals the agency of tourists within production worlds and their imbrication in industry power. While their presence may only support a fantasy or simulation of industry work, the collision of tourism and professionalism can simultaneously disrupt those boundaries between production and consumption. Yet the presence of the media industry tourist can also shore up existing institutional powers. As outsiders gaining privileged access to professional worlds, media industry tourists become audiences for performances of insider value and knowledge by those within this corporate world—participants in a branded work culture. Furthermore, to newly imagine themselves as insiders, media industry tourists may be asked to accept and endorse institutional systems of power and knowledge. The power of media industries may thus be produced and reproduced by tourists who play into existing corporate cultures or bend them through interactions in these spaces. Considered in this way, media industry tourism emerges as a crucial site for conceptualizing the production of power within and around institutions of media work.

Theme parks have historically proven central to these place-based consumer engagements with media industry. Examining the Disney media empire, Janet Wasko argues that the Disneyland and Walt Disney World parks sell access to the "backstage magic" behind onscreen fantasy worlds (2001: 163). While we might go to a Disney theme park to take an immersive walk through Sleeping Beauty's Castle or travel to the distant planet Tatoonine via the Star Tours ride, another draw comes from felt proximity to the work of manufacturing those fantasies. A visit to the Main Street Cinema enables tourists not just to watch Walt Disney's original cartoons but also to gain greater insight into the authorial legend of the man behind that work. Visitors to the Animation Academy can watch characters "brought to life" during presentations by Disney artists, take their own drawing classes, and generate their own sketches to imagine themselves as part of that industrial process ("Animation Academy" n.d.). Yet Disney has not cornered the market on media industry tourist attractions. The Universal Studios resorts in

Hollywood and Orlando provide a fantasy of geographical colocation in the professional space of the studio lot. Universal's Hollywood park in particular carries storied appeal, with the backlot tour providing a glimpse of historical sets and production spaces. Of course, this public-facing backlot does not overlap with spaces currently used by media professionals at the Hollywood park; yet the sense of a real world of production just on the other side of the park remains. The walls at the edge of the park reinforce the spacing between tourist and professional while reminding the visitor of their proximity to production. The technical imagination served by the Universal Studios experience undoubtedly shaped Disney's 1989 launch of the Disney-MGM Studios expansion in Florida (later renamed Hollywood Studios) as both a theme park and an operating studio. Several film and television projects would be produced on-site throughout the 1990s, a creative presence often highlighted in the backstage tours offered to visitors. The theme park experience has thus consistently served tourists a fantasy of entry into and participation in the professionalized world of media work. Despite being a fantasy, this tourism has supported production and development needs at an industry level too. Universal's Orlando tourists can visit the Studio Audience Center to sign up to serve as audience members for television productions taping on the adjacent lot, or visit a testing center to provide feedback on television pilots in development.

However, if the theme park often puts the media industry tourist in structured simulations adjacent to the places of institutional media power, other more straightforward facility tours allow visitors directly into the spaces of production bounded by gates and guardhouses. As early as 1915, Universal chief Carl Laemmle offered five-cent tours of his new studio facilities (before the advent of sound recording made audience presence more problematic) ("Universal Studios" n.d.). Many other Hollywood film studios, including Paramount and Warner Bros., continue to lure tourists to their production facilities. The marketing of such experiences often explicitly promises to transform visitors, affording them new "insider" status and professional potential after crossing the boundaries between consumption and production. Paramount, for example, runs daily tours of its Melrose Avenue facility, offering visitors a variety of packages at different rates and levels of industry access. For US$58 in 2017, Paramount promised any guest ten years and older "An Intimate, Behind-the-Scenes Experience" through a two-hour Studio Tour that takes the tourist "into the world of the industry's top talent, producers, and crew as they create today's award-wining television and feature films." An "Engaging Studio Page" would lead visitors through locales like the studio gate, New York Street backlot, and prop warehouse. Yet while the

Studio Tour asked the visitor to "Walk among Industry Talent," the higher-end, $178 VIP Tour prompted the tourist to actually "Meet Archivists and Backlot Tradesmen as they share their craft." Rather than just sharing space, VIP Tourists could anticipate meeting with professionals, gaining the "True, behind-the-scenes, 'insider' experience" at Paramount. Over the course of four hours, these tourists received "exclusive access to private areas" including special effects, the sign shop, sound stages, and archives that offered "hands on" experience plus interactions with real Hollywood professionals ("Studio Tours" n.d.). Industry tourism thus manifests as a means of producing hierarchies among consumers—where some have more access than others. Warner Bros. similarly differentiated between its standard Studio Tour and a Deluxe experience. Even the complimentary lunch meant to sweeten the $295 Deluxe package in 2017 figured as a means of providing access to the everyday work world of Hollywood Production: "A delicious three-course lunch is included in our Commissary Fine Dining Room—the place where producers, actors, writers and studio executives meet to discuss their latest projects or pore over top-secret scripts" ("Deluxe" n.d.). In the context of media industry tourism, mundane practices like eating can become part of a fantasy of privileged participation in and interaction with creative professionals on the institutional inside.

Whereas fan pilgrimages typically involve interaction with the spaces in which narrative events were staged, and the theme park experience links behind-the-scenes experiences to those fictive fantasies, these film studio tours foreground the industrial side of media tourism by focusing on a fantasy of participation in professionalized work. The invitation to tour industrial sites of production turns on the promises of interacting with specific classes and categories of industry workers, sharing their factories and commissaries, and participating in their workaday lives in those spaces. As such, media industry tourism demands attention as a space in which the relations of media industry labor are represented, identified, and performed in ritualized ways, while simultaneously offered to consumers as a site of structured participation. Media industry tourism reveals the interactions and blurred boundaries of labor across the divides of professional and amateur, producer and consumer, work and play. As such, media industry tourists are not merely consumers but collaborative subjects of production worlds (albeit temporary ones). Greater attention to tourism within institutional space provides deeper insight into the way media power depends on labor relations that extend across the boundaries of professional production and everyday consumption. At the same time, attention to tourist encounters in the studios, factories, and other locales of industrial cultural production encourage us to see these blurred boundaries as something more than the product of "new" media. Instead we should be increasingly attuned to the way in which the media power wielded by culture industries depends on a broad-based staging and management of participatory interaction by consumers with the spaces of creativity and production.

To consider the media power of LEGO—and the production and negotiation of that power by consumers as media industry tourists—the Inside Tour experience thus provides an instructive case study. While this tourist encounter offers entry to a "factory" that makes toys rather than film or television, LEGO's corporate headquarters has presented a comparable opportunity to "meet LEGO employees and especially LEGO designers, who will introduce you to their daily work at the LEGO Group" and "take part in a unique building experience together with LEGO Designers" ("LEGO Inside" n.d.). Like the deluxe Paramount and Warner Bros. tours, LEGO has promised its visitors the ability to interact with creative professionals in a participatory way. Moreover, just as LEGO can for all intents and purposes be considered a fully-fledged media company, the factory production of construction toys mirrors screen media as a creative, collaborative industrial effort. Most important to the focus of this book, however, might be a consideration of exactly what kind of transgenerational power these encounters afford LEGO, its employees, and/or the consumers who participate in these tourist practices. As a factory geared toward the production of playthings marketed to children, LEGO has sought to build value and claim legitimacy for cultural production in service to a specific, age-defined audience. Yet like the Paramount and Warner Bros. studio tours, the LEGO factory tour has also excluded visitors under a certain age and focused its touristic appeals on an older consumer market. In its efforts to claim institutional power in the production of childhood play and creativity, LEGO has invited adults to adopt their own playful positions of industrial subjectivity within its corporate culture. In this way, the participation of adults in the industry tourism experience offered by LEGO can be interrogated as a form of transgenerational brand management in which adult fans help produce corporate power in the production of childhood play.

Play and the Meaning of LEGO Work

Despite significant adult participation in tours of LEGO's global toy manufacturing headquarters, a branded emphasis on service to children and play otherwise insulates the company's products and consumer experiences from too close an association with adulthood. Take, for example, the story of John St-Onge, a LEGO enthusiast who, at the age of sixty-three, was denied entry to a Vaughan, Ontario, LEGOLAND Discovery Center in 2013. As reported in news coverage, St-Onge had a "lifelong dream" ("Legoland Dream" 2013) or "long-time dream" (Grenoble 2013) of visiting LEGO headquarters in Denmark, evoking the tourist fantasy of experiencing industry space. Whether St-Onge knew of the existence of the Inside Tour or not, health problems made such international travel impossible for him, so he and his daughter set out for the next best thing only three hours away: a LEGOLAND Discovery Center that condenses a theme park experience into a smaller commercial space. Upon arrival, however, St-Onge was turned away because of a policy that all adults must be accompanied by children. As center manager Lara Hannaford explained amid later press inquiries, "it is a child attraction so we do have this in place to protect the families and children that visit" ("Legoland Dream" 2013). This policy extended as much from concern about child predators as corporate branding; yet it nevertheless rendered LEGO experiences outside the context of family and child-rearing as a disruption of brand boundaries, where children were the only proper target for the LEGO tourism on offer. However, despite making use of the LEGO brand, LEGOLAND Discovery Centers and theme parks were at the time operated by Merlin Entertainment, an independent company licensed to use the LEGO name in tourist venues (until full acquisition by LEGO in 2019); this policy was less direct corporate dictate by The LEGO Group and more shared negotiation of child-centric branding across a host of different entertainment venues. Indeed, in the wake of press coverage sympathetic to St-Onge, Merlin paid for the LEGO enthusiast to travel (by car) to a full LEGOLAND park, where no similar policy existed (Thompson 2013). This policy difference suggests that LEGO and its partners have varied their market appeals across age boundaries, pitching the brand in different ways across different entertainment spaces.

In its own marketing, The LEGO Group has carefully managed the appeal of its products beyond a preferred emphasis on children. Although certainly informed by the collaboration of production partner Village Roadshow, the animation firm Lin Pictures, and for-hire directors and screenwriters, the 2014 feature film *The LEGO Movie* represents a branded attempt to negotiate the tensions inherent across adult and child engagements with LEGO product. What begins as a conflict between the mundane everyman minifigure Emmet and the evil Lord Business ultimately becomes a fourth-wall-breaking generational struggle between father and son, with the former prohibiting use of LEGO toys beyond the tightly controlled world of adult hobbyism. This narrative problematizes adult LEGO play as too driven by collecting and meticulous instruction, which is juxtaposed to the free, imaginative creativity of childhood. When the son reminds his father that the packaging marked these LEGO toys as intended for children 5–12 years old, the father's frustrated and comic reply "That's just a suggestion!" invites the audience to question adult-centric LEGO use. Ultimately, the father recognizes the illogic of confining LEGO play to an adults-only sphere, and the narrative conflict is resolved with affirmation of the child's place in a now properly transgenerational consumer relationship to LEGO. The father by no means relinquishes his own interest in LEGO, but that leisure pursuit becomes something to be enjoyed through support of his son's creativity, not as adult pursuit of an individual, generationally distinct LEGO fandom.

This is not to say LEGO has ignored the value of its adult consumers. On the contrary, although the company has continued to develop products primarily for children, it has openly communicated the importance of its adult fans in public relations campaigns and in internal disclosures to employees and corporate stakeholders in the business world at large. In 2018, for example, LEGO partnered with crowdfunding site Indiegogo to market LEGO FORMA, a "premium LEGO experience designed for adults looking for a fun, engaging way to reconnect with their creative side" (LEGO FORMA 2018). Yet this open acknowledgment of and service to the AFOL occurred in the niche space of online crowdfunding with small, limited production runs, communicating support in ways unlikely to interfere with the primary and far more visible focus on children on mass market retail shelves.

Other corporate statements have similarly acknowledged the significance of adult consumers while contextualizing them within the company's overall market outlook. According to *The Brick*, an annual publication highlighting corporate initiatives, creative roles, and work worlds within The LEGO Group, the company estimated in 2010 that "a little below 5% of the LEGO sales come from adults who buy the bricks for themselves" (*The Brick* 2010: 60). Approximately 5 percent of global sales is a significant amount of money—some US$111–142 million annually based on figures for 2010 reported elsewhere (Trangbæk 2012). Nevertheless, that number pales compared to other market indicators more visibly celebrated by The LEGO Group. In 2014, for example, the company's overall sales and net profit increased by 15 percent, a growth attributed in official press releases to the marketing of *The LEGO Movie*, as well as corporate dedication to creating "new products that are fun and appealing to children all over the world" (Trangbæk 2015b). That story continued into 2015, where an 18 percent sales increase and a 30 percent quarterly net profit increase compared to the previous year led president and CEO Jørgen Vig Knudstorp to exclaim "that we have again been able to develop exciting and fun play experiences that really appeal to children around the world" (Trangbæk 2015a). Nowhere are sales to adults—whether steady or rising—figured as part of these stories of phenomenal market growth. While the 2010 figures from *The Brick* did highlight the existence of adult consumers with a large pink headline "Adults Play with LEGOs too," this idea manifested as a factoid on the last page in the publication alongside "Did You Know?" notes about the number of bricks made per minute and the distance those bricks would stretch across the globe. The existence of adult consumers was not treated with the same strategic significance as topics like the company's digital initiatives, attempts to fight corruption, and education outreach given full article treatment. Instead, with the $111–142 million annual value of adults left unspoken, this disclosure framed the adult market as an important but still peripheral arena of corporate concern.

While some adult LEGO hobbyists have used that 2010 figure as evidence of how "important" and "influential" they must be (Millington 2010), others have more soberly read LEGO's corporate focus on children as an indicator that the age range printed on the product boxes may not indeed be "just a suggestion." Reflecting on the adult market, fan columnist Nick Martin (2015) concluded, "Most AFOLs seem to greatly overestimate the impact that we have on what LEGO does." While expensive, exclusive collector's items designated for builders fourteen- or sixteen-years-and-up did attract significant attention from adult fans, marketers, and journalists, Martin argued that LEGO's business model depended more significantly on consumer turnover, centered on "a narrow range of time when the majority of their consumer base is going to be using their products," after which the company would "need a new customer to step up and start purchasing." Martin suggested that rather than court the consumer continuity of AFOLs, LEGO combatted turnover by bringing new consumers into the fold earlier in their lives, particularly through the growth of the preschool DUPLO line. While AFOLs complained about rereleases or product offerings too similar to what came just a few years before, Martin saw that as irrelevant to a company that believes it has a "finite" time with one group of kids before product could be repackaged for another age cohort. What read as repetition to one surplus market reflected the company's regenerative reorientation to new consumers. In a market based on "churn," AFOL interest "doesn't matter all that much to their bottom line or product decisions."

From this perspective, it is little surprise that the strategies LEGO has shared with investors, employees, and other stakeholders position children as the company's primary and exclusive focus. The LEGO Group has consistently claimed a corporate "mission" to "inspire and develop the builders of tomorrow," within an overall "vision" of "Inventing the future of play" ("Mission and Vision" n.d.) Corporate documents like the *Responsibility Report* (LEGO Group 2013) have reinforced this child-centric focus and also offered insight into the roles that LEGO offers to adults (both consumers and professionals) in the pursuit of this moving target. The 2013 *Report* (shared with Inside Tour participants) opened by boasting of the seventy-five million children reached by the company that year, affirming this market focus as well as, by absence, the comparative marginality of adult consumers in corporate reporting (2). Similarly, an introductory letter from the CEO situated the company's priorities within the overall goal of "inspiring and developing children as they experience the joy and learning opportunity that creative play provides" (11). Supporting this corporate framework were results from a survey of consumers, employees, NGOs, industry associations, and other stakeholders in the corporate brand who confirmed the company's top three priorities as delivering safe high-quality product, "supporting children's right to grow," and communicating more broadly with children (14–15). In line with corporate social responsibility campaigns that emphasize the institutional capacity for "doing good" in branded environments (Ouellette 2018), the report asked readers to identify with the company's green environmental initiatives, the LEGO Foundation's philanthropic "Cultures of Creativity" project, and more. All these prosocial efforts found industry rationalization in the statement that "children deserve only our best" (3). Readers could find this corporate responsibility to children communicated on almost any page: "we see children as the builders of tomorrow and our primary stakeholders. To us, all investment in children is investment in the future" (18). LEGO also embraced in the report a leading role in developing a legal framework for "Children's Rights and Business Principles," centered on a commitment to human rights, the elimination of child labor, the creation of decent work for parents, the safety of children in business environments, and a respect for all these principles in marketing practice (48).

As this concern for parents suggests, LEGO's *Responsibility Report* did articulate—within the normative transgenerational framework of child-rearing—supportive roles that adults could play in this service of childhood creativity and human rights. While the welcome letter from the CEO foregrounded children, it did not entirely ignore adults; instead it imagined them as intermediaries involved in the consumer experiences of children: "Children—and their parents—should continue to have very high expectations of us" (10). A corporate emphasis on safety, in that sense, also met parental demand for protection of their children. Similarly, reflections on education and the virtues of creativity supported parents' hopes and dreams for their young. While the focus may have been on improving conditions of creativity for children, adults figured as the agents in a position to deliver that social good: "Adults can play a key role in enabling everyday creative behaviour for children" (24). However, in the LEGO Foundation's Cultures of Creativity initiative, where the company targeted "culture" as an arena for prosocial corporate intervention, creativity was figured as not merely something supported by adulthood but also something adults too might share with children. Through practices of playing, thinking, making, and sharing that grant children the "ability to stay creative throughout their youth and as adults," this initiative sought to create "a culture that accepts, acknowledges and nurtures creativity." This imagined social good also presented a market opportunity, insofar as a "creative culture" would provide a profitable context for a company that defines its cultural goods primarily in terms of the value of creativity. Yet it also acknowledged the potential for adults' creative interests to overlap with the child consumer churn at the heart of LEGO's business model.

LEGO thus ascribed creativity to both its employees and its adult consumers—seeking to harness both in service of its branded mission. Speaking to the role that LEGO employees might play in its corporate initiatives, the 2013 report celebrated the internal "LEGO Ideas" project that provided an online interface for workers to make bottom-up suggestions to serve these top-down goals. While comparable to any employee suggestion box, LEGO framed this feedback and input mechanism in creative terms: "Engaging with employees on an open online innovation and co-creation platform is a valuable way to leverage collective insights, experiences, and perspectives from LEGO employees" (95). Coincidentally, the moniker "LEGO Ideas" would be newly applied to another, separate initiative at the consumer product level in 2014. Beginning in 2008, the LEGO Cuusoo initiative had allowed LEGO users to submit concepts with sufficient fan community backing for review by the company to be considered as an official product. In 2014, products released under this umbrella adopted LEGO Ideas as a new brand name; while few if any consumers would recognize a connection to internal efforts to harness employee feedback, both "Ideas" initiatives turned on models of co-creativity and collective intelligence (Banks 2013; Jenkins 2006) in service of corporate goals. In both, adults emerged as the co-creative class engaged in the brand's service to children. The majority of LEGO Ideas submissions considered for production came from adult designers—surely a benefit for LEGO when it came to securing production rights and enlisting designer assistance in promotion (compared to the legal challenges of acquiring contractual consent from young children).[2] In fact, the LEGO Ideas rules posted as of 2017 restricted anyone under thirteen from submitting a concept ("Product Idea Guidelines" n.d.). Thus while AFOL's may not have been of significant concern to LEGO as a consumer market, they seem here to have had greater industrial utility as a force of co-creative labor.

Against the promises that LEGO makes about ethical marketing to children, the co-creativity of adult consumers may have an added advantage. In its *Responsibility Report*, LEGO directly wrestled with the incongruity of marketing to the children it purported to nourish creatively—acknowledging the longstanding concern of parents and regulators concerned with children's ability to distinguish commercial appeals from meaningful content (Seiter 1995; Hendershot 1998). Against these criticisms, the *Report* distinguished efforts to directly engage children in creative play from commercial exploitation: "We take a comprehensive approach to ensuring that our marketing materials and communication to children are ethical and legally compliant. We have a policy on Marketing to Children which lays down our internal rules and approach" (LEGO Group 2013: 50). Among these rules were dictates that LEGO's communication to children could not take advantage of children's "inexperience" to mislead them, portray "unsafe or harmful" scenarios, or "put pressure on children or parents to purchase our products" (51). Furthermore, the *Responsibility Report* affirmed a corporate commitment to gender equality in communication with and to children. Claiming that it did not want to preempt or limit children's building experiences "by defining in our marketing that some of our products are only for girls and some only for boys," the company's new Gender Marketing Guidelines "ensure that children are not being subjected to, or limited by, gender stereotypes" (55). Notably, these new communication guidelines emerged just after the launch of the new LEGO Friends product theme in 2012—a line specifically aimed at expanding market share with appeals perceived to resonant more with girls (Johnson 2014a). These rules framed the new product as not necessarily "for girls" but just one consumer choice in a larger portfolio.

Perhaps most importantly, these communication rules restricted the enlistment of child consumers in promotional and marketing labor. LEGO promised to prevent children under sixteen years old from becoming active promoters of the corporate brand (further suggesting that while LEGO Ideas allowed submissions from users as young as thirteen, those designers might not have served the company in a promotional capacity as effectively as their adult competitors). In other words, while LEGO aimed to support children's creative play, its support of co-creativity at the industrial level of production and marketing had to look to adults—lest it appear to exploit as labor the creativity of its core market. Altogether these brand values and corporate policies informed the context in which the consumer experience of the LEGO Inside Tour—and its overall presentation of a corporate culture based on children's creativity—could unfold as a site of adult participation. While not the core market, adult consumers of LEGO served a crucial industrial role as the co-creative workforce that children could not be asked to join in a corporately "responsible" way.

Professionalized Adulthood on the Inside

To understand the Inside Tour and the labor role-play it offers—and in particular the way that simulated work puts adulthood and childhood in tension—it is necessary to first consider the makeup of the tour group itself. Like most tourist experiences, the Inside Tour has depended on the economic and consumer privileges tied to fantasy vacations. Just as tourists visiting "exotic" foreign cultures can take pleasure in crossing cultural boundaries and experiencing a foreign world (no matter how constructed that experience might be), Inside Tour participants cross the boundaries of production and consumption to have an encounter with industry, thanks to economic and cultural capital that affords a similar colonial power. Attending the tour requires a significant investment. The 2014 cost of admission was 13,000 DKK, or approximately US$2,000; this included lodging at the Billund LEGOLAND Hotel and several meals but did not include airfare or any other travel costs. This expense made the experience accessible only to those of significant means or those with a sufficiently intense LEGO fan identity to rationalize the premium price. My informal discussions with participants revealed these class privileges at work: while some had clearly saved up to make the trip, participants describing themselves as consultants and contractors dominated the social makeup of our group. Attending the tour depended also on a certain degree of cultural capital, as having the funds to cover the costs of attendance did not alone guarantee the ability to participate. Aspiring participants had to keep tabs on the Inside Tour news site (buried fairly deep in the overall LEGO corporate website), perhaps following fan news about the registration process. On the appointed date prior to the 2014 event, participants had to be ready to submit their information immediately when registration began before all available spots were claimed. LEGO has held four or five of these events each summer, with a capacity of around thirty participants each. This limits access to less than two hundred participants per year—a far more exclusive tourist experience than the LEGOLAND theme park with millions of visitors a year, or even events like San Diego Comic-Con for which it proves notoriously difficult for some 130,000 fans to gain admission (Hanna, 2019). In 2017, LEGO experimented with changing the first-come, first-served registration, with applicants newly subject to selection by LEGO (leaving open the possibility the interests of brand management and fan engagement strategies could determine future admittances) ("LEGO Inside Tour" n.d.). The Inside Tour has thus been an exclusive experience afforded by economic and cultural privilege.

But these are not the only factors of exclusivity and exclusion to consider. Despite LEGO's branded emphasis on supporting the creativity of children, the Inside Tour has presented itself primarily as an adult, industry-oriented experience. While many of LEGO's most popular products target four-to-seven-year-old consumers, tour participants have skewed much older. The minimum age to participate in 2014, according to the tour website, was eight years old. By 2017, this minimum was lowered to seven but still represented a starting point at the end of LEGO's core consumer churn. Practically, the multiplication of the per-person admission fee has also presented a barrier to entry for most families. Considering the factory setting of the tour, it is easy to imagine corporate reluctance to let small children wander through spaces filled with running machinery. However, LEGO has occasionally demonstrated an ability to make its factory spaces suitable for occupation by children. The 2013 *Responsibility Report*, for example, described the opening of a new production facility in Kladno, Czech Republic, as a celebration in which two thousand visitors toured the facility, "eager to observe processing and packing lines and admire LEGO models in the halls" (LEGO Group 2013: 99). The report characterized this open house as part of a corporate interest in "Making children in Kladno happier"—efforts that continued throughout the year as the factory later hosted twenty-five "guided tours for schools and citizens in the community" (51). When aligned with its mission and its public relations campaigns, LEGO has used its factory spaces to cultivate tour experiences for the children it seeks to serve. The LEGO Inside Tour, however, appears to have served a different function.

The age thresholds that filter out young children instead speak to the interests and tastes to which the tour has been pitched—where the target audience appears to be an AFOL niche interested in industry rather than a child LEGO user interested in play alone. The Inside Tour group in which I participated in May 2014 consisted of thirty adults, as well as seven minors: one girl and six boys. As a teenager, the oldest of these boys was addressed and treated the same way as the adults on the tour (perhaps reflecting his status as having aged beyond the core LEGO market). The smaller children, however, made up a distinct group of tour participants—a cohort whose outlier status was often reinforced in presentations by adult professionals. Some of the LEGO employees we met explicitly acknowledged the potential for children to grow bored with the tour, recognizing a lack of fit between their address to adult fans and younger consumers' attention spans. A few presenters provided special activities for kids to work on, distracting them so discussion of life in the LEGO factory could continue as adult conversation. One provided the children in the group with a worksheet to help them follow along, promising them a reward for paying attention and filling out answers as they (quietly) listened. Others simply seemed resigned to the impossibility of holding kids' attention or soliciting relevant participation from them, unconcerned if children grew visibly bored. But whether children were ignored or given special support, the unfolding of the tour made clear that the adult participants were the primary audience. The industry encounter on offer was one between adult professionals who design children's product and the adults who consume that product.

This is not to suggest that consumption and play were absent in this factory experience. Quite the contrary, participants were repeatedly encouraged to continue and even intensify their consumer relationship with LEGO over the entire course of the tour. A collection of LEGO swag awaited participants upon their arrival at the LEGOLAND Hotel, for example. This included a brick-built LEGO rose souvenir, a three-foot LEGO duffel bag, and a season pass to the LEGOLAND theme park (the grounds of which lay just outside my hotel room window). The bag was meant to facilitate purchase of LEGO product during the trip, removing luggage capacity as a barrier to greater consumption. The orientation packets waiting for us similarly emphasized the tour as an opportunity to purchase product: careful explanation of how the visit to the employee store would unfold (far more detailed than discussion of any other agenda item) underscored that the logistics of buying should be a primary concern for any tour participant. The season pass, too, framed the participant as a consumer beyond any focus on the inside world of the company. While my visitor badge permitted me to visit the theme park as often as I liked during downtime while on the tour, its continuing function as a season pass presumed that I might return to Billund to resume my consumer role much like any of the other thousands of everyday park visitors. For the rest of the first day on site, there was also little to do besides visit the adjacent LEGOLAND park. This offered a particularly odd experience for one traveling without children, as the theme park's attractions skewed toward young riders and, of course, a family dynamic in which solitary adulthood seemed out of place (if not as forbidden as at a LEGOLAND Discovery Center). Through this awkwardness, however, the Inside Tour's encouragement to visit the park reinforced LEGO's branded articulation to childhood play.

Another experience that oriented me toward the corporate culture of LEGO before the tour began in earnest was my decision to spend day one familiarizing myself with Billund—a true company town of slightly over six thousand people. As I approached the town square, I found it under construction, with signage featuring LEGO logos, minifigure images, and other corporate iconography. Public space and corporate space overlapped, and as I would learn later in the tour, this construction site would soon house a mixed civic center, art space, and LEGO attraction. This mix between the public and private loosened the boundaries around the work culture of LEGO. In addition, signage in these public spaces frequently referenced the civic "vision" for Billund as the "Capital of Children"—an urban development plan to support "effectively designed spaces for play, social interaction and experiences" ("Billund City Vision" n.d.) (fig. 4.1). This civic vision thus mirrored the local employer's corporate brand, a "public-private partnership" that LEGO highlighted in stakeholder documents like its *Responsibility Report* as "a common ambition to develop a strong society where children are the center of attention" (LEGO Group 2013: 28). While these visions linked LEGO to a host of top-down neoliberal forces and branded prosocial corporate actions, they served at the ground level to position the occupant of civic space as a potential corporate subject. In exploring Billund, the Inside Tour participant could occupy the geography of expansive corporate identities and visions built on the values of childhood—values that adults could help produce.

In providing unstructured time to experience LEGOLAND and Billund alongside thousands of other consumer visitors, the Inside Tour generated by contrast a more exclusive sense of "real" industry access when participants finally assembled as a small group on the second day. As these exclusive activities began, we modulated between inside and outside, between consumer identity and a more authentic (or authenticated) sense of belonging within a production world. The generational awkwardness felt in walking through the theme park became reframed as the insufficient and childish consumer illusion against which insider corporate access appeared more genuine and well-fitting to an adult. The trappings of the tour similarly marked participants

Figure 4.1. Signage at the under-construction LEGO House at Billund town center reinforces the values of childhood linking corporate and civic visions. (Photo by author.)

as different from and more privileged than the consumers who surrounded them on the LEGOLAND grounds. The tour organizers distributed to each of us a visitor pass complete with lanyard, designating our special status. This designation intensified as we moved between different production facilities and work sites on the Billund campus, where despite our special lanyards we were given additional visitor passes to wear. While this seemed redundant—our lanyards marked us as different from real LEGO employees and from park attendees—it symbolically acknowledged our entry into each space typically closed to consumers. Throughout the program, our guides made repeated comments about our "privilege" to have access to genuine LEGO employees and spaces. During a Designer Dinner session in which we had the opportunity to converse with employees responsible for creating new LEGO construction products, these efforts to distinguish our group from typical consumers continued. Whereas some fans are very "intense," one designer told us, our group was "down to earth." This flattery distanced us from fans looking in from the outside and made us feel a greater sense of belonging on the industrial inside.

Having invited participants to distance themselves from consumption and adopt subject positions attuned to the insider realm of production, much of the Inside Tour proceeded to orient us to identification with professionalized labor within the LEGO factory. Unsurprisingly, we were asked to sign a nondisclosure agreement that explained that any idea we shared with LEGO employees during the tour would become the company's property to exploit as it pleased. We were then shown a corporate training video called "The LEGO Story" that recounted the history of the company, but just as crucially the branded values supporting it. Our discussions with the LEGO designers, meanwhile, zeroed in on the everyday life of creative labor under the corporate umbrella. While designers described twelve-hour days as routine, for example, acknowledgement of labor struggles was rare. Instead designers oriented us to the corporate culture of LEGO by celebrating its cheery, pleasant atmosphere, with the caveat that not everyone thrives in such an environment. Once again, their casual conversation with us drew boundaries between an industry inside and outside, while inviting us to imagine ourselves belonging as insiders.

During this exploratory, orientation phase, it was difficult to miss the branded emphasis on childhood cutting across cultures of production and consumption alike. As the three primary tour organizers introduced themselves, each claimed an explicit connection to childhood while describing their work history at the company. Two of the three framed themselves as mothers who had raised their children on LEGO products and theme park experiences. This child-rearing authority naturalized their professional knowledge and expertise (much as the identity of industry mother emerged in the performances of Kidscreen trade show presenters in chapter 3). The youngest of the tour organizers, however, presented herself as more directly embodying the subjectivity of a playful child. While many AFOLs describe their fan identities in terms of a "dark age"—a period of disinterest in LEGO products typically extending from adolescence to the later embrace of LEGO play as an adult hobby—this tour leader claimed to be a perpetual child who had never stopped playing with such toys. In each case, professional authority extended from a connection to childhood identities and experiences. As the organizers asked each participant to introduce themselves to the group by sharing thoughts about their favorite LEGO product theme, I offered without too much thought that I enjoyed the "modular buildings" because of the experiences they had allowed me to have "with my daughter." Only later on did it occur to me that this seemingly offhand disclosure meshed with the dominant child-centric marketing and labor culture that we were all entering.

This emphasis on childhood continued in the spaces of the tour experience too. The factory corridors we walked through, for example, displayed images of children as well as art made by children. In the Hauremarken factory—a central hub of production for the ubiquitous LEGO minifigure—placards posted to communicate quality guidelines reminded employees to "Look Out for the Little Guys." This slogan captured both the size of the anthropomorphic product and the special needs of its consumers: all "little guys" in need of special care and protection. Elements of the physical factory environment such as these emphasized the connection between adult work and the child needs served by it.

Each major stop on the tour drew participants into this culture of professionalized creative labor. This included the LEGO Idea House, described as a space accessible only to employees when they need to find inspiration for new initiatives and product concepts. To transmit that inspiration, the Idea House offers a material media interface to the corporate culture, melding curatorial museum spaces about company history with meeting spaces in which its future might be imagined by its present employees. We were first shown a bare, white meeting room that offered a blank slate upon which creators could develop new ideas from scratch. Yet in contrast to this unwritten creative future was a corporate history manifest in tangible artifacts. As we moved past the meeting room, our guides revealed a series of exhibits preserving the earliest works of company founder Ole Kirk Christiansen—including design sketches, wooden toys predating molded plastic, and early machines designed to produce LEGO bricks. Indeed the Idea House had been built within the structure of the original Christiansen family home and factory space. This sense of corporate nostalgia continued as we moved into the basement; there we could visit "Memory Lane"—a vault preserving a pristine copy of nearly every LEGO construction set ever released (fig. 4.2). After touring the vault, we entered a multiroom exhibit chronicling the history of the LEGO brick, the development of new product lines and marketing innovations, and the values driving the company throughout this process. If the Idea House was a space to which present employees might go to find inspiration, it privileged creation and innovation extending from awareness of and harmony with the company's history and core brand values. The structure of the house could transmit corporate culture to its occupants—and here in the context of the Inside Tour, that culture opened to the tourist consumer. This invitation to take up corporate subjectivity did not constitute a complete dissolution of the boundaries between professionalism and consumer tourism, of course; our continued outsider status reasserted itself when we were told that the second floor of the Idea House

Figure 4.2. Visitors to the "Memory Lane" vault can share in nostalgia for the corporate past represented by preserved product releases. (Photo by author.)

was off-limits because of the secret 2015 product on display for industry buyers. This teasing management of boundaries emphasized how close we were to secret, insider knowledge while at the same time kept at arm's length.

Moreover, while this visit to the Idea House was framed as an employee-only experience to which tour participants were exceptions, the reality was that LEGO fans could already enjoy detailed glimpses of this space. The Idea House has maintained its own Facebook page, for example, where social media users can tag posts about the museum and share descriptions, images, and videos of their visit ("LEGO Idea House" 2017). While only 926 users as of September 2017 had ever "checked in" to this page to report visiting in person (with the vast majority claiming LEGO employee status in their profiles), their discussion of the Idea House made its transmission of corporate culture accessible to a wider audience than professionals or Inside Tour participants alone. The producers behind the documentary *Beyond the Brick: A Lego Brickumentary* (2014) also provided mediated access to the corporate culture of the Idea House. The *Beyond the Brick* YouTube page features a twenty-minute virtual tour, in which presenter Joshua Hanlon walks the viewer through the same exhibits described here; a separate a thirty-minute YouTube tour focuses solely on the Memory Lane archive (Beyond the Brick 2017a, 2017b). While visiting the Idea House in person provided a tactile advantage, of course, these YouTube tours have actually allowed longer, extended looks at these spaces than the organized schedule of the Inside Tour would necessarily allow. The in-person Idea House tour has remained an exclusive experience available only to LEGO employees, Inside Tour participants, and other "VIP" guests, but its function as a transmitter of corporate culture could extend beyond on-site visits.

What does seem significant and distinct about the in-person nature of the Inside Tour, however, is the way in which our presence as tourists positioned us to take up professionalized roles once we were oriented to this corporate culture. As newly initiated corporate subjects, our role as tourists was not simply to consume corporate narratives but also to partake in material actions and engage with the corporate world of LEGO as increasingly professionalized participants in that creative culture. In his welcoming speech, general manager and vice president of LEGO House Søren Lund directly asked our group, "What can you do to promote LEGO House?" Not to be confused with the Idea House, LEGO House is a mixed civic center, public art space, tourist attraction, and LEGO retail outlet in Billund—the construction of which had just begun at the time of our visit. Perhaps like a public-facing Idea House in its attempts to communicate the meanings and ideals of the LEGO brand at a civic scale, this new facility was clearly a corporate priority in 2014. When prompted to serve as promoters for LEGO House, then, Inside Tour participants transformed from tourists visiting the exclusive sites of LEGO work to enculturated subjects who might contribute something to the company mission.

Some of this work closely resembled focus group testing. On the last official day of the tour, Lund returned to mine our collective intelligence for our thoughts about LEGO House. He asked us what we wanted to see the space accomplish and what kinds of functions we could imagine it serving. He presented a marketing campaign strategy that had been prepared by an outside agency, in which the LEGO House was positioned as "the only place" where LEGO dreams happen. Our group represented a captive audience of potential consumers who could assess that campaign's potential. If this was focus testing, however, our particular group was one that had spent days embedded within the LEGO corporate culture, with a potentially greater capacity to filter our consumer interests in the LEGO House space through the internal values and priorities of the company. The tour participants proceeded to provide insightful, critical feedback about how the exclusivity proposition in the campaign ("the only place . . .") would discount all the creativity, imagination, and other forms of LEGO dreaming that occurs on a daily basis for all product users outside Billund. Of course, our group also provided many irrelevant, pie-in-the-sky suggestions for the building that would have made it less of a civic center and more singularly a theme park experience. Nonetheless, our ability to serve as a test audience seemed somewhat enhanced by our collective orientation to the values and needs of the company. At the same time, Lund's interest in our role as promoters of the LEGO House imagined us as ongoing agents of the company that would perform important work after the tour's conclusion. In fact, he framed our imperative to promote LEGO House—presumably, to our families, friends, and any fellow LEGO fans with which we might interact online—as our "responsibility," because the new facility would be "your House too."

Yet while our interaction with executives like Lund may have served somewhat productive ends for LEGO, the tour much more significantly invited participants to directly imagine ourselves as professionalized consumer-employees. Throughout the programmed course of events, we were continually encouraged to adopt the role of aspiring LEGO employees and inhabit the fantasy of the worker subject positions offered to us. The most involved, time-consuming, and spectacular of these role-playing events was a design challenge in which each tour participant had the opportunity to demonstrate their creative acumen by constructing a LEGO model of their own. Beyond an opportunity to play with LEGO bricks, this competition took on a veneer of professionalization, as organizers described the competition format as similar to that used by the company to evaluate the worthiness of designers seeking employment. The tour competition, as reported to us, simulated interviewing practices in which LEGO provides a set of guidelines or constraints to would-be designers (a target size, piece count, or price point, for example), asking them to come up with the best, most innovative creation possible. As told to us, these interview competitions sometimes take place in group situations similar to ours, where applicants out-design one another to get hired. And so, as tourists inhabiting this industry space, we were set loose at the end of an evening of programming to design our own LEGO creations, with access to several cabinets full of seemingly every possible part and color, restricted only by reminders that the judges would give priority to cost-effective, marketable models that would support significant play by children. Importantly, the sense of play here prioritized design oriented toward the needs of child consumers (rather the adults doing design work). "Your model must be built for the purpose you intended," we were told, which meant avoiding a situation in which "a model you want to actually play with falls apart every time you touch it." The purposes we intended were therefore prescribed for us, making the rough and tumble demands of kids' play paramount over adult practices of collecting and display.

Furthermore, the tour organizers repeatedly reinforced the fantasy that our creative labor in this context could have very real professional stakes. Making repeated references to our nondisclosure agreements, they claimed that sufficiently impressive entries could become real LEGO releases in the future. While this was surely a bit of theater meant to lend authenticity to our simulation, one of my fellow participants expressed ambivalence about the possibility that his efforts could become uncompensated labor. Meanwhile, as a structure for making work meaningful, this theatricality signaled the significance of contests and competitions as industry rituals of professionalization—making playful and fun the prospect of success or failure in a creative labor market. Much like the "Big Pitch" session at the Kidscreen trade show in chapter 3 that pitted aspiring television writers against one another, LEGO's design challenge engaged tour participants in a competitive industry process while bringing them together as a community. Our time to work came at the end of scheduled events for the evening, and we were promised that the workshop created for us in the LEGOLAND Hotel would remain open throughout the night. This implicit encouragement to pull all-nighters naturalized overnight "crunch time" as a character of creative work (Consalvo 2008); but it also created an opportunity for members of the tour to bond with one another as part of a creative community, sharing ideas, offering feedback, and collaborating in the course of design work. As an academic whose research agenda initially put me somewhat on the fringes of the group, my own participation in this work session well past midnight helped affirm my membership in the simulated creative community under construction.

The next day, our designs were subject to review by LEGO's professionals. Reinforcing the idea that our creative labor mattered, the organizers held an evening awards ceremony to identify and rank the value of that work. This was no egalitarian, "everyone gets a trophy" event. Instead the organizers clearly marked out winners in our group, highlighting what work would have industrial value. With a handful of children present on the tour, it would be easy to imagine LEGO choosing to validate child submissions over those of their parents—if only to affirm corporate support for the creativity of kids. However, in this case, the awards ceremony focused exclusively on the value of adult work. The organizers went one by one through ten models they found most outstanding, evaluating and describing the merits of each before asking the tour participant who had designed them (notably, all men) to take the stage to receive a prize. This left out more than half of our group, including all the children on the tour who had participated in the design challenge the same as their parents. These children did receive a collective award—a group honorable mention in recognition of their shared efforts—but the specialized attention paid to individual creations focused entirely on work adults had done. This collective exclusion from awards consideration made clear that this comparative evaluation focused on the potential of adults to design in a professionalized capacity. Another design activity that had served as a warm-up for the competition similarly illustrated this exclusion of children from assessment of professional aptitude: the tour organizers had broken us into teams, challenging us to build the most stable, load-bearing bridge possible using only preschool DUPLO blocks. Neither adult participants nor organizers, however, paid much attention to how the competitive dynamics ironically sidelined child participants, whose input became less vital for teams most concerned with winning. For the adults under evaluation, meanwhile, these competitions further affirmed or denied their potential professional value to industry (especially against the surplus nature of their consumer interest in playing with these toys as adults).

In addition to this simulation of the designer evaluation process, our group was also invited to step into the shoes of other LEGO employees. When visiting with managers in Children's Community and Moderation—a group responsible for maintaining a safe online space for children to engage with the brand—our interactions unfolded under the conceit that we had arrived to join in their work. In fact, these employees framed our labor potential as quid pro quo for the small promotional LEGO items handed to us upon arrival; we had been paid with this consumer collectible, and now it was time to put us to work. Our tour guides emphasized this professionalized framework by asking us, "do you have what it takes?," "do you think you could be up to the challenge?," and "will you help do the work of moderating?" their online community. As we soon learned, this work was significant, as every single comment posted at LEGO.com required moderation and approval before becoming visible to all users—a policy meant to provide children special protection from the risks of online interactions. In encouraging children to interact with LEGO online, the company was responsible for delivering a safe space; yet its desire to provide users with participatory agency in that space required prompt moderation.[3] Our tour guides explained that LEGO received nine thousand comments on the average day, each moderated within fifty minutes of their submission (resulting in a 98 percent approval rate). These community managers then presented us with a role-play scenario, asking

Figure 4.3. Models constructed by Inside Tour participants await evaluation by LEGO's professional designers. (Photo by author.)

us to decide in a series of hypothetical scenarios what action, if any, to take to best manage the interactions of children in LEGO's online community. Asking us to try our hands at their jobs, they proceeded to evaluate our ability to internalize corporate principles and policies governing the labor of managing online communities for and of children.

Some of the situations presented to us tested our ability to identify off-topic discussions in need of intervention by LEGO management. Others focused on the difficulties of protecting children from outside marketing, prompting us to police external links to commercial sites like eBay. The imperative to protect children also produced scenarios in which we had to moderate comments and links that might inadvertently disclose users' identities, email addresses, or other private information. Other points of potential intervention focused on the degree to which LEGO could support kids' desires to freely create with corporately owned intellectual property, especially when owned by other media companies. Community moderation here was not just about providing safety but also managing the creative energies of children. Somewhat surprisingly, the solutions advocated by LEGO's managers supported a liberal interpretation of kids' creative rights to remix culture, rather than an attempt to police creativity that fell outside of LEGO's sphere of ownership and licensing agreements. A final type of scenario similarly prompted us to affirm that kids had the right to be critical of the products created by LEGO, and that approval for any such comments need not be withheld. Whether we were being trained to be permissive or restrictive in moderating children's online interactions, the exercise made clear that the work of adult moderation and deliberation had to be done in each instance that a child consumer had something to contribute. By the end of the session, it seemed, we had gained the training to do that work, newly minted as "honorary moderators." Of course, LEGO need not depend on tourists for this labor, as its community management team continued to handle this ongoing stream of submissions. Yet this stop on the tour emphasized the positioning of tourists as industry workers in an imaginative, speculative, and playful way. In this case, moreover, the branded participation of child consumers demanded a significant amount of mediating adult work, where our role-play as agents of the LEGO factory meant taking up a position of professional moderation and management of kids.

This suggestion of the tour as a path to potential professional employment with LEGO's child-centric corporate mission reemerged when one of the three primary organizers revealed that she was a former tour attendee who had subsequently pursued a professional path with the company. The final session on the Inside Tour schedule also highlighted this linkage between our tourism and the fantasy of our newfound professional capacity. One of LEGO's human resources recruiters spoke directly on the aspirational theme of becoming a LEGO designer. She explained how the process of becoming a designer works, and even encouraged us to apply in the future if we were interested. Until this point in the tour, we had been invited to consider our professional potential through play; but now we were directly prompted to consider formalizing such industry relations. The recruiter affirmed that the design competition workshop we had experienced mirrored what real applicants endure, but she prepared us to expect that we might be assigned "homework" to design beforehand as well. Tying together many of the experiences we shared as a tour group, the recruiter also noted that every prospective employee who interviews on the Billund campus visits the Idea House too. Her comments thus made explicit the articulations between professionalism and tourism that had been suggested throughout the event. She also addressed our potential status as fans of LEGO and assured us that such fandom had both utility and potential in the professional interview process. As she recalled, fans without formal design schooling or professional experience often won the chance to interview; and even when they failed to land the job, she added, fans played a vital role in the competitive interview process. While some applicants with impressive industrial design credentials had not had prior familiarity with LEGO elements, fans possessed an expertise that productively pushed the entire group to do better work. Overall, this recruiter reinforced the impression that applying to work for LEGO would very much resemble the tourist journey we had experienced, revealing a path (however unlikely) through which fans could belong in this corporate world.

Thus while the recruiter framed our tourist experience as part of an aspirational professionalism, her comments also reinforced the boundaries of that corporate culture and the exclusions that keep some on the outside. Professional entry into the work world of the factory was by no means guaranteed, as she explained how LEGO uses a personality test to assess who is and is not a "fit." Instead of seeking a singular personality type to produce a homogeneous corporate culture, she stressed, these assessments identified the unique qualities that workers brought to the table to fill gaps in the existing labor force. She also asked us to consider that the designers we had met over the course of the tour did not represent the whole of that corporate culture, selected instead because they were most extroverted and able to entertain a tour group. Notably, this selectivity did not directly reflect LEGO's more public ambitions to demonstrate commitment to diversity and bring gender balance to its workforce at all levels of the organization. Although we had met many women in administrative and managerial positions, the recruiter responded to pointed questions about the lack of female designers in creative roles selected to interact with us. She acknowledged that a predominance of male designers followed the company's long-standing marketing focus on making toys for boys. A gender-imbalanced production culture, in other words, extended in part from gender-exclusive marketing. The recruiter noted, however, that the growing success of LEGO Friends—a new product theme aimed at providing more inclusivity for girls—would create more equal employment opportunity, given her belief that designers worked best when making products for people like them. These comments stood in some contrast to official statements in the *Responsibility Report* that promised universal, gender-neutral forms of play. This notion of a natural fit between female designers and female-targeted product also conflicted with promises made in the report about new hiring policies ensuring "appeal to both genders in any position" (LEGO Group 2013: 49). However, the recruiter's reflection on who was and was not suited to make product for LEGO consumers held additional significance in the context of the tour, in that it identified participants' gender as a consideration in their potential entry into the LEGO work world. At the same time, these statements revealed contradiction between the belief that gendered workers were best suited to design cultural goods for gendered subjects and the tour's focus on the work that adults do across generational lines to design playthings for children.

This dialogue with human resources highlighted other tensions during the course of the tour pertaining to LEGO's branded commitment to gender equality in its construction of childhood creativity. With LEGO Friends having launched less than two years prior, many of the presenters' talking points celebrated its early successes—sharing that the product line already accounted for a full 10 percent of all LEGO construction set sales. Amid this excitement, numerous employees made the sole girl tour participant into the target of a Friends marketing blitz. At various stages throughout the tour, LEGO employees would hand out promotional polybags and other swag, seemingly drawn at random across LEGO themes, including City and Super Heroes. Yet the professionals interacting with us consistently offered Friends swag to our girl participant, giving her a Friends-specific LEGO Club Magazine, a Friends polybag, and a Friends-branded visitor badge. With no other participant did I see an employee push Friends product as a point of identification. This pigeonholing led to some parental frustration: in a LEGO Technic presentation framed as "for the guys" in the room, this child's parent also piped up to add "girls too!" Despite corporate rhetoric and communication policy, LEGO employees used Friends as a gender-specific, compulsory offering in their interactions with children, suggesting that gender relations on the ground differed from marketing promises.

Overall, much of the tour experience geared itself toward building and assessing participants' fit with the community of creative labor upon which the company depended. LEGO's specific reasons for doing this appear diffuse. This opportunity to engage industry tourists did have some potential to generate productive labor. On the one hand, even though our group's simulated labor had little immediate use value, our orientation toward the corporate culture could pay later dividends if we reentered that world as designers, tour guides, or aspiring applicants whose presence in the interview process would drive innovation within the professional applicant pool. Yet make no mistake: no evidence confirms the Inside Tour has actually become a reliable path to employment by The LEGO Group. Beyond generating revenues from admission fees, the tour has remained most centrally a promotional tool that propagates corporate brand identities and values. In this case, that brand pedagogy has operated through support for fan fantasies of crossing professional-amateur boundaries to enter the LEGO workforce. On the other hand, the tour encouraged participants to be better promoters (if not producers) of LEGO product. Whether that promotion centered on new corporate initiatives like the LEGO House or simply new product, the tour organizers urged participants to return home and act as fan evangelists and influencers for the LEGO brand (evoking the transgenerational industry participation of the "Marvel Dad" explored in chapter 2). As an experience directly tied to the company's community engagement strategy, the Inside Tour granted access to exclusive industry spaces not merely for fans' gratification but as part of the management of the larger LEGO brand through its fan community. Just as these community engagement strategies include reaching out to provide access and perks to fan blogs and other social media influencers in that community, our tour experiences might have led participants to spread brand values and consumer goodwill within the larger group of fans with which we would later interact. A senior designer I spoke with during the tour affirmed this need to bring fans in line with the company's preferred values and market emphases, specifically citing the incongruence of adult fans with the primary corporate brand and mission. In this sense, much of the tour communicated those preferred corporate values to a surplus audience beyond the primary focus on children; it reoriented adult consumers toward the labor of creating for children and moderating the community in line with branded corporate needs, refiguring adult consumption as something compatible with these foci. By asking adults to participate in the work and promotion of making children's culture—rather than just consuming it—LEGO built a more industrially useful set of transgenerational corporate relations.

A process of assessing and validating participants' fit for the industrial inside, this tour ultimately modulated the boundaries of cultural work and figured the adult tourist as a part of the factory constructing childhood consumption, rather than a parallel site of surplus consumption. Of course, the simulated professional subjectivities on offer to the tourist never became mutually exclusive from consumption. The tourists willing to pay to visit the industrial inside were also a target market for LEGO's products—captive audiences for presentations that could serve as glorified sale pitches for high-end products with price tags of US$200 or more. We also were explicitly reminded of our consumer status during our visit to the customer service office that fulfills requests for missing and broken pieces, where we were held more at arm's length than at any other stop on the tour. While our hosts were welcoming and gracious, they bluntly communicated that they "needed to keep an eye on us" around the many bins of LEGO elements warehoused in their workspace. Even if playfully delivered by these customer service agents, instructions to "keep your hands in your pockets" reminded tourist consumers of the potential crisis of boundary maintenance that our presence could represent. Perhaps appropriately, it was when interacting with customer relations specialists that our status as customers could be most keenly felt.

Our trip to the LEGO Employee Store also emphasized the persistent primacy of our consumer role on a more spectacular level. Although the role-play of visiting a retail outlet only accessible to LEGO employees (and shopping with their employee discount) extended our simulated fantasy of professionalism, the experience emphasized our power to spend over our power to work. LEGO provided each participant with a giant box that would be shipped for free to our home address, encouraging us to fill it up before the fantasy of being a part of the LEGO factory ended. Moreover, the articulation between adulthood and consumption persisted in other moments, such as my observation of a participant insisting that their child pick something out from the Employee Store, despite the child's disinterest. Reversing the dynamics of pleading child and annoyed parent, the AFOL drove consumption first and foremost. Several participants also appeared to be buying two of every item they selected—one to keep for themselves and another to sell on the aftermarket. While an industrious form of investment and retail labor taken on by the consumer, such work did not directly benefit LEGO (aftermarket sales of old product on eBay could in fact compete with the company's attempts to push new product). As a result, tour rules explicitly forbade its consumer-workers from purchasing more than two of any item, recognizing and regulating this potentially productive and entrepreneurial practice. While we may have entered the store through the fantasy of being an employee, this moment at the end of the tour reoriented us to consumption—suggesting that, in the end, LEGO was happy to maintain its surplus market even while reframing adult consumption to match its branded corporate culture.

Conclusion

To conclude, let us return to the Wonka Chocolate Factory. As the honest, loving child that Willy Wonka idealizes, Charlie Bucket seems the perfect successor and embodiment of corporate culture to chart the factory's future. Yet what if Wonka realized that handing this labor responsibility over to a minor sat somewhat at odds with the playful, Technicolor, carefree, child-centric ethos for which his company seems to stand? What if Wonka considered the potential incongruity between serving the child's desire for magical taste adventures and installing children as workers in that system (subject to the same questions of labor and exploitation that Oompa Loompas might be)? What if he decided that perceptions of the Wonka brand's social responsibility to children would be better served by cultivating adult consumers as aspiring professionals in that service? In that case, it would perhaps be Grandpa Joe to whom Wonka could have turned instead of Charlie. Yet unlike Charlie, who already embodied the brand ideal, Grandpa Joe might require some reeducation: his selfish adult consumer interests would require reorientation to the values of Wonka corporate culture (after all, it was Joe who tempted Charlie with the Fizzy Lifting Drinks and encouraged Charlie to sell his Everlasting Gobstopper sample to the competition). Thus the tour of the Chocolate Factory might have been an opportunity not to assimilate the ideal child consumer into the world of industry, but instead to transform the surplus adult into a professionalized subject of the child-centric corporate culture.

Willy Wonka may not have been operating from these principles, but global companies like The LEGO Group do, recognizing that their corporate focus on children constitutes a transgenerational brand culture in which the valuable labor of producing play requires the vested participation of adult professionals and adult consumers. Branded tourist experiences like LEGO's Inside Tour represent a blurring of boundaries through which we can see the role of consumers as participants in the corporate cultures at the heart of industry. As outsiders, tourists can serve as audiences for the ritualized articulation of corporate cultures whose interest and attention validates brands' value; those tourists can then return to the outside world as potential advocates for the branded cultures in which industry has invested. Yet at the more specific level of the transgenerational, this case study reveals that these boundary crossings are more complex than unfettered, remaining subject to persistent juxtapositions between childhood and adulthood. The Inside Tour transmits a corporate culture across the boundaries of production and consumption, but in its articulations of adulthood and childhood at that intersection it ultimately reinforces the exclusion of children from the world of industry, insisting on the participation of adults as professional subjects. Through a simulation of life in its factories, LEGO has transformed its adult tourists into subjects of corporate culture because it cannot similarly professionalize children amid corporate commitment to the ideologies of childhood specialness and extraindustrial innocence. The prosocial corporate responsibility to children so perceived demands a transgenerational reliance on adults to coinhabit its child-centric brand culture.

Of course, LEGO can hire adult professionals to do most of this work. And thus the additional significance of tourist experiences like the Inside Tour—where consumers are only invited into a fantasy of professionalization—

resides in highlighting the transformational capacity of transgenerational strategies. By inviting tourists into the space of pediocular industry, LEGO transforms play into work, amateur sensibilities into professional aspirations, and adult fandom into corporately responsible stewardship of branded child creativity. This case thus reveals the boundary crossings at the heart of transgenerational media industries to be a crucible of articulations and rearticulations in which meaning and value can be made and remade through the branded relations of childhood, adulthood, and the production of culture across them. Nevertheless, LEGO's transgenerational strategies do turn on a corporate refusal to disrupt the generational boundaries between amateur and professionalism in respect of the perceived special needs of children that adults should serve. The next chapter will directly confront the possibilities of such disruption, asking what happens when media industries recognize children as a source of labor and enable cultural work to cross these generational divides.

CHAPTER 5

Child Labor

Testing the Limits of Transgenerational Media Industries

In the 1988 comedy *Big*, twelve-year-old Josh Baskin makes a wish on a magic Zoltar machine to skip past his frustrating childhood. When Josh wakes the next morning—now fully grown and played by Tom Hanks—he discovers that his adult status comes with new responsibilities. Chased out of his home by a mother who does not recognize him, Josh must find a job to provide himself with food and shelter. Drawing on his digital savvy and familiarity with children's consumer products, Josh applies to work as a data entry clerk at the MacMillan Toy Company in New York City. He holds this position until a chance encounter with the company owner in the iconic retail space of FAO Schwarz on Fifth Avenue. Mr. MacMillan is the pediocular adult professional, roaming the store to learn what kids want from their toys. Yet Josh proves to be something more, impressing Mr. MacMillan through his ability to engage the space of the toy store *as a child*. Transplanted to work in an adult body and industry, Josh's child mind contains a perspective and enthusiasm that even MacMillan lacks; yet Josh can also share that insight, leading the industrialist in a virtuosic duet on the store's giant "walking piano" (fig. 5.1). MacMillan quickly moves Josh out of data entry to become vice president of product development, where his new responsibilities include product testing—determining through play what toys and games are fun, which are not, and why. This professional success temporarily distracts Josh from his quest to reverse his transformation and ultimately return home to his childhood. Until that reversal at the end of the film, however, Josh's status as a professionalized child makes him the idealized but magically impossible labor subject of this entertainment sec-

Figure 5.1. The iconic "Walking Piano" scene in *Big* hints at the value of the professional child laborer to the pediocular toy executive. (Screen capture.)

tor: a source of child insight and productivity to be mined by industry once transformed and transported into the adult world of labor.

Josh Baskin represents the transgenerational industry subject par excellence. He occupies a space between adulthood and childhood, and in building bridges between them, reinforces this central binary of age-based distinction. As perceived by his colleagues, Josh evokes the pediocular adult professional explored in chapter 3 who can see through the eyes of the child. Yet even if his coworkers are fooled by his adult body, Josh also represents the potential value of children's direct participation in the production of their own consumer culture—where child participation, engagement, and play can provide vital industry input that professional adults cannot. Of course, Josh's transgenerational transformation occurs within a literal wish-fulfillment fantasy and does not represent actual employment practices in the culture industries. Yet this fantasy labor figure speaks to meaningful values and ideals circulating within this transgenerational industry context. While television, comic, and toy industries cannot rely upon a labor pool of children posing as adults to meet their creative and managerial needs, they do nevertheless develop strategies to otherwise employ childhood as a source of productivity. If previous chapters have explored the cultivation of adults as consumers (chapters 2 and 4) and as professionals (chapter 3) who can support the strategies of making and transmitting popular culture across generational boundaries (chapter 1), this final chapter grapples with the work children themselves might do as a part of these transgenerational industries. Instead of focusing on adults' orientation to childhood ideals and identities, it examines how transgenerational dynamics transform children into professional subjects, troubling the presumed exclusion of children from the industries that have reproduced divisions between child and adult as a gulf between consumer and producer.

In doing so, this chapter sits somewhat at odds not just with previous chapters but also with previous scholarship that has recognized children's media industries as expressions of adult cultures, presumptions, and hopes for the next generation rather than the desires, practices, and agency of kids (Buckingham 2000; Kline 1995; Rose 1992; Seiter 1995). Recognition of the child labor that would seem to be excluded from the professionalized culture industries does not refute these previous arguments, but instead offers a contradiction that affirms them: while the boundaries of adult professionalism and child consumerism can be bridged, that transgenerational relationship requires—like Josh Baskin—a transformation. Children can participate in media industries when their labor is reoriented to accommodate the persistent boundaries of professionalism and ideals of generational distinction upon which those industries are built. In this sense, the question of child labor in transgenerational media industries confirms the arguments at the heart of this book, in that it transcends and troubles boundaries within the matrix of adulthood, childhood, professionalism, and amateurism—all while reasserting the power of age and generation over participation in cultural reproduction.

To explore these issues, this chapter examines how and why toy testing—the industry practices for which Josh Baskin's child subjectivity provided so much talent—supports a culture of child participation in industry work. While many contemporary industries have come to rely upon the cocreativity of their consumers as enabled by digital media platforms (Banks 2013), the participatory work of consumer product testing has proven particularly useful for mature, legacy industries like toys facing their own generational crises, as analog, material playthings increasingly compete with immaterial, digital ones. Toy testing enlists the child to identify emerging consumer desires in this context while also producing innovative promotional content that can circulate as "spreadable media" (Jenkins, Ford, and Green 2013) throughout the digital networks of social media in which young consumers increasingly participate. Toy testing is treated here as a broad category encompassing many different kinds of cultural practices, including scientific evaluation of consumer products to meet safety standards, market research gauging children's response to playthings in development, user reviews of product meant to generate trust in product, and unboxing videos that turn children's responses to playthings into a new form of screen content. With the exception of scientific testing (largely bracketed here), these practices represent industrial attempts to harness the productivity of children—often, though not exclusively, framing that work in the playful context of participation in "fun" games and contests. Crucially, these toy testing practices also figure that child work in transgenerational relationship to the parent who must at the very least grant permission but is also frequently framed as a collaborator in this productive sphere. Furthermore, the hands-on work of toy testing often requires children and their parents to be savvy digital media users, making critical perspectives on participatory media work in online environments vital to understanding how consumer product manufacturing sectors adapt to the immateriality of the digital economy (and particularly as they use transgenerational strategies to do so).

To access this intersection between toy testing practices, consumer product industries, and the digital media economy, this chapter puts several different kinds of sources in dialogue. It considers the materials through which toy industries solicit participation online and via social media, as well as the applications that it asks children to submit to become toy testers; it examines the popular discourse around toy testing, particularly as it manifests as advice for securing opportunities to participate; it explores trade reporting in which economic value is imagined, negotiated, and affirmed; and it interrogates the statements that adults make about the value of their children's participation in this economy as well as their own parental roles in it. Although it will be important to recognize the participatory media practices of children as a vital productive input in this industry sphere, it is also necessary to read this "free labor" (Terranova 2000) alongside gift economies (Jenkins, Ford, and Green 2013) and other frameworks that relate work to the "fun" of play (Bulut 2014).

From this theoretical perspective, the chapter first explains how and why toy industry stakeholders—from manufacturers to retailers to research marketers—have cultivated toy testing as a way of harnessing children's engagement in media culture as a productive form of industry participation. The chapter secondly considers how the toy industry recruits, compensates, and professionalizes child participants as media producers responsible for providing feedback, writing online reviews, and creating video content. Yet this enlisted workforce of content generating toy testers can also develop their own channels and revenue streams on digital media platforms like YouTube, further troubling the ideological boundaries between adulthood and childhood, commodified industry labor and noncommercial innocence.

Thus the chapter also reveals the deployment of an ideology of "fun" to manage these disruptions of professionalized labor and identity. On the one hand, despite the value of this work, the toy industry often presents toy testing as part of a *prize economy* in which consumer participation is commodified not as labor but as a form of play structured by rules and contests in which participation gets rewarded with token gifts rather than wages. On the other hand, the autonomy and agency with which children productively participate in these industrialized economies is often discursively disavowed in favor of the consent, collaboration, social influence, good parenting, and managerial labor that adults provide in and over this digital media work. Toy testing unfolds within transgenerational relations that ascribe its labor potential to adult participation and reproductive notions of family while containing child participation within the realm of "fun" organized by prizes and other alternative forms of economy.

On the whole, toy testing reveals how the labor implications of child media production—particularly its disruption of boundaries between adult industry and child consumption—get managed through transgenerational relationships. Children make valuable contributions to industry research and development, but the prize economy maps that work onto the fun of taking part in contests and vying for prizes as authorized and supervised by parents. Kids can anchor multimillion dollar YouTube channels, but the value of that work has been articulated by parents who claim to insulate children from the specter of labor by foregrounding fun. While children perform important work for these industries, their imbrication with transgenerational industry relationships enables parents to remain idealized adult labor subjects with managerial agency over that child participation. Child labor disrupts the boundaries of generation that define these industries while also instigating their transgenerational reinforcement within the digital economy.

Kids at Work

To grasp the significance of toy testing and its mediation as a form of participatory culture online, one must contend with its status as a form of work that can be lucratively commodified and exchanged by the culture industries. In the broadest sense, labor refers to the activities of producing goods or services; within capitalism specifically, labor has the potential to be commodified as an object of exchange (Marx 1847/2009; Appardurai 1986). However, in what she calls the "digital economy," Tiziana Terranova identifies as "free labor" those exchanges in which "knowledgeable consumption of culture is translated into productive activities that are pleasurably embraced and at the same time often shamelessly exploited" (2000: 37). Many other scholars, including Marc Andrejevic (2010) and Axel Bruns (2008), similarly understand the Internet as animated by the efforts of users who add and update the content to which distributional gatekeepers provide us access. However, critical recognition of this user productivity does not mean that users understand themselves as exploited or even as participants in a labor economy. David Hesmondhalgh (2010) calls the reduction of free labor to exploitation "unconvincing and rather incoherent" because it ignores forms of unpaid labor that stand in opposition to capital and it valorizes paid labor despite the oppressive working conditions of paid employment in creative industries. Meanwhile, John Banks (2013) and Hector Postigo (2007) reveal how video game players engage in unpaid co-creative labor because of the social payoffs of participation in productive fan communities. These claims reinforce wider research in digital game studies that builds on and complicates Johan Huizinga's notion of a "magic circle" that creates boundaries between everyday life and the meaningful rituals of play (1938/2004: 103). Pointing to the permeability of play within the magic circle and work outside of it, Nick Dyer-Witheford and Greig de Peuter identify in digital games a "playbor force" of worker-players whose participatory engagement can be harnessed as a form of productive input by developers, publishers, and other institutions (2009: 23). Participation in the digital economy can thus constitute the labor of work and the "fun" of play simultaneously.

This perspective enables us to consider how legacy industry institutions in the business of play, including toy manufacturers like Hasbro, Mattel, or LEGO, might embrace digital media platforms like YouTube and others to harness this user power as work. Ergin Bulut (2014) has already identified professional video game testing as a form of precarious employment for adult professionals, defined by what he calls a "degradation of fun" that transforms previously pleasurable forms of play into commodified labor in the production of digital commodities. While consideration of toy testing in this chapter extends that work by asking how industrial productivity is generated from fun, it also shifts focus to ask how the valorization of fun (rather than its degradation) enables children (rather than adults) to engage in productive forms of participation on behalf of culture industries in the digital economy.

Toy testing is not native to the digital economy, of course; it emerged in twentieth-century manufacturing contexts out of the twinned concerns of protecting the safety of child consumers as well as conducting corporate research to measure and meet the expectations of that growing consumer culture (Burton 1997; Crossen 2007; Curran 2017). As consumer products, toys undergo rigorous scientific testing of all kinds by adult engineers to ensure that they meet at a material level the different regulations and safety standards imposed throughout the world. In terms of testing the experience of pleasure these products provide, however, this industry has commonly relied upon children to provide more direct consumer insight. In the contemporary culture industries, children participate in play testing in at least three different but overlapping ways. First, toy manufacturers gather their consumers to play with their products as part of their market research strategy, inviting children into industry space to provide feedback on in-development product. At The LEGO Group's corporate headquarters in Billund, Denmark, for example, designers position their own creative work as part of a dialogue—and even struggle—with play testers brought in to evaluate their concepts. Respecting the need for consumer feedback but challenged by testers who fail to appreciate design elegance, abuse or destroy prototypes, and reveal inadequacies in adult work, these designers tell war stories that frame children as important if disruptive participants in the creative process.[1]

However, child consumers also participate in a second type of industrial toy testing practices in spaces outside of the factory—particularly as enabled by digital media. In an online reviewing economy that extends well beyond toys, retailers like Amazon.com depend on their users to produce a significant amount of sales support content. When retail consumers post online reviews, they add to a detailed array of information that encourages others to trust in online transactions dependent on virtual evaluation of products. Instead of waiting for consumer reviews to emerge organically in the process of purchase, use, and feedback, many manufacturers and retailers seek to incite that consumer feedback, recruiting customers to receive product in exchange for providing reviews. Third-party intermediaries often coordinate these practices; ProductTestingUSA.com, for example, solicits participants to test a wide range of products from video games to cosmetics ("How It Works" n.d.). Toy testing thus represents only one small part of the reviewing economy—yet its remains significant as a key point of participation for child consumers. In this reviewing economy, moreover, the function of toy testing changes compared to the product development model: the child's valuable consumer feedback is not just used internally for product improvement but is also shared with a wider audience of consumer peers through online media platforms. Such toy testing evaluates play appeal, but it also serves as a form of external marketing to circulate claims about that appeal to other potential consumers.

A third type of toy testing might be considered more independent—at least insofar as its participatory practices are not conducted explicitly under direction by toy retailers, manufacturers, and the research firms they hire. By circulating "unboxing videos" and other consumer analysis of toy products, YouTube channels like EvanTubeHD, KidToyTesters, and more have created an entertainment genre out of toy testing. In these video reviews, kids document their initial reactions to consumer products as they first open and play with them; the most popular unboxing videos can attract millions of viewers. On the YouTube platform, children act as literate content creators with agency over their work (Burgess and Green 2009; Lange 2014), and as viewers they also seek out unboxing videos and other media created by their peers to contextualize their consumer desires and experiences in a form of collective engagement (Marsh 2016: 371–72). Beyond peer-to-peer relationships, David Craig and Stuart Cunningham (2017) situate children's participation in unboxing video production and consumption as part of the creative labor at the heart of "social media entertainment." They argue that the unboxing video requires us to consider children as producers and entrepreneurs in this emerging industrial context; the makers of unboxing videos are "professionalizing-amateur content creators and YouTube partners" (83–84).

While unboxing videos are only one part of the larger field of toy testing that this chapter investigates, they demand recognition of children's creativity as it unfolds in relation to professionalized industrial spheres. Andrew Zolides similarly frames as "child media production" a discursive formation and visual aesthetic in which media brands like *Axe Cop* and *Kid President* foreground the agency, autonomy, and participation of children in the highly publicized creation of valuable content (2017a: 150). Meanwhile, as emerging "micro-celebrities" in the space of YouTube (Marwick 2015), child media producers increasingly circulate as commodities in their own right, transgressing the boundaries between childhood and career-oriented adulthood, much like child stars have long sat in uneasy relationship to their status as industry professionals (Cary 1997; O'Connor 2008; O'Connor 2011).

The visibility of unboxing videos and the talent behind them has captured industry attention—not just as a lucrative part of YouTube's content-driven advertising market but also as marketing collateral by toy manufacturers seeking to harness this participatory power. According to Samantha Cheh (2017) of *Techwire Asia*, this "next generation" of YouTube content producers has drawn significant attention from the toy industries: "Major toymakers such as Mattel Inc., Hasbro Inc., and MGA Entertainment Inc. are now turning to these pint-sized stars to help create content and market their latest products." Particularly as ongoing changes to YouTube algorithms make advertising revenues unpredictable for content providers, channels like KidToyTesters have increasingly cultivated relationships with toy industry stakeholders that provide direct payment for producing sponsored content. Although toy testing therefore fits snugly within the larger digital economies of online reviewing, streaming video advertising, and sponsored content production, unique conditions within the toy industry motivate intense interest in the voices and productive capacities of its consumers. As Cheh (2017) also notes, the value of online reviews and unboxing videos as market indicators has risen in an industry facing significant disruption. In 2017, major global retailer Toys "R" Us announced bankruptcy, while industry leading manufacturers Mattel, Hasbro, and LEGO reported disappointing earnings—all amid fears about digital playthings shrinking the market for more traditional consumer products. This climate also disrupted toy advertising logics, with the power of traditional television marketing in doubt. According to Nielsen ratings shared with *Bloomberg Businessweek*, The Disney Channel saw a 53 percent decline in viewership among six-to-eleven-year-olds between 2008 and 2017, while Nickelodeon faced a similar 54 percent loss (Stratton 2017). Those viewers had not lost interest in video content altogether but followed their interests to new platforms beyond broadcast and cable television platforms upon which toy marketers have long relied. Yet amid this anxiety, the participatory culture of online reviewing and unboxing videos provided new promise, with millions of kids watching their peers discuss, open, play with, and interact with toys—proof that even traditional playthings could remain a crucial component of the new media environment. Already by 2014, CNN reported that the number of unboxing videos on YouTube had increased 871 percent in four years, with users having produced 6.5 years of footage in the previous year alone (Kelly 2014).

In this context, toy companies saw significant opportunity for user-generated digital media content themed around consumer toy testing to help secure and maintain their market. MGA Entertainment, for example, began developing products specifically to take advantage of this culture of peer-to-peer production (Cheh 2017). LOL Surprise!, for example, was a blind-buy item in which the toy was fully concealed by its packaging. This mystery—and the suspense that could accompany the act of opening it—encouraged consumers to record and share their experience of surprise when discovering which of fifty possible toys they received. Beyond developing new product, the toy industry has also recruited its consumers as a driving force behind its marketing efforts. In that sense, what is most significant about LOL Surprise! is not the item itself but instead its incitement of consumer participation in its mediated marketing. According to Hasbro's senior vice president for digital marketing, Victor Lee, these digital platforms supported a force of consumer "influencers" whose power lies in their status as peers who "are able to relate better to kids than a scripted or overly produced traditional TV advertisement would" (Cheh 2017). Confirming this industry logic, a "holiday spending survey" by firm PwC LLP reported that 72 percent of "young Generation Z consumers" saw YouTube as the social media outlet with the most influence over their purchasing decisions, because they would be "far more likely to buy a product if an influencer they follow shares a product review or uses that product on social media" (Stratton 2017). In this market for influence, online reviews and unboxing videos represented a new evolution of toy testing practices compared to internal forms of playtesting research: beyond testing the viability of the product to induce fun, these new media forms mediated that test as a form of publicity which in circulation online could buy significant visibility and influence for products. Whether produced for a new toy concept or an established property, the video that documented the initial reaction of its child subject to its play possibilities created an opportunity for market impact proportional to the influence of the child (where the number of views a video received or followers a user had could measurably test that impact).

Attempts to harness the peer-reviewing practices of influencers have not been confined to the toy industry. Looking at the packaged consumer products industries more broadly, trade publication *Packaging Digest* reflected on the promise of unboxing videos, attributing their value to "consumers' interest and, most importantly, trust in online reviews." Social media has emerged as "a major influencer of purchasing decisions," thus representing "opportunities for brands to reach consumers in ways not previously possible" (Luttenberger 2016). Similarly, Laura Zielinski wrote in *Brand Packaging* that the unboxing video could give "brands' potential customers access to their peers' perspective on products" (2016: 22). She quoted marketing executive John Ball to argue that this peer-to-peer mediated engagement with packaged goods enabled a "third-party credibility" that could substitute for the traditional role of the brick-and-mortar retailer. Instead of going to a store to make consumer decisions, online users could rely upon one another's mediation of the shopping process. As a result, Ball argued, many brands were "catching on and creating their own unboxing videos and/or featuring the trend in their advertising to control the experience" (Zielinski 2016: 24). Following these wider trends, toy manufacturer MGA Entertainment decided in 2014 to shift its marketing budget away from television in order to commit a full 90 percent of that budget to digital platforms. Larger manufacturers like Mattel remained comparatively invested in traditional media, yet by 2017 it too had shifted an estimated half of its marketing budget to digital media (Stratton 2017).

What remained unique about the participatory culture of peer-to-peer toy testing reviews, however, was its reliance upon children to take part in this work—a potential disruption of the generational boundaries around adult professionalism and commodified industry labor. By looking at how children have been invited and incentivized to participate in toy testing—and how that potentially professionalized labor has been reframed as part of a "fun"-based prize economy—the remainder of this chapter explains how transgenerational industry relations have contained this potential disruption.

Now Hiring

Although toy testing directly supports the needs of culture industries and constitutes a significant amount of work from the children who make unboxing videos and other digital reviews, its productive practices have not been uniformly valued as a labor commodity traded for the economic capital of wages. Instead the work of toy testing has circulated with alternative forms of valorization and exchange as supported by the digital economy. Building on early digital theorists who understood knowledge work as a process of giving back to a larger community (Rheingold 1993/2000), Henry Jenkins, Sam Ford, and Joshua Green situate user participation in media distribution as part of a "gift economy" based in social conventions, repaid obligations, and a sense of "worth" over "value" (2013: 63–65, 67). While this ethos offsets unpaid participation in the digital economy with the pleasurable affective motivations of community and collaboration, the practices of gifting can nevertheless intersect with capitalist forms of commodified exchange. As Jenkins, Ford, and Green write, "Objects in movement—media that spreads—thus may travel across different systems of exchange, often multiple times in the course of their life cycle" (66). Not quite pointing to exchanges fully beyond labor, then, gift economies invite reflection on the wider, intersecting systems of exchange imbricated in media use under digital capitalism. In this light, toy testing supports economic exchanges shaped both by the terms of commodity labor and those of gifting. By looking at the recruitment rhetoric and compensation strategies that have been used to encourage participation in toy testing, a clearer picture of this hybrid economy can emerge.

The experience of toy testing varies, of course, across in-house play research, online reviewing, and video content production. Yet in each case, participation has typically been framed as an exchange. In order to manage the expectations of participants in on-site market research sessions conducted at the Mattel Imagination Center facilities in El Segundo, California, the 2018 application for aspiring toy testers offered a detailed description of what the experience would involve as well as what compensation the company would offer. "Each session usually takes approximately 20 to 60 minutes," the application explained. "The children are shown new toys and their play activity is observed. We can then determine if changes are needed to simplify the operation and/or increase the enjoyment of the toy based on feedback from the children. . . . After the session, each child is given a gift for helping in the development of our products" ("Imagination Center" 2018). Parents who let their children participate therefore received a very clear explanation of what their children would and would not be doing. On the one hand, children would provide feedback that Mattel would capitalize in the course of product development. On the other hand, children would not be performing labor; instead their productive participation was explicitly valued as part of a gift economy requiring token acknowledgment of their contributions. At the other end of the spectrum—where toy industries make deals with YouTube influencers to produce sponsored unboxing videos—children's productive activities have been compensated in far more commodified terms. As toy companies replaced traditional ad expenditures with sponsored video content, they spent anywhere from a couple thousand dollars to US$200,000 to entice social media influencers to engage with their product (depending of course on follower reach and the quality of engagement via comments, likes, and shares) (Stratton 2017). The play of toy testing thus sits in an uneasy, unfixed relationship to labor—sometimes directly compensated as such but other times disavowing the idea of commodified work. Indeed, since toy companies' investment in unboxing videos has targeted a relative handful of producers with the most measurable influence, most children making unboxing videos on YouTube never see any kind of direct payment for their participation in this work, settling instead for other kinds of rewards and motivations. Yet whether the work is done for wages or for gifts, participation operates similarly according to an economy of exchange.

This quid pro quo can be seen in other calls made for toy testers by retailers and manufacturers. In 2015, online retailer The Hut promised to send its online toy testers free product, proposing clear terms of exchange in which "You and your child can play with and use the toy as it is intended, followed by providing a review on exactly what you thought of it" (Costello 2015). Here the participant was figured not as a child alone but as a transgenerational team of child and parent working together (where the parent would likely author the review). Similarly, manufacturer Step2 made very clear in 2018 the duties it expected toy testing applicants to perform. Those selected to participate could keep the test product in exchange for their participation, and the application detailed the terms under which participation would be satisfied. Upon receipt of the product, the tester had no longer than fourteen days to complete a product review on Step2.com as well as to share images of the toy on Facebook, Instagram, and/or Twitter using the specific hashtags #Step2Kids and #ToyTester ("Step2 Toy Tester" 2018). In earlier years of this toy testing program, participants were also responsible for submitting thirty-second videos in addition to their written reviews (Lill 2017). If these terms were not met, the application explained that "Step2 has the right to charge you the cost of the product plus the cost of freight." Beyond their contributions to the production of this review content, parents were also expected to take on financial responsibility for their child's participation. Embedded in these terms was a fluid, dynamic economic relationship between the tester and the industry: the tester had the potential to engage in productive industry work based in the obligation of gift exchange, but he or she could also be remanded back to the realm of commodity exchange if that work was not completed. At the same time, the expectation that social media would play a role in this work figured toy testing as a productive activity to emerge in transgenerational collaboration; while the review produced might benefit from a child's perspective, its distribution on social media would likely require adult help (particularly given Step2's focus on toddler toys). In this way, the terms of these applications structured toy testing practice as transgenerational by prescribing who would do what kind of work as part of what type of exchange.

Perhaps one of the best examples of toy testing as an exchange-based practice was ToyTesters.tv, a British web portal active from 2013 to 2016. Created by Gemma Gallagher, a television and digital media strategist, the project emerged from "creative industries" policies dominant in the continental context at that time. Funded by iNets South West Creative Industries and the European Regional Development Fund, ToyTesters.tv also drew from leadership by Creative England, a not-for-profit company that "accelerates talent and ideas across tech, games, film and TV" ("Creative England" n.d.) ToyTesters.tv was thus positioned to take advantage of policy priorities as well as shifting relationships between traditional culture industries and emerging digital economies. Serving children, parents, and industry stakeholders alike, ToyTesters.tv provided video reviews of toys and games, generating media content and a community of users from engagement with consumer products. This community was to be united by the belief "that children should be able to review toys, games, apps and products that are made for them. We also love the idea of children being instrumental in concept creation and product development" ("Information" 2013). The mediated production of video reviews, in this climate, aimed to initiate children within the otherwise closed and adult space of toy development, placing specific emphasis on the industry value that could be found in children's productive participation. The review process worked similar to the toy testing models used by Step2: select applicants would be sent free products in exchange for producing video reviews (called "testing reports") and/or answering questionnaires. But whereas Step2 solicited reviews on its own website to directly stimulate sales, the third-party ToyTesters.tv model positioned itself between the consumer and manufacturer as a third-party market research conduit. Testing reports would be "passed on to the companies so they can use this information to refine the product or enhance future products. Aggregated information may also be used in order for a toy or game company to publish information on their products" ("Information" 2013).

This aggregation of children as a community of market research subjects produced a commodity that the site could sell to manufacturers and advertisers alike. This sales pitch was often quite explicit. On the one hand, the areas of the ToyTesters.tv website that explicitly addressed industry users demurred that any content available on the site was "strictly for ToyTesters.TV Club members. That's because we only want children to participate in our activities. They are, after all, TOP SECRET." This claim reinforced the company's emphasis on the productive agency of children while imagining a space inaccessible to the adult industry professional (and thus inflating its potential value). On the other hand, ToyTesters.tv clarified that this boundary between industry and the participatory world of kids could be crossed for the right price. "If you're interested in entering the top secret world of TTHQ, we can provide adults with a sneaky peek behind the scenes," the site teased. Driving home the exclusive nature of this access to a closed community of child users, ToyTesters.tv requested that its potential industry partners send emails similarly marked as "TOP SECRET" ("Toy Companies" 2013). ToyTesters.tv thus adopted an intermediary role between participatory children and adult industry, generating economic exchange out of the transgenerational value proposition of enabling professionals to cross these boundaries. A similar promise was made to help marketers "connect with your target audience" by facilitating the production of sponsored video content centered on their product offerings ("Advertise" n.d.). Industry partners were instructed to reach out to arrange to have their toys tested and featured in review videos, as well as to commission short documentary content and participate in interview features.

One of the most significant boundaries under negotiation in these exchanges, however, concerns the determination of which children could provide the most industrially valuable participation. These play testing economies have rarely proven open to all, depending instead on closed and hierarchical communities of child participants. These boundaries have been largely produced through the search process in which children are recruited to participate in this work. According to Oisin Curran (2017) of *How Stuff Works*, toy companies have rarely advertised their internal play testing positions "for fear of being overwhelmed with preschool resumes." Although The LEGO Group did rely on play testers, for example, a February 2018 search of the corporate website revealed more than 180 types of marketing, manufacturing, and retail openings in the global organization—with toy testing not listed ("Careers" n.d.). On its Frequently Asked Questions page, manufacturer Hasbro explained to aspiring toy testers in Canada that they should look instead for opportunities to participate in tests run by the national Toy Testing Council and Protégez-Vous/Options Consommateurs—deflecting rather than soliciting direct interaction with consumers on this level ("Customer Service" n.d.). Hasbro limited its direct play testing interests to the preschool market, explaining that its Playskool division alone might have been interested in getting feedback from parents who tried out toys with their little ones. These boundary drawing practices have made opportunities to participate scarce: enthusiast blogs like *All Best Toys* suggested that aspiring toy testers should look for opportunities to do focus group testing throughout the market research economy more broadly, where opting into contact lists for research companies like Volition could eventually lead to toy-related opportunities. "While none of these companies can assure that you will get a survey or toy-testing possibility," it advises, "you will certainly never obtain the possibility if you do not subscribe" (arenahes 2016).

The competition to become a toy tester has persisted in online toy reviewing. Despite the fact that anyone can post online reviews of products, toy retailers and manufacturers have conducted very public, promotionally minded searches for child consumers who can be officially authorized as product testers and reviewers. In 2017, Kmart Australia sought children aged four through eight to take on the responsibility of becoming "official toy reviewers," in which applicants had to submit detailed applications that included a one-minute video explaining their qualifications for the position ("Kmart" 2017). The aspiring toy tester was thus evaluated on the basis of

Figure 5.2. The ToyTesters.tv application lays out the terms for child participation and prompts aspirants to consider sending proof of their on-camera presence. (Screen capture.)

their photogenic personality. Similarly, to win the position of chief play officer for Toys "R" Us Canada in 2016, young Émile Burbidge had to respond to a call on the retailer's website by producing a two-minute video detailing his fit for the position and discussing the finer points of his favorite toy (Woods 2016). In addition to sharing the age, gender, and national identity factors that would help match product testers to market categories (fig. 5.2), ToyTester.tv applicants were asked to explain their interest in the position—with those over thirteen years old being able to send in a video in addition to their written responses ("About You" 2013).

Perhaps most importantly, these recruitment efforts have sought to identify potential child toy testers with the greatest influence on social media platforms. Nancy Baym (2015) describes participation on digital media platforms in terms of a "relational labor" that commodifies our social connectedness. The digital economy thus rewards practices of self-branding in which so-called social media influencers can leverage their relational labor (Khamis, Ang, and Raymond 2016), commodifying their identities as brands sold to advertisers and brand partners. By building a platform and a network of followers for one's self via social media, digital celebrities can commodify identity as a brand to be sold to advertisers and brand partners.[2] As participants in this digital economy, toy testers, too, have accrued significant labor value through their use of social media. Catherine Alford (2017) advised that children who want to be selected must be comfortable on social media and in front of cameras, as these mediated performances of identity prove crucial to being noticed and securing the work.

While these companies have all sought to harness the participatory practices at the intersection of toy play and Internet use, they have also enclosed these productive energies within a corporately authorized and exclusive work community. As described on *How Stuff Works*, the application process is "an audition" in which children will be evaluated for their capacity to do the work of evaluating product.[3] Although the terms of participation do not explicitly communicate an expectation that the child's enthusasm must generate glowing reviews, it seems likely that the savvy parent would help suppress negative responses in the production of the review or video, realizing that future participation could depend on providing the kind of content and influence that the industry wants.

The result of this audition process has been a professionalization of child toy testing practices. Even if not explicitly figured as commodified labor exchange, the work of toy testing has taken on the values and meanings of employment, where securing participation often amounts to a job search. In its list of strategies for finding toy testing opportunities, the enthusiast blog *All Best Toys* equated aspiring applicants to typical job hunters: "treat it like any other kind of various job," the blog recommended. "MySpace maintains a list of available placements in the toy group, with the alternative of looking by city, state, or zip code to limit the outcomes. You could additionally see SearchTempest, CareerBuilder and also Monster. Every one of which post notices of toy-industry work every so often" (arenahes 2016). Directing the aspiring toy tester to the same online resources with which users position themselves in a labor market, this advice granted a professionalism to the participatory practices of consumers. Moreover, the job hunting framework imposed upon this application process emphasized a politics of precarity and scarcity that could lead aspirants to disappointment. "Remember, nevertheless, that bigger toy firms may not wish to be bothered, and you might often walk away empty-handed," the blog concluded. "Try to stay upbeat and understand that a [*sic*] work as a toy tester does not come effortlessly" (arenahes 2016). These efforts to manage applicant expectations revealed real perceptions of emotional and economic stakes in this professionalized consumer economy.

Of course, sometimes this professionalization has been conveyed in a tongue-in-cheek manner. Reporting on Fisher Price's 2017 search for an Australian-based "Top Toy Tester," the website *Essential Kids* offered a gently satirical critique of the tendency to treat child toy testers as aspiring professionals. Describing the search as one for "a toy connoisseur, a trendsetter even, when it comes to the latest gadgets and must-haves," it offered the advice: "brush up your CV and update your LinkedIn profile, kids, because oh-boy do we have the ultimate job for you." Imagined as part of this employment was a plastic company car, flexible naptime hours, and a "generous remuneration package" of free toys (Beeston 2017). This report mocked the professionalization of child toy testers, and yet it recognized the grueling audition processes, connoisseur consumer identities, and economic exchanges at odds with the assumed innocence and extra-commercium status of children. In evoking social media platforms like LinkedIn, meanwhile, it echoed *All Best Toys*' efforts to situate toy testing within the labor identities and practices of the digital economy. Toy testing has participated in a wider discourse of professionalized employment and job hunting advice, despite its focus on exchanges outside of waged labor and the productive activities of children instead of adults.

This professionalization of child productivity has also been produced by the social and economic capital accrued to those who secure participation in these industry practices. The titles given to child toy testers, for example, have afforded honorary insider status within the corporate hierarchies of adult labor. At the conclusion of its 2016 search for a toy tester in the Canadian market, Toys "R" Us bestowed upon twelve-year-old Émile Burbidge the title of chief play officer (CPO) and assigned him the responsibility of "passing judgment on gadgets, games and various other plastic playthings on behalf of legions of Canadian kids." Supporting the company's market research and promotional aims, Burbidge described his job as one in which "different vendors come and show me the toys. So I play with them and try to find out what's cool about that toy. Then I go on interviews and talk about them" (Woods 2016). As CPO, Burbidge served as a resource for gauging consumer interest and as a marketing poster-child to be deployed by the retailer in interviews and other promotional outlets. Yet his CPO title granted this work a professional weight beyond his status as surrogate consumer. Toys "R" Us conducted a similar search in the United States later that year—this time looking for a "President of Play" between the ages of nine and thirteen who was "well spoken" and "comfortable on camera." In addition to the professionalized social capital provided by the title, however, the position was described as "a paid job and the winning kid will receive a variety of toys across all product category" (Kell 2016). Whether conflating free product with payment or revealing the company's willingness to directly engage children as paid laborers, this insistence on toy testing as a "job" with a title and wages constructed child toy testers as participants in the adult economies and social relations of industry. The potential for toy testing to be a professionalized practice was also highlighted on the ToyTesters.tv platform when it implied that its interface between industry and young consumers carried educational and occupational value. Taking a long view, the website figured interactions between industry and child consumers as one with instructive potential for those who might grow up to be professionals. ToyTesters.tv promised parents of its child users that it was "busy making an online TV show that will feature educational content such as career advice in the toy and game industries, interviews with toy makers, designers, producers and manufacturers, behind the scenes at toy companies and much more" ("Information" 2013).

Professionalization of child participation in toy testing can most clearly be seen in the entrepreneurial and celebrity-driven streaming video economies of YouTube. Popular and industry discourse on unboxing videos has insisted on the agency of children as drivers of this economy. Samantha Cheh (2017) described the YouTube channel KidToyTesters as one created by a group of five siblings aged thirteen-and-under from Omaha, Nebraska. In 2016, Australian journalists marveled at sixteen-year-old Ben Pasternak, who had leveraged his success in the world of unboxing videos six years prior as venture capital to support the development of his own app (Vincent 2016). Pasternak represented the potential for professionalized child YouTube creators to build their own media empires on the foundation of toy testing in unboxing videos. Similarly, Oisin Curran (2017) invited his readers to stand in awe of Elliot Cowan, who as a nine-year-old started his own product testing consultant business, "headhunted" his peers to take part in focus groups, and charged toy and app companies no less than US$300 "plus the brand new toys and games they play with" per session of access to those consumer perspectives. When child toy testers have been recognized as professionalized entrepreneurs in these economies, they have also been increasingly viewed as paid labor professionals—where their potential power as social media influencers commands commodity value within wage-based media production economies.

Child toy testers have driven at least two potential revenue streams in the streaming video economies of YouTube. On the one hand, YouTube has shared a percentage of its advertising revenues with its partnered content creators. *Toy Insider* editor Marissa DiBartolo estimated in 2015 that the portion of advertising revenues shared with child entrepreneurs could be in the range of US$5 per one thousand impressions. At that rate, if a YouTube channel could attract one million views per video and post just one such video each day, its annual share of the advertising revenue could reach $1.825 million (ABC News 2015).[4] Of course, not every user could capture this kind of audience, leaving these kinds of economic returns to a few standout producers alone. Changing platform algorithms have also imposed significant consequences on these economics flows, making advertising a significant but unpredictable revenue source even for those users with large followings. Therefore YouTube video entrepreneurs have, on the other hand, pursued direct payment from toy companies and retailers in exchange for producing sponsored content. Some online toy review sites, like "The Noise on Toys," frowned on this practice and saw themselves as independent checks on the marketing excesses of the toy industry. Nevertheless, the YouTube economy has supported paid brand partnerships, simply requiring that any such content be disclosed, flagged as "sponsored content" (Stratton 2017). Even so unappealingly designated, sponsored toy reviews and unboxing videos have been very lucrative for some of the content creators engaged in its creation. YouTube channel KidToyTesters revealed to *Techwire* that its videos could earn anywhere between US$3,000 and $20,000 when sponsored by the toy industry (Cheh 2017). Similarly, Catherine Alford (2017) reported that The Warehouse toy company, based in New Zealand, entered into relationships with toy testers that provide them with free product and NZ$8,000 cash. In combination, these advertising and sponsorship economies added up to a significant amount of direct payments for the commodity of kids' media labor. One of the most prominent unboxing channels, EvanTubeHD, was credited with earning some US$1.3 million from video work on YouTube in 2014 alone (arenahes 2016). Speaking on behalf of his son, Evan, who created the channel and provided the celebrity influencer image at its center, father Jared concluded, "You can make a pretty good living from these YouTube videos if you can get the viewership" (ABC News 2015). The unboxing video thus pushed toy testing into a realm that we might recognize as waged creative labor exchanged as a commodity in the digital economy.

Nevertheless, the emergence of play testing, reviewing, and video content creation as labor has unfolded in tension with its parallel participation in other kinds of economies too. As we have seen, the application and audition process discursively professionalizing children's productive activities also set very clear terms, social roles, and expectations for a quid pro quo gift economy. The industrial value of toy testing, in other words, is overlapping and complex: exchangeable as a commodity but also a form of volunteerism recognized with obligatorily gifted consumer products—all embedded in a culture of professionalization that has authorized and qualified children to evaluate consumer products in the peer-to-peer influence networks of digital media.

Despite these many efforts to recruit and reward toy testers, however, popular discourse about this industry sector has continued to reinforce boundaries between adult labor and child's play. Oisin Curran (2017) of *How Stuff Works*, for example, juxtaposed the toy testing work that children did—which is "really a form of market research designed to help toy companies fine-tune their products to meet consumers expectations"—to that of "grown-ups in lab coats" employed to do the more complex and technical work of scientifically testing toys for safety. To Oisin, children remained end-users, not participants in the more technical world of adult work. By contrast, companies like Intertek involved in toy testing conducted "toxicity assessments" and "chemical certifications" based on the various regulatory provisions governing toy markets globally (such as the Consumer Product Safety Improvement Act in the United States, the European Union's Toy Directive, or GB 6675 in China) ("Toy Testing" n.d.).[5] Through its technical expertise, the scientific work adults did with toys distinguished itself as work from the assessments kids made as consumers. The child work of toy testing is thus polysemic, polyvalent, and contradictory, with the professionalization of kid creators unfolding in tension with persistent ideological assumptions about childhood innocence and nonparticipation in industry and legitimate forms of labor. These tensions have not gone unmanaged, however. As the remainder of this chapter explores, the "fun" of toy testing as a means of both winning prizes and subordinating child work to family togetherness has helped to resolve these contradictions.

Transgenerational Relations in the Prize Economy

Instead of situating toy testing exclusively within systems of labor or gift exchange, the idea of a prize economy can capture both the overlap between these logics and their dependence on the values and ideologies of "fun" to make sense of that overlap. In this prize economy, children operate not as laborers analogous to adults or as industry outsiders granted gifts but instead as active participants competing in the fun of trying to win contests. Competitive contests have recurred as a significant industrial practice throughout this book—whether in Marvel's search for an ideal transgenerational evangelist in chapter 2, the ritual competitions between aspiring creators at the Kidscreen Summit in chapter 3, or the design challenges used by LEGO to measure professional potential in chapter 4. In this chapter, the contest motivates the productive activities of children in the digital economy, where the possibility of winning prizes disavows child labor, transforming it into an exciting and potentially rewarding game. Contests have long been used to promote and cultivate children's participation in popular media. As Avi Santo notes in his history of transmedia branding, children's radio frequently held contests that gave listeners "structured and limited opportunities to affect the story" by suggesting names for new characters and other narrative elements (2015: 46). Despite this long history, promotional contests have taken on new significance in rewarding children's productivity and creativity on digital media platforms. At the intersection of online participation and toy industry marketing efforts, this prize economy valorizes children's contributions to the culture industries beyond labor value or gift worth, recognizing them as efforts freely exchanged on digital platforms in the course of competitive fun. This ethic of fun is vital to the economic valorization of children's digital production practices like toy testing. As Andrew Zolides argues, the aesthetics of child media production privilege "fun over professionalism. Children are encouraged to produce and create, but not to hone their craft in any professionalized capacity" (2017a: 152). As we will see, the prize economy has helped to manage persistent anxieties about child professionalism, shunting that productive and creative agency into more playful, fun, and less ideologically disruptive contexts of cultural exchange. Yet kids' creative agency and digital savvy means that their capacity for professionalized labor persists, never fully erased by the potential to play for fun prizes.

Similarly, the ideologies of fun extend to the transgenerational relations of production through which children have engaged in creative work within the digital economy. Typically requiring adult consent, collaboration, and oversight, the creative practices of child toy testers have often been linked by the structures and practices of the digital economy to the efforts of parents who have shared in that productive responsibility. In that relationship, insistence on child participation as the pursuit of fun and prizes leaves any potential labor value as the domain of the parent, thus insulating the child from the professionalized realm.

While the fun of the prize economy recasts children's work as nonlabor, that work can yet transform into an exchangeable commodity through the authorization and authority of a parent, who is not only asked to grant permission for their child's participation but is also frequently implicated in the work of securing these opportunities, writing reviews, and managing kids' visibility on social media. In their study of labor in the creative industries, David Hesmondhalgh and Sarah Baker encourage us to consider what constitutes "good work," placing significant emphasis on the idea of autonomy, where the laborer can be one's own person with self-determined goals and desires (2011: 39). Yet the transgenerational relationships between child and parent collaborators in toy testing can obscure the former's potential for autonomy, subjecting creativity and agency to the managerial approval of adult guardianship. These transgenerational relations of production thus smooth over potentially transgressive intersections of childhood and professional work. The practices of toy testing evoke the relational character of digital labor (Baym 2015) by nesting the productivity of children within their transgenerational relationships to parental figures, who are granted greater agency and autonomy to participate in the professionalized realms of labor outside the scope of "fun."

This is not to say that parents merely insulate children from labor in service of the higher calling of fun. The relationality of transgenerational production instead turns on the value of parents themselves as digital media users and active participants in the commodified exchange of social influence through their child-rearing identities. The collaborative transgenerational production practices of toy testing intersect with the online culture of "mommy blogging" that, as Lori Kido Lopez argues, enables women to publicly reassert the value of their roles as parents while offering an entrepreneurial means of monetizing that voice and influence as a lucrative magnet for advertisers (2009: 740–41). Commodified parent labor supports the fun by which children might participate in a prize economy—where parenting is not unpaid work but a potential source of economic capital through the relational labor of the digital economy. Even when that digital work remains unpaid and unrecognized by industry, Brooke Erin Duffy (2016) reminds us that users' productive activities in the digital economy constitute "aspirational labor" motivated by the hope of future social and economic capital. Thus, just as Craig and Cunningham (2017) consider the child creators of unboxing videos to be aspiring professionals, so too might we conceptualize the parents who manage that child work in terms of their entrepreneurial aspirations. Ultimately, these transgenerational relations square the fun of the prize economy with the industrialized labor entrepreneurialism of participants in toy testing practice. As the assignee of an adult, the child toy tester becomes a subject not of industry but instead a family in which parents manage the child's nonautonomous productive energies while commodifying their own relational labor. Through these transgenerational relations, the unpaid labor of parenting can be transformed into a potentially lucrative form of media management work, where good parenting is a process of managing a child's engagement with the fun to be had in the prize economy.

The "fun" of toy testing as a system of exchange between industry and child participants has often depended on the game-like logic of the contest—

where value is earned not through work but competitive play. Labor markets, of course, depend upon competition too; and as we have seen, aspirants have sometimes turned to self-help tools used in employment searches to secure the chance to participate in toy testing. In the fun of play, however, the contest has become something other than the unfair exploitation of children in an oversupplied labor market. As contests, and not capitalist competition, toy testing has imagined into being a system of exchange irreducible to the logic of the waged labor commodity or the gift. To apply to become a Fisher Price "Top Toy Tester" in Australia, for example, applicants agreed to a long list of terms and conditions that explicitly framed participation as a contest to be rewarded with prizes. Per national regulations for promotional contests, these terms carefully noted the retail value of the prizes offered to its entrants, tallying the complete AU$14,294 cost of hotel accommodations and economy-class flights for a toy tester and three other family members selected to travel from Australia or New Zealand to Fisher Price's corporate headquarters in the United States ("Terms & Conditions" 2017). These same terms also insisted that the opportunity was part of "promotion" as an outward-looking marketing campaign aimed at attracting consumers; this promotion was thus not presented as a professionalized, industrial work relationship. Toy retailers, too, have embraced this promotional, contest-based approach. In 2017, UK retailer Hamley's sought to build a team of in-house "VIP Toy Testers" who would "star in videos broadcast online and report your findings to the world" ("Toy Testers" 2017). This search adopted the usual professionalizing promises—but beneath the surface, the creation of these celebrity retail VIPs was simultaneously structured as an in-store competition with an explicit set of rules. Collaborative encounters between children and professionalized adult work cultures have also been figured through these contest dynamics rather than as a form of productive work. In 2007, LEGOLAND California started hosting monthly Junior Master Builder competitions in which children competed to win "a private working session with a master model builder" responsible for creating distinctive brick-built objects throughout the theme park (Pesquera 2007). In these contests, children entered industry not as laborers but as prize winners.

Beyond refiguring labor potential, the game-like structure of contests and prizes has also provided a powerful means of revalorizing and motivating work that could otherwise be understood in terms of a gift economy of social participation. As an extrinsic reward for good play, the prize can encourage child participants to do their best work possible. In 2015, for example, online retailer The Hut measured and distributed toy testing rewards proportionally to the quality of participants' online reviews. While all reviewers could retain the toys they tested upon completion of their reviews, the program promised that "really great reviews" would earn additional prizes—thus providing added incentive for participants to offer their best effort (Costello 2015). The Hut remained vague about what those prizes were; yet this arguably enhanced the fun of the game-like exchange. Participants were not laboring for set wages but playing with toys in an unpredictable but rule-structured system of feedback and surprise rewards.

ToyTesters.tv used the rewards-based prize economy to deepen its pool of participants through an ethos of fun while maintaining the industrialized hierarchies of status and exclusivity upon which claims to status and professionalism could also be built. Although it selectively considered applications for children to serve as on-screen talent in its video reviews, ToyTesters.tv simultaneously cultivated a secondary class of participants to sustain its user community and be mined for its value to the toy industries. While a select few would become featured reviewers and regular recipients of toy product, failed applicants and general website users became members of the ToyTesters club through which they could generate valuable content and consumer data. Club members were incentivized to contribute through a system of trophies attached to their digital profiles, as well as entry in random drawings for a limited number of physical prizes. To earn these rewards, participants could answer marketing questions about existing toys (two hundred trophies each), write their own toy reviews (three hundred trophies), or even submit ideas for new toys (three hundred trophies) ("Information" 2013). As barely disguised market research and intellectual property development strategy, these online activities positioned the user as a contributor not just to the ToyTester.tv community but also to the needs of industry. Disclaimers to parents made this productive role clear: "The information your child provides in this section may be sold, disclosed, shared or published to or with third party companies" ("Information" 2013). Yet the prize structure framed this work as something other than labor: a form of play in which digital ephemera might be won. The collective creative labor of children was still very much a commodity that ToyTesters.tv could sell to consumer product manufacturers, but that work unfolded in the context of a shared game in which players competed for social standing and rewards.

In the prize economy under construction here, children's creative work has undergone the process of "gamification" that Ian Bogost (2011) critiques as harnessing the power of game structures to "make them accessible in the context of contemporary business." From this perspective, we can understand the gamification provided by these prize systems as transformative—working to package player input as a valuable commodity while embedding it alternatively within the values of fun accompanying play. The point, however, is not that the participation of children in the work animating sites like ToyTesters.tv is definitively a form of labor or gift exchange that these prize incentives have misrepresented as play. Instead it may be most helpful to read the prize economy as something that turns on a different kind of exchange—where work has been valued not only because of its ability to be exchanged as a commodity or gift but also for enabling entry into a rule-based system of play that provides affective pleasure or engagement for the worker-player. Gamification is the paradox of free labor, in which work is a commodity exchanged not for capital but for the affect of play.

Such a prize economy imposes an explicitly national and regulatory framework upon the exchanges of toy testing. In adopting the structure of the contest, toy testing participation has become subject to the various rules and laws governing games and gambling in each nation. As such, these structures of participation have been almost uniformly organized within national scopes to steer clear of incompatible regulatory schemes and to offer uniform rules and disclosures to participants. The terms and conditions that users read as a precondition to participation have effectively served as the rules of play that govern the gamified exchange of prizes at a national level. On ToyTesters.tv, for example, application materials restricted participation in its prize economy "to residents within the United Kingdom only and excludes our employees and their families, our agents or anyone professionally connected with the organisation of the company" ("Terms & Conditions" 2016). Applicants also had to affirm their understanding on the online submission form by ticking a box that confirms "I live in the UK" ("About You" 2013). The rules that govern the prize economy thus determine who can participate—not only restricting it on the basis of nationality but also in terms of corporate employment relationships that would threaten a sense of fair play in that contest. Whether at the level of the nation or otherwise, the prize economy has depended on the creation of boundaries of eligibility—a magic circle—to participate in and generate value from the fun of gameplay.

One might assume, then, that the prize economy of toy testing has erected boundaries that exclude adults from participation in the creative fun had by children. Indeed, as one parent described the Mattel Imagination Center toy testing facilities, mirrored walls separated children at play from adult observers, allowing researchers to be discrete and preventing parents from intruding on their activities (Lipmen 2016). The prominence of unboxing videos and child celebrities on YouTube, too, has signaled the value of toy testing as a direct expression of young consumers' unique identities and distinct desires. And yet the economies in which toy testing has circulated have not precluded adult participation; on the contrary, they have oftentimes prescribed a set of transgenerational relations in which children's participatory practices must unfold. In this way, the persistent labor potential of children—and its disruption of adult-centric models of industry and professionalized cultural production—has been managed not just by its embeddedness within a "fun" system of prizes but also within the transgenerational relations of family. These have defused the economic implications of creative work as part of the affective bonds (also often "fun") shared between adults and their children. So while Jackie Marsh (2015) describes the economy of unboxing videos as a "peer-to-peer cultural industry" in which children have found a way to generate value from their ability to influence one another's consumer decisions, the digital work of toy testing is also the product of transgenerational relations involving nonpeer adults.

Indeed some of the most popular YouTube influencers in this sector have not been children. By 2014, Melissa Lima, at the time a twenty-one-year-old from Brazil, attracted a significant following for her DisneyCollector channel, producing unboxing videos that had garnered up to ninety million views. According to *The New York Times*, she was "very likely the most successful auteur" working in the genre (Silcoff 2014). Suffice it to say, adults too contributed to the creative practices of toy testing through unboxing videos. Yet specific consideration of parental participation in these endeavors reveals not only adult presence but also the ways in which productive child activities have remained entwined within transgenerational relationships. Across play testing, reviewing, and video content creation, parents have participated by providing consent, collaborating directly in creative endeavors, generating the value of their own influence, and situating child creativity within the discourses of good parenting. All these practices unite to produce a form of transgenerational media management in which parents have reshaped the value of their children's participation in the digital economy as "fun."

Whether children participate in internal market research sessions, online reviewing, or video content creation on YouTube, they have typically required parental consent to engage in that work. While parents must fill out release forms on their kids' behalf, those documents have also called for parents to provide their own service to industry. The 2017 "Child Testing Agreement" Mattel required of its participants, for example, asked parents to extend permission for their children and themselves to be observed and engaged by Mattel personnel, to surrender ownership over any "ideas or opinions expressed by my Child and/or myself," to agree to nondisclosure of proprietary information to which they might be exposed in industry space, and to avow that their testing relationship with Mattel did not conflict with a prior parental relationship to another toy company, entertainment company, or research group. Contractually speaking, the parent granted Mattel the same kind of power over their child's contributions that the company had over for-hire creative laborers. Although for-hire laborers have legal standing to enter into such agreement, here the parent stood in for a nonautonomous child. Considered another way, child participants figured as a part of the network of economic relations and legal rights of the parent rather than as participants in their own right. If there has been a consideration of labor here in these consent instruments—and indeed, "prior relationships" with other companies implicitly included labor employment—it has relegated labor to the autonomy and agency of parents and denied its possibility at the level of childhood participation.

Beyond these required permissions, the work of toy testing has also directly cultivated adult participation alongside that of younger consumers. As Mattel explained, "In some instances, we may also ask parents/guardians, either alone or with children, to participate in a focus group session" ("Imagination Center" 2017). In this way, the applicant of the toy testing audition process was not a child but a transgenerational subject constituted across family relations. When advertising internal toy testing opportunities, toy companies have often directly acknowledged a desire to measure parental perspectives alongside those of kids. On the Facebook page for its Imagination Center facility, Mattel encouraged parents of children up to thirteen years old living in the Los Angeles area to sign up to become part of their testing program (Mattel Imagination Center n.d.). As much as the company's regular status updates called for child toy testers, they also figured parents as valuable inputs into this testing economy. On January 26, 2018, for example, Mattel advertised a "PAID FOCUS GROUP OPPORTUNITY" for "first time Moms of boys or girls." The previous call on November 28, 2017, similarly hailed "all Dads with sons who love action figures! We are looking for Dads of Boys ages 4–7 years old to participate in a PAID focus group." Not all announcements figured the parent as the research subject; but even in those cases, these posts envisioned the parent as a Facebook user keeping tabs on toy testing opportunities on their child's behalf. An August 2016 call for fans interested in My Mini Mixie Q and DC Super Hero Girls asked parents to consider if "your child is a good match for this study" and if "your child is collecting or thinking about buying" (Mattel Imagination Center 2018). At the very least, the parent served as the booking agent for the testing work their children might do.

The most common kind of call on Mattel's Facebook page, however, centered on the figure of the mother—especially "first time expecting moms" whose brand allegiances were likely less formed. Similarly, the willingness of Toys "R" Us to recruit children into this kind of work "pre-birth" ("Apply" n.d.) signaled the transgenerational character of this labor. Through the parent who chose this option on an application and enrolled their children in this work before they were even born, toy testing became a site of transgenerational collaboration, where a gestating child was the only prerequisite for adults to seek entry into the economy. This was a work relationship that the parent might begin and children might continue after birth as they adopt their own consumer subjectivities. As those transformations unfolded, the parent and child could continue to be figured as a collaborative subject of these participatory exchanges and productive activities. The call for participants issued by online retailer The Hut in 2015, for example, figured the parent-child team as a collective creative subject that would navigate the participatory economy of toys and digital media together. The Hut sought "Enthusiastic parents and children who would love to be involved in our 'tried and tested' campaign" (Costello 2015). Meanwhile, Curran (2017) described the moment in which toys arrive at an online reviewer's home for evaluation as one of excitement shared across generational lines, with the child excited to engage with a new object of play and the parent "in hot pursuit, video camera in hand" to fulfill the economic obligation of mediating these experiences. In her advice on securing toy testing work, Catherine Alford (2017) suggested a similar generational division of labor in which the child would typically do the work of playing, with the parent responsible for delivering required reviews. By placing responsibilities for productively satisfying the economic exchange upon the parent, these transgenerational relations of collaboration have insulated the child's fun enjoyment of prizes from a persistently adult realm of labor. The toy testing economy has worked by marrying children's engagement with toys and digital media to parents' willing collaboration in the packaging of that participation within systems of mediated communication and exchange.

Through parental participation in the influence economies of contemporary social media platforms, meanwhile, toy industries have evaluated individual children's capacity to valuably engage in toy reviewing and video content creation work. Children have not simply competed with one another in these audition processes. Instead their relative values have been assessed according to the social media clout of their parents in a transgenerational influence economy. Oisin Curran (2017) argued that children interested in product reviewing "need mothers and fathers who will doggedly pursue any opportunities they can find. It comes as no surprise that, these days, social media plays an important role in the process." Alford (2017) echoed this, suggesting that parents must "prowl" social media to find fleeting opportunities. Parents' social media savvy has extended beyond catching calls for participation, however; the child's ability to participate has frequently depended on the value of what parents themselves did and said in digital spaces. As interviewed by Alford (2017), blogger Krystal Butherus credited her own social media footprint for granting her child access to the toy testing economy: one needed to "show influence if you're interested in being a toy tester. Word-of-mouth marketing still seems like a big deal to brands, and it's worthwhile if you actually use the product and enjoy sharing information with your family and friends." From this report, Alford concluded, "The bigger online reach you have, the more likely it is that you will be selected as a toy tester." The operative "you" in these statements was not the child. Social media platforms like Facebook and Twitter have technically prohibited users under the age of thirteen ("Terms of Service" 2018; "Twitter Terms of Service" 2018), limiting (though certainly not curtailing) the ability of the youngest consumers targeted by toy companies from accruing influence comparable to their parents. YouTube similarly asked that "If you are under 13 years of age, then please do not use the Service" ("Terms of Service" n.d.)—meaning that even its unboxing video child entrepreneurs should have technically relied upon the consent and collaboration of parents to set up accounts and manage channel profiles. The "you" in the best position to provide influence, therefore, was typically the parent.

As a result, toy testing applications have often measured the social media influence of parents as much if not more than the traits of would-be child reviewers and video creators. For example, although toy manufacturer Step2 used its Facebook page to pitch its search for Toy Testers to "little ones" (Step2 2018a, Step2 2018b), the linked application asked for details well beyond the age and gender of aspiring child participants. Step2 inquired about parents' use of a variety of social media platforms including Facebook, Instagram, Pinterest, Twitter, YouTube, Google+, and Snapchat. For each platform, the application instructed parents to provide their user handles so that evaluators might directly assess their social media profile and quality of interactions with followers ("Step2" 2018). These application questions naturalized the premise that any qualified child applicant would have a parent of significant influence. In the case of testing for products aimed at younger children, demonstration of social media influence has also preceded delivery of a child. In the United Kingdom, Toys "R" Us recruited "Toyologists" two to four years old and "Babyologists" aged "pre-birth to 24mths." Just as with the Step2 application, parents provided links to their social media profiles across a number of different platforms, empowering

Toys "R" Us to assess the value of that child's participation on that basis. In the case of Babyologists, however, that child could still be unborn: the parent had to demonstrate influence upfront but could prove the existence of the child later ("Apply" n.d.). Child participation in these economies, in other words, has depended on embeddedness in the transgenerational relations of parental influence.

While child participation is enabled by parental consent, collaboration, and influence, parents themselves have also acted as full participants who navigate the industrial demands of toy testing as part of their child-rearing responsibilities and identities. On the one hand, the "fun" of toy testing could serve parental desires to provide kids with rewarding, enriching childhood experiences. The LA Dads Group, for example, is "a diverse community of fathers who take an active role in their children's lives" by organizing regular events for father-child bonding. These have included trips to the Mattel Imagination Center's toy testing facilities that offered children the opportunity to learn about these industry processes (Lipmen 2016). As part of the public performance of good parenting in which these dads have been invested, industry participation provides a learning experience less valuable for its labor power than for its capacity to draw fathers and children together. On the other hand, child involvement in toy testing has often manifested in more explicitly economic terms as part of a demanding consumer culture in which middle-class parents seek exploits and workarounds. Here exchange value is economic, where parents' toy testing labor has operated in concert with the consumer thrift of bargain chasing. Sites like Extreme Couponing UK, for example, publicized toy testing opportunities as part of its mission to help users stretch their resources, figuring the quid pro quo of "free" product for reviews as a good deal ("Toys 'R' Us" n.d.). Websites like Penny Hoarder similarly recommended enrolling children in play testing as a more affordable alternative to buying new toys (Alford 2017). Bargain hunting blog *Eat, Drink, and Save Money* and motherhood blog *Domestic Mommyhood* added to this a recommendation to keep an eye on the Facebook pages of major toy manufacturers for potential toy testing gigs (Rinaldi 2016; Bekki n.d.). Bargain hunting and good parenting discourses intersected through toy testing participation.

Participation in toy consumption economies has also provided a means of transforming the unpaid work of parenting into more lucrative, entrepreneurial forms of commodified relational labor. Manufacturer Discovery Toys! used its Facebook page to reach out to parents looking to identify the economic opportunities to be found in their children's consumer lives. Soliciting parents to participate in a direct sales model (like Mary Kay or Shaklee), Discovery hailed its consumers as potential retailers. In advertisements that featured mothers from diverse racial backgrounds, these Facebook posts encouraged parents to hold sales parties with their friends and turn the communities of child-rearing in which they were embedded into distribution networks for Discovery product. "If you have a passion for making a difference in the lives of children and would like to earn some extra income," one 2017 post read, "there's never been a better time to join Discovery Toys! All Consultants earn 25% Sales Commission starting Day 1 with no Sales Requirement!" Another post promised that an "Online Party Specialist" could help the parent-salesperson to embed this work into their everyday social relations: "you gather the people, we'll throw the party!" (Discovery 2017). Although not a practice of toy testing per se, here the relations of parenting became a form of social media labor that could be commodified through toy industry participation.

In the transgenerational relations of toy testing more specifically, this industrialization of parenthood has manifested as a form of media management in which adult consent, collaboration, influence, and avowed commitment to good parenting produced commodity value out of the child's participation in these productive but fun practices. Through interviews with unboxing video channel creators, David Craig and Stuart Cunningham reveal how parents Brian and Lori envisioned their sons' YouTube channel, Gabe and Garrett, as a way of absorbing creative media labor within the relations of family. By "turning his children's videos into a business," Brian could leave his day job to manage an enterprise that afforded more time to be a father (2017: 84). This role of parent-manager can be traced throughout the economy of unboxing video production. As the father of the child celebrity at the center of the EvanTubeHD brand, Jared has been credited with managing the business of coordinating with YouTube as well as advertising firm Maker Studios (ABC News 2015).[6] In these reports, Jared managed the industrialized side of the work and appeared to insulate Evan from it, freeing his child celebrity identity from questions of commodification and industry labor.

Meanwhile, siblings Maya and Hulyan (born in 2012 and 2010, respectively) were credited as reviewing toys on their eponymous channel to the tune of US$1.5 million in 2015. It was the oversight of their parents, however, that managed the business operations as well as the values and meanings of this massive industry enterprise as a form of economic exchange. Their parents described toy reviewing as something they started as "just a hobby," thus retaining a sense of the noncommercial despite lucrative potential as commodity work. As managers of their children's time, Maya and

Hulyan's parents explained that their role was to motivate and pace the creative work of making videos—keeping the kids productive while making sure they did not approach a point of excess. The reported secret to their success was "making sure the kids are having fun while shooting the videos and keeping the videos short to avoid bored and cranky kids" (ABC News 2015). The subtext of their managerial disclosure about the potential for children to grow tired of the rigors of video production certainly invites questions about transgenerational media management pushing children to complete valuable commodity work. Nevertheless, these parents framed their managerial priorities not as exploiting child labor but quite oppositely as protecting a sense of "fun." Their job as transgenerational creative managers meant ensuring that child productivity respected the relations of family pastimes rather than labor (or perhaps, more accurately, to ensure through these kinds of disclosures that this was perceived to be the case). The transgenerational manager-parent has thus served as a wrangler of kids' participatory practices and a producer of meaning and value from them, directing and containing their potential within a number of different, overlapping kinds of economic exchanges.

The values of family togetherness, fun, and bonding time also underwrote kids' creative labor practices in an October 2017 story about the father who managed the KidToyTesters YouTube channel. As reported by *Bloomberg Businessweek*, Lee served as the de facto publicist and business manager for his children, protecting their interests and, of course, their safety in the face of economic possibilities posed by their industrial participation. As in most popular reports about child YouTube stars, *Bloomberg* made special mention of Lee's request to have his last name withheld to protect the identities of his kids (Stratton 2017). Not protecting them from requests by toy manufacturers for sponsored videos in support of their end-of-year holiday retail season, however, Lee also described how his children operated within what he called "crunch mode"—recalling the periods of intense work and labor exploitation that plague the digital media economy (Dyer-Witheford and de Peuter 2009). He estimated that his children would produce content for seven or eight companies over the course of the season, contributing to earnings of approximately US$140,000 annually. Lee even described this work in explicitly labor-oriented terms. To dispel the idea that this was "easy money," he instead reported "15-to-20 hour workdays . . . seven days a week every day of the year," with marathon all-night postproduction sessions. "A lot of time we don't see sunshine," he added (Stratton 2017). Lest these disclosures open themselves to a grim reading of child exploitation, Lee remained vague on who the "we" invoked here actually included. Indeed it is much easier to imagine these all-nighters as adult collaboration at a postproduction level than it is to think that Lee could successfully wring that much sustained cooperation from his kids.

Moreover, against the hard labor implied to be required of him as a parent, Lee positioned this creative enterprise as one of transgenerational professionalism where the family that works together plays with toys together. He explained how the flexible schedules afforded by home schooling allowed his children to engage in these complex creative practices while he himself spent only a half-hour per day on his own marketing business in order to fully support his children's professional efforts (Stratton 2017). Through these transgenerational relations, the fun work of production was imbued with additional educational value, whereas fatherly managerial efforts absorbed the commodified adult labor economies of industry. As a transgenerational media manager, Lee acted not just as businessman, publicist, and child wrangler but also as an insulating force between his children and full exposure to industry, containing their participation within the hegemonic ideologies of childhood and family. At the same time as he facilitated his children's creative participation in the economies of toy testing, he smoothed over that disruption of boundaries by reinscribing children's productive activities within the supervision of an adult who could engage in nonfun commodified labor exchanges on behalf of the family. Lee adopted a position of authority over labor so that children could remain nonautonomous in that field and subject to relations of fun and family instead. It is through the parent, in other words, that the creative work of toy testing and reviewing has not only been consented to, collaborated in, granted influence, and situated within child-rearing practices but also that the value of child participation in industrial forms of economic exchange has been managed.

Conclusion

Consider once more the story of Josh Baskin and the magical bodily transformation through which a child gains entry to the culture industries. Although the protagonist of *Big* is the transgenerational labor subject par excellence, he nevertheless looks quaint compared to the child producers of unboxing videos that have increasingly dominated the contemporary streaming video economy. In the fictionalized toy industry of the late 1980s, Josh enters a professional economy in which the boundaries between adult industry and child consumption are quite secure; nothing short of magic intervention will allow him to participate in that industry world. Without the body of an adult, Josh cannot legitimately perform work in that professional space. His child identity must be rendered invisible to maintain those industry boundaries even as his transgenerational body moves across them.

Yet in the toy testing, reviewing, and sponsorship economy of the digital era, different transgenerational labor relations have played out. While Josh Baskin's professionalized childhood had to remain a secret, the child participants of the toy testing economy have been hyper-visible. The search for children as market research subjects has received heavy publicity on social media; through the production of online reviews, the voices of children have become central in the marketing apparatus of the toy industry; and the streaming video market has supported a childhood of celebrity entrepreneurship and peer-to-peer influence. As children become increasingly professionalized, traditional industry boundaries tied to adulthood are troubled. Yet whereas the transgenerational body allows Josh Baskin to engage in labor, the professionalized child's embeddedness in transgenerational relations enables these disrupted labor boundaries to be reaffirmed. Placed in relationship to prize economies and the labor of parents, these hyper-visible child participants can appear *not* to be autonomous workers; instead their productivity and participation in economic exchanges comes from engagement in the fun of contests and family togetherness. Baskin possesses the transgenerational body that allows the child to engage in commodified labor; but the digital toy tester occupies transgenerational relations of production that revalue child labor. As this chapter has argued, the adult parent has figured as a crucial participant in the toy testing economy, providing consent, collaboration, influence, and the assurances of good parenting to act as a manager of childhood productivity, containing its economic potential within less disruptive frames.

Further dating *Big* are its representations of technology in relation to childhood productivity: among Josh's innovative contributions to MacMillan Toys include his attempt to prove the interactive storytelling potential of digital games based largely in text. These products remain a far cry from the digital playthings of today. Nevertheless, in its recognition of children's new media savvy as a valuable source of innovation and productive disruption for culture industries, *Big* demonstrates prescience. Of course, the contemporary toy industry continues to face the threat that digital worlds and devices hold compared to the decreasing appeal of injection-molded material plastic playthings. In response to the continuing threat of digital technologies, as seen here, the toy industry has embraced consumer participation in market research, online reviews, and sponsored unboxing videos as a way of adapting to new cultural contexts. The work of children may be ascribed meaning and value through transgenerational relations with adults who can mediate between childhood and the commodity logics of the culture industries—but it is at the same time a valuable form of cultural labor that capital has worked to harness. The process of auditioning children as toy testers, reviewers, and media makers aims to assimilate the next generation of cultural production into the strategies of industry. The professionalization of child participants, even as they are not paid as laborers, also reproduces industry cultures into that future. In the end, this child labor both disrupts industries and points to the means of their continuation.

Conclusion

Reproducing the Future

As part of an effort to transform the materiality of the printed comic book by intertwining it with the affordances of new digital media devices, Marvel Comics introduced in 2012 a new promotional platform called Marvel AR, or "Augmented Reality." Although new distribution via the Comixology app and directly on the Marvel.com website made digital comics available to a new, potentially younger market, the AR initiative seemed aimed more at attracting those who still read physical comic books to those digital platforms. Marvel hoped that its traditional comic book readers would download the new Marvel AR app onto their phone or tablet reader in order to integrate that device into their engagement with print media. Throughout Marvel's superhero titles, readers could now find special AR banners embedded in the layout at some point in each issue; when these banners appeared, the Marvel AR app could be used to scan them. Uniting media analog and digital, old and new, the app recognized the comic title in question and linked the reader outward to some additional digital content meant to deepen the experience of reading that story—typically a short YouTube video.

The hype surrounding the Marvel AR launch suggested that these features could be used to develop new interactive narrative worlds and story structures that would spill into the spaces of users' physical reality as they used digital devices; but in practice the links that readers followed offered an augmented insight into the industrial world of creative work at Marvel. According to one report, AR would enable the publisher to circulate "commentaries from the writers and artists behind the stories—sort of like DVD bonus features for comics" (D'Orazio 2012). In this behind-the-scenes commentary, writers and editors offered recaps of past storylines to help readers remember where, how, and when they last saw various characters, filling in the gaps in reader knowledge inevitable in long-form storytelling. Sometimes video commentary would grant these creative practitioners visibility as author figures with the power to arbitrate meaning and authorize particular interpretations. The AR video that accompanied the fifth issue of his *FF* series, for example, enabled artist Mike Allred to affirm the thematic centrality of "family" to all stories featuring the Fantastic Four, identifying it as his favorite part of working on the title. Beyond narrative world building, "AR" engagement in instances like this meant readers could interface with the professional world of thoughtful creators that gave structure, meaning, and value to the work. Nevertheless, Marvel AR proved fairly underwhelming. If anything, the process of flipping through a comic book in one hand and, in the other, following links to video content on one's digital device posed a rather overengineered means of engaging consumers. This gimmick evoked the familiar economy of "viral marketing" through which industries deploy making-of specials and other glimpses of authorship behind-the-scenes to support media sales (Caldwell 2008: 274). Indeed, within a few years, Marvel had discontinued its support for the AR app, dropping the conceit of interactive scanning as a means of accessing this kind of material—which it simply continued to post directly to its YouTube channel and Marvel.com ("Hey!" n.d.).

Yet amid this attempt to marry print and digital materialities via discourses of industry authorship was a recurring reflection on children and their potential presence in the creative world of Marvel. These AR videos often imagined children as unruly, uncontrollable forces occupying the Marvel offices and revealed individual Marvel professionals to be participants in adult-child relationships. The AR video for *All-New X-Men* #13, for example, begins simply enough as editor Nick Lowe summarizes the basic premise of the series and its focus on younger, teenaged, time-traveling versions of mutant heroes formerly portrayed as adults. As Lowe continues, however, he jokingly proposes that Marvel will take the aged-down premise one step further to introduce a new cast of "Kid X-Men." Lowe then pulls into frame a boy wearing an oversized yellow visor in addition to his street clothes and introduces him as "Kid Cyclops," an even younger version of the mutant hero known for his ability to shoot blasts of concussive force from his eyes. Bringing this attempt at humor to a quick end, Kid Cyclops uses his superpowers in a simple bit of physical comedy (rendered via computer effects) to knock Lowe out of frame ("Marvel AR: The Kid X-Men" 2014). Meanwhile another series of videos presents a different child as a recurring menace for professionals working within Marvel's editorial offices. "Sydney's Don't Try This at Home," the AR video attached to *Superior Spider-Man* #6, features the eponymous girl repeatedly punching different male editors in the crotch, building to the comic affirmation that "editors WERE harmed in the making of this video" (Marvel Entertainment 2013c). In another video for *Nova* #4, Sydney asks several male editors which titles they work on before using new lightning powers to zap each of them (Marvel Entertainment 2013b). At the end of each video, a woman who identifies herself as Ellie Pyle passes money to Sydney in apparent payment for her editor-maiming services. The potential alliance depicted in these videos between girls and women against male editorial power takes on additional meaning to fans who might recognize Pyle's name as an associate editor working under that authority. In these cases, professional tensions and creative conflicts—breaking along gendered lines—play out in a fantasy of children let loose in industry space to violently assault creative management.

Other AR videos imagine relationships between children and editorial authority in more collaborative terms. In "Sydney's Sound Effects," attached to *Avengers* #8, assistant editor Jake Thomas prompts the girl to provide her own sound effects to complement the visuals of the issue and to share her general reaction to the scenes as drawn (Marvel Entertainment 2013a). Through this contribution, the video imagines children not just as having access to the editors and spaces of the Marvel offices in which these videos are shot but also as participants who can add something of value to the creative work on the comics page (both in sound work here and participation in AR video production more generally). At the same time, the video models the relationship between Thomas and Sydney as one that consumers might emulate, with comic books pleasurably shared across generational lines. Another AR video positions the child subject in the role of interpretative authority typically inhabited by adult professionals in behind-the-scenes features. In the "Intro to Nova by Zack" video for *Nova* #1, the eponymous boy speaks to viewers from behind his computer to ruminate on the reasons he and his friends enjoy the series ("Marvel AR: Intro" 2014). Although Zack does not share space with adult professionals in this video, he adopts their authority as arbiter of value in creative work. Yet the video also puts Zack in a position of peer-to-peer influencer, perhaps, making an appeal that might bring other children within the shared space of online video into the fold of *Nova* fandom.

Finally, these kid-oriented AR videos construct children's participation and collaboration in the professional world of comics editing as an extension of their relationships with parents. While not made explicit on screen, Sydney and Zack gain access to this space as children of one of Marvel's editors. The comic bits and vignettes of the AR videos cheekily represent the chaos, conflict, and collaboration that could unfold from the participation of children in this workspace, but the production of the videos also reflects the possibilities of everyday transgenerational relations within this professional space. Although the exact circumstances of their participation is unknown, it is easy to imagine Sydney and Zack pulled into the orbit of producing these promotional videos while a parent juggled another professional project nearby. Perhaps they had begged to accompany that parent to work, or perhaps they had been dragged into the office because of a lack of child care, suddenly finding themselves with little more interesting to do than help generate the significant amount of video content required by the AR program. Zack's *Nova* video appears to have been shot in a home office, also suggesting the capacity for the professional work of a parent to bleed into the domestic sphere and family time in that space. Perhaps these children were excited to participate, or perhaps they did so begrudgingly. Whatever the scenario, their participation helps us imagine the Marvel editor as a parent whose professional work is imperfectly contained within the bounds of industries and instead extends to relationships with children—who gain their own access to and participation in industry through those family relations. In this context, the "Don't Try This at Home" disclaimer in Sydney's videos takes on new meaning, where relationships between children, parents, and other adults take place in a world of industrialized creative labor beyond the domestic sphere.

Although these AR videos may, by virtue of their corporate branding, most obviously recall Marvel's transgenerational comic publishing strategies as discussed in chapter 2, I close this book with detailed discussion of these otherwise throwaway promotional efforts because they subtly intertwine many of the forces that have been under examination throughout. At its core, this book has explored the boundaries that constitute the media industries and participation within them, focusing on the way in which those borderlines have been constructed, managed, and transgressed through the relations between adults and children. On the one hand, this book has engaged with the "extra-commercium" status of children (Cook 2004) that excludes them from participation in the professionalism and labor practices of industry, exploring the need for adults to create, distribute, and promote popular culture on kids' behalf. On the other hand, these efforts to work on consumers' behalf across the generational lines of demographic categories have required a constant negotiation of adulthood and professional subjectivity in relation to childhood. As shown in chapter 1, transgenerational marketing strategies figured "co-viewers" as consumer subjects whose television tastes could be reproduced across their transformation from child to adult to parent. Moreover, industrial efforts to engage adult consumers as a promotional force in chapter 2 depended on granting reproductive subjects (often distinguished by their gender) the power to share culture as an inheritance passed to the next generation of consumers. Within media industries, meanwhile, the professional identities of adult producers examined in chapter 3 depended on "pediocular" claims to knowledge and authority over childhood. Adult fans of LEGO in chapter 4 blurred these boundaries of both age and production; but in becoming industry tourists they participated in a scripted brand culture that reoriented their transgenerational boundary crossing within the corporate interest. While online toy reviews and sponsored video production similarly enabled toy manufacturers, retailers, and streaming platforms to assimilate the creative media work of children in chapter 5, the redrawn boundaries of labor in that digital environment articulated distinct positions of industry participation for children—as prize winners and nonautonomous family members rather than fully-fledged industry professionals.

Looking across all of the generational boundaries that media industries construct, transgress, and then shore up anew, this book has argued most centrally that the ongoing reproduction of popular culture depends on the formation and management of transgenerational subjectivities that govern who can participate in what industry practices of reproducing the future, in which kinds of ways, and why. Many different types of transgenerational subjects have been revealed over the course of this argument, from the co-viewing consumer who links adult markets to those for children, to the promotional evangelist who shares culture within the relations of heterosexual reproduction, to the pediocular professional who sees through a child's eyes, to the adult fan who problematizes the demographics of children's markets, to the child laborer whose professionalized peer influence in the digital economy requires management by adults to be commodified. Yet each of these idealized industry subjects supports the reproduction of culture through participation in transgenerational relations and identities that affirm and bridge the gulfs between present and future, old and new, adult and child, amateur and professional. At the heart of this transgenerational industry matrix lies a paradox of continuity and change, where the reproduction of media culture operates both by building oppositions between adulthood and childhood and by encouraging participants within these industrial oppositions to blur the lines, creating, promoting, and spreading culture across them. In this context, the subjectivities of transgenerational media matter because they have produced the power of different industry participants to facilitate this crossover and shape the future reproduction of popular culture.

In this light, Marvel's AR videos reveal the transgenerational relations in which comic book culture might be produced and its industrial subjects imagined as the agents of that process. They represent, on the one hand, the persistence of adult male professionals in a position of creative authority as editors. As "augmented reality" extensions of the representation of this male-dominated industrial community, on the other hand, the AR videos quietly imagine that authority as one increasingly contested in and by the future represented by these children. Calling attention to the prevalence of derivative concepts like "Kid X-Men," the AR video recognizes the challenges editors face in sustaining superhero franchises over time, inevitably making and remaking them in pursuit of finding new youth appeal. Moreover, these videos figure editors as easily dispatched by figures like Kid Cyclops and Sydney, who enter industry space as forces of violent disruption in generational and gendered alliance with creative voices on the margins. These comedic videos grant children the power—often literally the superpower—to disrupt aging, stagnant industry spaces. Crucially, this comedy frames that power as a playful one, befitting the child subject as easily as the many gamified contests and competitions that have emerged in this book as a means of managing entry into transgenerational industry communities.

Yet this prospect of playful, disruptive industry participation by kids is not without limits. Instead these videos fold the discontinuity of children empowered as industry subjects within the hegemonic continuity of family relations, social reproduction, and patriarchal authority. Linked to the company through the employment of a parent, kids like Zack and Sydney lend Marvel a bridge between generations. While a few adult editors might be comically hurt in the process, the participation of these children remains subject to authorization and management by this older generation. When Zack sings the praises of *Nova*, he not only participates in a transgenerational economy of online peer-to-peer product reviewing but also validates the aesthetic sensibilities of contemporary superhero comics, deeming them worthy of reproduction in the tastes of younger readers like himself. More than representing child creative laborers, children in these videos serve as a special kind of transgenerational industry subject authorized to endorse adult authorship and contain industry power within the reproductive trajectories of family.

This is not to say that as transgenerational industry subjects these child participants failed to perform any real creative labor of their own. These videos anticipate the same kind of child reviewer-influencers explored in chapter 5 and suggest that Marvel might have drawn upon child creativity to support viral video content that could circulate in the same digital economy as the unboxing videos that serve toy industries. The actual influence and impact of Marvel's AR videos, however, was questionable. Buried within the arcane analog-digital AR scheme and only later released more widely in spaces like YouTube, these videos were anything but popular. Almost half a decade after its release, the "Sydney's Don't Trust This at Home" video posted to YouTube by Marvel Entertainment had received only 6,084 views by February 2018. Perhaps due to a lack of comparably broad physical comedy, Sydney's sound effects for *Avengers* #8 had attracted an even fewer 2,684 hits. While videos hosted directly on Marvel.com do not similarly display viewing numbers, it seems unlikely that any larger viewership would have been found there—especially considering these videos' function as part of an app supporting comic titles purchased by considerably less than one hundred thousand people each month. Viewed in this way, a few thousand hits constituted a fairly significant proportion of the existing readership. This limited impact also indicates the gulf a legacy company like Marvel would have to cross to integrate comic book publishing with the massive participatory video economy of YouTube (where kid-produced unboxing videos can attract millions of views).

Thus, while pointing to the multiplicity of subject positions shaping participation in transgenerational media industries, these AR videos capture another tension running throughout this book—that is, the management of relations between adults and children as a means of negotiating industry change in a digital age. This book began by looking at the television industries, focused on how co-viewing emerged as a means of adaptation to changing distribution systems based in streaming delivery and subscription service. Industry disruption motivated the development of new logics for leveraging familial relationships across different generations of television viewers rather than dividing them up into separate markets. After exploring the role of inheritance and sharing as key generational relations to be exploited by the similarly aging comic book industry (in part through cross promotion with television), this book considered how pediocular professional identities and practices emerged in the professional communities shared by television producers and toy manufacturers. This concern for toys carried the book through to its conclusion, not just in the exploration of adult fandom and industry tourism but also in revealing how manufacturers and retailers shifted focus to user-generated streaming video in lieu of the dynamic marketing support television once provided. Here the digital video economy inherited the role that legacy television industries once played. In this way, the status of television as an unstable, disrupted industrial formation has provided a framework for conceptualizing the transgenerational media industries as a whole.

Indeed all of these media industries—television, comics, toys—have in the twenty-first century grappled with shifts between the analog and the digital (as well as the material and immaterial) that often manifest in professional and popular discourses as a function of generational change. Just as superhero comic book publishers confront the existential crisis of an aging industry—and thus a dying one necessitating transgenerational strategies for sharing and reigniting consumer practices in younger readers—so too have television industries struggled with the abandonment of traditional broadcast, cable, and advertising economies by a generation of consumers perceived to be more interested in social media and YouTube. Toy manufacturers and retailers have perceived the same kind of generational threats, not only losing the power of traditional television platforms as an advertising apparatus but also facing competition for kids' attention from online games and other digital playthings that increasingly circulate outside of the brick-and-mortar retail economy. The struggles of the comic book industry to secure its future in the face of media change is thus part of a larger story of transgenerational industry management in which television and toys have played equal roles. These AR videos—and many industrial experiments like them—aim to redraw the boundaries around industries in order to build bridges between the consumer cultures of the past and the present. Transmedia attempts to incorporate digital platforms operate hand in hand with transgenerational efforts to build crossover audiences; and in that sense, it is through greater attention to transgenerational dynamics that media scholars might better understand why industries pursue these convergences and blurred boundaries. As the old and the new collide (Jenkins 2006), and analog industries face digital disruption, media industries court a new generation that will allow their institutionalized practices and forms of power to be reproduced into the future.

It is this question of industrial reproduction—and power to participate within it—that is ultimately of greatest concern. At stake throughout each of these chapters has been the capacity for media cultures and institutions of media power to be reproduced through generational relations that span the age boundaries between children and adults. In this sense of negotiating media change on an institutional level, these transgenerational dynamics are indeed all about top-down strategic efforts by legacy companies like Marvel or LEGO to maintain the status quo of their market power. However, in terms of bottom-up participation in that process by industry professionals, parents, adult consumers, as well as children themselves, transgenerational media also represent a negotiated terrain in which the power to participate in cultural production is arbitrated by access to valuable industry subjectivities. Because this book has focused primarily on the construction of these subjectivities as offered to participants by the media industries, there remains much more work to be done to understand how and why they have been embraced by producers and consumers alike. The pleasures and lived experiences of participating in transgenerational media industries demand equal attention in future research, and will likely lead to powerful revelations about the strength of the affective relations that form between parents, children, and other adults as they try to make sense of, share with, and collaborate with one another. The realms of inheritance and investment in the future present arenas in which intense cultural struggle for agency, voice, and participation unfold in diverse ways too numerous to be captured here. More such work could also explore how generational positionality and identities are felt across lived experiences differentiated on the intersectional basis of race, gender, class, and sexuality.

In terms of idealized participatory roles as imagined by media industries, however, it has already been possible to grasp the strategies by which institutions of cultural reproduction position producers and consumers to occupy the borderlands between generational identities. As explored in the preceding chapters, the capacity to engage in play has often empowered the transgenerational subject within these industry cultures. Adult entry into the professional communities of children's television production and toy development has hinged on their performance as players in competitive rituals and reality television series formats. The capacity of adult consumers to participate in industry spaces—whether as agents of promotion or tourists—often turned on their ability to perform within structured, game-like competitions in which they could prove themselves to be the best corporate spokesperson or the most qualified industry applicant. Meanwhile the power of play has inscribed the alternative values of "fun" upon child participants in digital economies in order to disavow their participation as a form of labor. The ideal transgenerational industry subject, in these cases, has often been a player that can cross boundaries between adulthood and childhood as well as amateur and laborer. Articulated to the ideologies surrounding childhood, the industry power that accrues to and through play could almost seem utopian or even innocent—where the capacity to participate in the industry work of reproducing culture turns on pleasurable and meaningful engagement rather than commodification.

Nevertheless, as the previous cases have shown, not all potential participants are equally valued for their capacity to play, share, or otherwise engage in practices that forge relations across the boundaries of childhood and adulthood. In the introduction, I drew upon queer theory to consider the politics of reproduction as part of the generation of futures that extend the privileges and orientations of the past (Ahmed 2006; Edelman 2004; Halberstam 2011). The chapters that followed revealed very little of the utopian queer futures envisioned by Jose Muñoz (2009), more consistently offering stories of industrially preferred and privileged forms of participation. In these stories, the reproduction of popular culture turned on idealized industry subject positions dependent on relations of family as defined by the heterosexual reproduction of people. Perhaps the most "queer" subjects under examination throughout this manuscript were the adult fans of LEGO in chapter 4 whose interest in childhood playthings represented a "failed" form of adulthood and child-centric play (Halberstam 2011). Nevertheless, the transgressive potential of those nonconforming consumer subjects was corporately recuperated throughout a process of industry tourism that encouraged adult fans to adopt more professionalized identities defined by service to the branded corporate ideals of childhood play. Through that process, these fans became more aligned with the many other adults in other chapters whose participation in transgenerational media industries is validated by their reproductive status and their capacity to support children. In chapter 3, parental identity authorized some professionals' knowledge of the child consumer, leaving nonparents to seek alternative means of establishing their own expertise in that space. The figure of the parent as media manager loomed large in the exploration of toy testing in chapter 5, too, enabling the participation of children in digital media economies through consent, collaboration, and commitment to "good" child-rearing, while also providing social media influence with which kids' reviewing and video work accrues additional value. In chapters 1 and 2 both, industry strategies of television co-viewing and comic book sharing depended significantly on the valorization of the parent as the agent of generational transmission of culture. While the winner of Marvel's transgenerational marketing spokesperson contest may have been another potentially transgressive industry subject—given her interest in sharing comics with kids as an adult mentor and friend rather than as parent—the company's ultimate failure to fully embrace her affirmed the difficulty with which transgenerational media industries have been able to imagine cultural reproduction in any terms outside of family reproduction. In these instances, the reproductive status of the industry subject takes on two linked valences—that of a parent and that of participation that feeds the transgenerational economies under construction.

As a result, this examination of transgenerational media industries has decentered kids in the study of children's consumer culture and its production, gravitating toward greater focus on adults and, more specifically, the parents to whom the conservative cultural politics of industrial reproduction have repeatedly looked. Even the child unboxing video creators of chapter 5, like the industry disruptors represented in Marvel's brief AR videos, must be understood in relation to the industrial power of their parents. If the subject positions offered to media industry participants (professional and amateur alike) constitute invitations to help do the work of cultural reproduction and the labor of transmitting popular culture across generational lines, then parenthood has been repeatedly and consistently invoked as a means of value, privilege, and management in that work. Transgenerational media industry strategies and practices need not be inherently conservative; but as currently developed by the television, toy, and comic book industries, continuity of power for legacy institutions manifests through investment in the heteronormative power of family structures to secure existing orientations and cultural inheritances (Ahmed 2006). In this story about the transgenerational destabilization of industry boundaries, the privilege accorded to family imposes hegemonic stability over the new industry formations that result.

While this book has pointed on occasion to alternative industry subjectivities that support the work of cultural reproduction, my hope is that future work can use it as a springboard for developing more detailed visions of what queer transgenerational industry subjects could look like—outside parenting and also potentially beyond play, fun, or even sharing. At the very least, such industry subjects would be antipatriarchal and nonheteronormative, extending from strategies that envision a future that can more definitively diverge from the past. Instead of bequeathing or sharing that which already exists, these subjects might steer the future toward that which does not. In that sense, the most radical industry subjects would be nonreproductive—and, of course, that is what makes them currently so difficult for media industries to support. For the moment, one might continue to look for the seeds of their emergence in the surplus markets that rest entirely outside of intersections of generations and industry participation currently envisioned by media industries. There, relationships to new and old, digital and analog, producer and consumer may be articulated in ways that push against and fail to serve prevailing industry logics. It would also be productive to consider how nonheteronormative consumer families negotiate the logics of inheritance and reproduction as constructed in the participatory roles offered by the industrial formations examined here. It will also be worth asking whether the logics of reproduction, however nonradical, might nevertheless introduce possibilities for industrial change and adaptation over time, allowing us to imagine futures that start to steer away from the past even as they continue to resemble it.

Similarly, as much as the more conservative investment in parental participation within transgenerational industry formations has required a focus on adults in this book, there remains room to explore in more detail the participation of children outside of these industrially privileged adult and parental subject positions. Discussion of children's productive participation as toy reviewers, sponsored content creators, and subjects of AR videos is a start, but researchers in children's media literacy and celebrity studies from which I borrowed inspiration will hopefully take these ideas in turn to explore the persistent if less industrially valued participation of children in these transgenerational practices of cultural reproduction—especially when it operates beyond the scope of the work so eagerly harnessed by industry here.

In detailing how the boundaries and subjectivities of industry participation have been constructed, I have frequently looked to the perspectives of scholars like Vicki Mayer, Miranda Banks, and John Caldwell (2009) who help us to understand labor under capitalism not just as a realm of economic exploitation but also as a site of identity formation and community where the cultural value of work is also produced. Among the many methods embraced here, my interest in such "production studies" has led me to engage in participant observation research at industry sites like Kidscreen and the LEGO factory, while also looking to "deep texts" (Caldwell 2009) that communicate the values, meanings, and identities through which these cultures of work take shape. At the same time as I borrow these methods, however, I have stopped short of aligning this book too closely with production studies, preferring to imagine my contribution as one that can help a critical media industry studies more broadly to see relationships and connections that exceed the boundaries of a production culture—where industry subjectivities and professionalisms intersect with those of consumers across the boundaries of adulthood and childhood both. I have sought to put production in greater dialogue with consumption cultures and practices in order to assess how the power to participate in the cultural work of media industry follows other kinds of privileges beyond belonging to a professionalized class. From this framework, I have approached questions of labor not just from a concern with who can be exploited through formal employment but also who can be empowered to participate in industries on the basis of what kinds of subjective privileges. In zeroing in on the transgenerational industry subject, my concern for labor has been one not just of production but more broadly of reproduction in which professionals and amateurs, adults and children alike participate in significant but unequal ways.

As a means of temporary closure, then, it seems appropriate to reflect one last time on the relationship between labor and reproduction. In the privilege accorded to parents as managerial agents transmitting culture from one generation to the next, labor is not just productive but reproductive—where biologically procreative subjects regenerate industries too. The literal labor of birthing children, followed by the unpaid labor of raising them, brings with it a privilege of greater participation in a process of cultural inheritance. In that sense, I do not leave questions of media labor to production studies, but instead consider its centrality to an ongoing *study of media reproduction* more broadly conceived. Continuing attention to transgenerational media industries will grant insight into the labor of cultural reproduction while also revealing the power dynamics through which participation in that reproductive work turns on privileged relations between the old and the young as those identities intersect with gender, class, sexuality, race, and more. Ironically, it was as a parent and through my consumer participation in these transgenerational practices that I started writing this book; but at the end, I must acknowledge that this regime of media reproduction grants industry subjects like myself a privileged power to claim culture as an inheritance I might pass down—while denying that same participation to others.

Here, then, is where something as simple as Marvel's AR videos can serve as an indicator of both the disruption of that status quo and the continued health of this regime of media reproduction. There is a visceral joy in watching the kids take over and literally knock the old generation and its privileges from view. However, as part of a staged, managed representation of industry culture deployed as promotion, the transgenerational participation of these unruly kids manifests through the patriarchal power of the industry and an invitation to the progeny of the powerful to enter the professional sphere. In that sense, the possibilities of reproductive participation extend the legacies and inheritances of the (white, middle-class, and heterosexual) family rather than support for anything revolutionary. Transgenerational media industries often seek to transform adults and children into different kinds of participant subjects—from parent to promoter, from creative laborer to parent-managed child, from adult fan to pediocular professional—but that does necessarily not make them transformative of existing power structures. Going forward, our attention should focus on what other kinds of transgenerational media reproduction can be envisioned, and with them, what other kinds of futures.

Notes

Introduction

1. In their critique of Disney comics, Dorfman and Mattelart argue that adult and child "fuse in a single embrace, and history becomes biology. The identity of parent and child inhibits the emergence of true generational conflicts. The pure child will replace the corrupt father, preserving the latter's values. The future (the child) reaffirms the present (the adult), which, in turn, transmits the past" (2012: 113).

2. Notably, Halberstam identifies childhood as a queer experience that produces "subjugated knowledges" from which new social relations might be imagined (2011: 3, 11).

3. Through historical analysis of the merchandising and retailing of children's clothing in the early twentieth century, Cook reveals the emergence of "the child as an individuated, volitional, and socially legitimate commercial actor—that is, as a consumer" (2004: 67).

4. This move away from exclusive focus on children also sidesteps some of the more common debates shared across childhood studies, media studies, psychology, and other disciplines. Sonia Livingstone and Kirsten Drotner describe a tension in this research between those who imagine the "vulnerable child" prone to exploitation by the commercial market forces, on the one hand, and those who envision the "competent child" empowered by the savvy literacies afforded through media use, on the other (2008: 9).

5. In writing her book on girls' media production, for instance, Mary Kearney writes that describing the project to new acquaintances often meant correcting assumptions that she studied media texts produced for or about girls by adults (2006: 292).

6. Mindful of the production of childhood by industry, Cook also argues that "'adult' industries, structures, and economic arrangements temporally and structurally precede and encompass any one child or any particular historical manifestations of childhood" (2004: 5).

7. Against scholars, activists, and regulators who aim to protect children from consumer culture, Buckingham hopes to "*prepare* children to deal with these experiences"

(2000: 16). As part of that preparation, he wants to interrogate the barriers of appropriateness that separate the mediated lives of adult and children.

8. Havens, Lotz, and Tinic nominate the methods of production studies as "entirely consistent with our proposed research framework," drawing on "close readings of industry discourses, interviews, and ethnographic participating in industrial practices" (2009: 245); as such, the following chapters adopt many of the same "midlevel" industry fieldwork strategies.

9. As Stig Hjarvard argues, the "mediatization" of society has broadly integrated the forms, institutions, and practices of media culture within other social and cultural realms, including politics and religion but also, notably, everyday practices of play (2013: 103).

10. In his landmark study, Dan Fleming demonstrates that toys are culturally meaningful objects interpreted in different ways by children and their parents alike (1996: 57, 60).

Chapter 1

1. As Lotz writes, "viewers now increasingly select what, when, and where to view from abundant options," shifting power away from the programming executive (2014: 28).

2. In this model, the open and participatory affordances of the networked era provide more than choice to support new, independent modes of production and distribution that give voice to those previously ignored.

3. Elsewhere I have argued that these new "portal" functions need not be considered a fundamental break from the earlier "channel" logics structuring the television industry (Johnson 2018).

4. Although society-making and segment-making media could in principle work in equilibrium to support both the strength of smaller interest groups and their ability to interact and connect with one another, Turow argues that they work in practice to produce a divisive imagination of the social world.

5. Equally sociological is the circulation of these stories about new generations of television viewers as a form of "industry lore" (Havens 2006: 123) used as the basis for new business action and to regulate practice within professional communities.

6. Disney Junior claimed a greater overall daytime and primetime co-viewing percentage of 57 percent, due in significant part to greater parental supervision of preschool television viewers ("Catering" 2010: 13).

7. Although Netflix had previously partnered with Italian animation studio Rainbow to acquire the rights to the six earlier seasons of *Winx Club* first carried on Nickelodeon in the United States, *WOW* would represent the first exclusive arrangement as a Netflix original series. This expansion of the *Winx* franchise would offer a "serialized storyline designed specifically for online viewing" (Fisher 2014d).

Chapter 2

1. John Banks (2013) similarly proposes that video game users' productive contributions to the commodities sold by publishers be considered in terms of a rewarding "co-creativity" rather than mere exploitation. In my own research, I identified dynamics whereby media industries were "inviting audiences in" to play meaningful roles in the creation and promotion of media content, focusing on the way in which it played into the pleasures of media fandom (Johnson 2007).

2. Half of the top ten 2013 bestsellers in the United States carried an M or A rating (*Grand Theft Auto V*, *Call of Duty: Ghosts*, *Battlefield 4*, *Assassin's Creed IV*, and *Call of Duty: Black Ops*) (Crossley 2014).

Chapter 3

1. Havens describes industry lore as the product of the beliefs and ideologies that underpin production and distribution practices, constituting commonsense assumptions among practitioners about how the industry in which they work operates.

2. Including professional anecdotes, trade publications, how-to manuals, and other artifacts within industry sectors, deep texts both make sense of the industry world and provide shared stories, symbols, and "willed affinities" around which communities can form (Caldwell 2008: 201).

3. Sherry Ortner (2010) notes the challenge that accompanies attempts to enter the often-secretive worlds of media industries.

4. Reflecting on the "buffet" of deep texts accessible by consumers, Caldwell also notes that these artifacts perform important reflexive boundary work that "unseats traditional anxieties about gaining access to industry's guarded center. This, in turn, makes the self-referencing borderlands between industry and audience a compelling question to be solved" (2008: 361).

5. Against this adult industrial power, Buckingham hopes to establish a better "means by which children themselves can speak more directly, collectively, and loudly to producers and policy-makers" (2000: 204).

6. In her articulation of a feminist production studies project, Banks imagines work that can pay attention to the voices and experiences of producers situated within labor hierarchies that gender professional positions, governing both the access individuals have to that work and the value such work can accrue (2009: 96).

7. This situates the reality series within a tradition of marketing toys through television that has long been a concern of parents, regulators, and scholars alike (Seiter 1995; Hendershot 1998). The build-up to the reveal of this new Mattel product over multiple episodes also recalls the "total merchandising" strategies employed by Disney in the course of its 1955 *Disneyland* series, the first season of which chronicled the design and construction of the theme park, culminating in its opening (Anderson 1994).

8. Neither Mattel nor Toys "R" Us have released any significant sales data for Artsplash, but given that the retailer declared bankruptcy less than four months after release in September 2017 and began closing all its stores early the next year, the prod-

uct's initial market impact will likely have been impaired by the exclusivity at the heart of these industry partnerships.

9. While McCracken's status as scholar might make him seem somewhat of an outsider in this professional space, his work as a consultant for companies like Netflix, Google, and Amazon—leading out of well-received business books like *Chief Culture Officer* (2009)—speaks to the compatibility of his knowledge production with industry cultures.

10. The 2017 conference theme "Rainbow Rangers" emphasized the linkages between generation, gender, and race in this project, visualized in a poster that shows ten superheroes in action, of which one is a robot, another had blue skin, and one in the far background could be read as white, with the other seven all visually marked as black, Asian, Latino/a, or Arab (Giarusso 2017).

Chapter 4

1. I shared a draft of my findings with Inside Tour representatives who kindly provided feedback and pushed back in instances where my descriptions appeared inaccurate. I have incorporated that valuable perspective in the analysis of this chapter; however, LEGO's representatives stressed that this productive dialogue did not represent any kind of validation of my claims or conclusions.

2. Prominent Ideas designers include adults with professional status in other fields, such as Dutch geochemist Ellen Kooijman, US science writer Maia Wienstock, and Pixar filmmaker Angus MacLane.

3. The broader importance of moderation in kids' consumer culture reasserted itself in 2017 when YouTube sought ten thousand new content moderators to help it reensure trust and safety in content aimed at kids following concerns about inappropriate material (Dickson 2017b; Ducard 2017).

Chapter 5

1. This insight is drawn from my fieldwork with The LEGO Group in Billund, as described in the previous chapter.

2. Alice Marwick describes as "micro-celebrity" the marketable practices of "creating an easily consumable persona, responding directly to readers, and sharing personal information to enhance emotional ties with fans" (2015: 341). Andrew Zolides (2017b) frames these entrepreneurial endeavors as part of an "influence economy" in which one's ability to connect with other social media users can be directly measured and commodified as sold to media marketers.

3. Even for internal market research sessions in which children are not expected to produce their own online reviews or videos, the blog describes a process of selection in which researchers observe the child's interaction with toy products in order to "scrutinize and record his every move" in selecting from a pool of potential participants (Lipmen 2016).

4. CNN reports shared similar estimates in 2014, although with slightly more con-

servative estimates of US$2–5 per one thousand impressions and acknowledgment that not all views are "monetized" (watched long enough to expose viewers to embedded advertisements) (Kelly 2014).

5. The US Consumer Product Safety Commission's (2010) ninety-one-page "Laboratory Test Manual for Toy Testing" lays out detailed protocols and procedures to organize this kind of work.

6. Maker works with a wide range of social media celebrities, including PewDiePie.

Bibliography

"2017 Comic Book Sales to Comic Shops." n.d. Comichron.com. http://www.comichron.com/monthlycomicssales/2017.html.

ABC News. 2015. "How YouTube Kid Toy Testers Make Millions." *ABC News Business*, March 24. http://abcnews.go.com/Business/youtube-kid-toy-testers-make-millions/story?id=29864873

"About CBW." n.d. *Book Week Online*. http://www.bookweekonline.com/about

"About You." 2013. ToyTesters.tv. https://toytesters.tv/Become_a_toy_tester.aspx?ad=topad

Acland, Charles. 2004. "Fresh Contacts: Global Culture and the Concept of Generation." In *American Youth Cultures*, edited by Neil Campbell, 31–52. Edinburgh: Edinburgh University Press.

Aden, Roger. 1999. *Popular Stories and Promised Lands: Fan Cultures and Symbolic Tourism*. Tuscaloosa: University of Alabama Press.

Adorno, Theodor W. 1963/2000. "Culture Industry Reconsidered." In *Media Studies: A Reader*, edited by Paul Marris and Sue Thornham, 31–37. New York: New York University Press.

"Advertise." 2013. *ToyTesters.tv*. https://toytesters.tv/Advertise.aspx

Ahmed, Sara. 2006. *Queer Phenomenology: Orientations, Objects, Others*. Durham: Duke University Press.

Albiniak, Paige. 2011. "Kids Programming More Competitive Than Ever." *Variety*, March 12. http://variety.com/2011/tv/features/kids-programming-more-competitive-than-ever-1118033474

Alford, Catherine. 2017. "Parents: Tired of Paying Big Bucks for Toys? Sign Your Child Up to Test Them." *The Penny Hoarder*, June 21. https://www.thepennyhoarder.com/life/parenting/toy-tester

Alonso, Axel. 2014. "In-Depth on 'Avengers NOW!' and New Takes on Captain America, Thor, and Iron Man." CBR.com, July 18. http://www.comicbookresources.com/?page=article&id=54183

Alters, Diane, and Lynn Schofield Clark. 2003. "Introduction." In *Media, Home and Family*, edited by Stewart Hoover, Lynn Schofield Clark, and Diane Alters, 3–18. New York: Routledge.

Anderson, Benedict. 1983. *Imagined Communities: Reflections on the Origins and Spread of Nationalism*. London: Verso.
Anderson, Christopher. 1994. *Hollywood TV: The Studio System in the Fifties*. Austin: University of Texas Press.
Andrejevic, Mark. 2010. "Exploiting YouTube: Contradictions of User-Generated Labor." In *The YouTube Reader*, edited by Pelle Snickars and Patrick Vonderau, 406–23. Stockholm: National Library of Sweden.
"Animation Academy." n.d. *Disneyland Resort*. https://disneyland.disney.go.com/attractions/disney-california-adventure/animation-academy
Appadurai, Arjun. 1986. "Introduction: Commodities and the Politics of Value." In *The Social Lives of Things: Commodities in a Cultural Perspective*, edited by Arjun Appadurai, 3–63. Cambridge: Cambridge University Press.
"Apply to Join the Programme." n.d. Toys "R" Us UK. http://blog.toysrus.co.uk/apply-to-join-the-programme
arenahes. 2016. "7 Best Tips on How to Become a Toy Tester." All Best Toys. http://www.allbesttoys.com/7-best-tips-on-how-to-become-a-toy-tester
"Artsplash Is the Winner of ABC's Hit Series, 'The Toy Box.'" 2017. PR Newswire, May 19. http://www.prnewswire.com/news-releases/artsplash-is-the-winner-of-abcs-hit-series-the-toy-box-300460869.html
Atkinson, Claire. 2008. "Co-Viewing: No More Fights Over the Remote." *Broadcasting & Cable*, April 21: 9.
"Avengers & Hulk Animated Series Get Premiere Dates." 2013. Marvel.com, March 8. http://marvel.com/news/tv/2013/3/8/20256/avengers_hulk_animated_series_get_premiere_dates
Banet-Weiser, Sarah. 2007. *Kids Rule! Nickelodeon and Consumer Citizenship*. Durham: Duke University Press.
Banet-Weiser, Sarah. 2012. *AuthenticTM: The Politics of Ambivalence in a Brand Culture*. New York: New York University Press.
Banks, John. 2013. *Co-creating Videogames*. New York: Bloomsbury.
Banks, Miranda. 2009. "Gender Below-the-Line: Defining Feminist Production Studies." In *Production Studies: Cultural Studies of the Media Industries*, edited by Vicki Mayer, Miranda Banks, and John Caldwell, 87–98. New York: Routledge.
Baym, Nancy. 2015. "Connect With Your Audience! The Relational Labor of Connection." *The Communication Review* 18.1: 14–22.
Becki. n.d. "How to Become a Toy Tester and Get Free Toys!" *Domestic Mommyhood*. http://domesticmommyhood.com/how-to-become-a-toy-tester-and-get-free-toys
Beeston, Ariane. 2017. "Dream Job Alert: Fisher-Price Seeks 'Top Toy Tester.'" *Essential Kids*, March 20. http://www.essentialkids.com.au/entertainment/toys-products/dream-job-alert-fisherprice-seeks-top-toy-tester-20170320-gv1vxg
Beeton, Sue. 2005. *Film-Induced Tourism*. Clevedon: Channel View.
Benedetti, Angelina. 2011. "Not Just for Teens." *Library Journal* 136.11: 40–43.
Berenson, Tessa. 2015. "Here's Where to Get a Free Comic Book Today." *Time*, May 2. http://time.com/3844238/free-comic-book-day
Berlant, Lauren, and Michael Warner. 1998. "Sex in Public." *Critical Inquiry* 24.2: 547–66.

Beyond the Brick. 2017a. "Inside the LEGO Archive Vault." YouTube, June 26. https://www.youtube.com/watch?v=EgFvzpB6BsQ

Beyond the Brick. 2017b. "Rare Look Inside LEGO's Private Museum." YouTube, July 3. https://www.youtube.com/watch?v=T-O1mRL1DNU

Bielby, Denise, and C. Lee Harrington. 2008. *Global TV: Exporting Television and Culture in the World Market*. New York: New York University Press.

"Billund City Vision." n.d. Capitol of Children. http://www.capitalofchildren.com/projects/billund-city-vision

Bogost, Ian. 2011. "Gamification Is Bullshit!" *Ian Bogost* (blog), August 8. http://bogost.com/writing/blog/gamification_is_bullshit

The Brick. 2010. The LEGO Group.

"Bring the Kids! Comic-Con's Child Care Has You Covered." 2015. Comic-Con. http://comic-con.org/cci/child-care#sthash.iteWqPrv.dpuf

Brooker, Will. 2007. "Everywhere and Nowhere: Vancouver, Fan Pilgrimage, and the Urban Imaginary." *International Journal of Cultural Studies* 10.4: 432–44.

Brookey, Robert Alan. 2010. *Hollywood Gamers: Digital Convergence in the Film and Video Game Industries*. Bloomington: Indiana University Press.

Bruns, Axel. 2008. *Blogs, Wikipedia, Second Life, and Beyond: From Production to Produsage*. New York: Peter Lang.

Brustein, Joshua. 2015. "Why HBO, Netflix, and Amazon Want Your Kids." *Bloomberg Business*, August 14. https://www.bloomberg.com/news/articles/2015-08-14/why-hbo-netflix-and-amazon-want-your-kids

Bryant, J. Alison, ed. 2007. *The Children's Television Community*. Mahwah: Lawrence Erlbaum Associates.

Buckingham, David. 2000. *After the Death of Childhood: Growing Up in the Age of Electronic Media*. Cambridge: Polity.

Buckingham, David. 2008. "Children and Media: A Cultural Studies Approach." In *The International Handbook of Children, Media, and Culture*, edited by Sonia Livingstone and Kirsten Drotner, 219–36. Los Angeles: Sage.

Bulut, Ergin. 2014. "Playboring in the Tester Pit: The Convergence of Precarity and the Degradation of Fun in Video Game Testing." *Television and New Media* 16.3: 240–58.

Burgess, Jean, and Joshua Green. 2009. *YouTube: Online Video and Participatory Culture*. Cambridge: Polity.

Burton, Anthony. 1997. "Design History and the History of Toys: Defining a Discipline for the Bethnal Green Museum of Childhood." *Journal of Design History* 10.1: 1–21.

Burton, Bonnie. n.d. "Welcome to GRRL." *GRRL*. http://www.grrl.com/newhome.html

Burton, Bonnie. 2013. "A Little About Me." CNET, October 24. https://www.cnet.com/profiles/bonniegrrl

Caldwell, John. 2008. *Production Culture: Industrial Reflexivity and Critical Practice in Film and Television*. Durham: Duke University Press.

Caldwell, John. 2009. "Cultures of Production: Studying Industry's Deep Texts, Reflexive Rituals, and Managed Self-Disclosures." In *Media Industries: History,*

Theory, and Method, edited by Jennifer Holt and Alisa Perren, 199–212. Malden: Wiley-Blackwell.

Caldwell, John. 2013. "Para-Industry: Reseaching Hollywood's Blackwaters." *Cinema Journal* 52.3: 157–65.

"Careers." n.d. LEGO.com. https://www.lego.com/en-us/careers/search-jobs

Carl, Daniela, Sara Kindon, and Karen Smith. 2007. "'Tourists' Experiences of Film Locations: New Zealand as 'Middle Earth.'" *Tourism Geographies* 9.1: 49–63.

Cary, Diana. 1997. *Hollywood's Children: An Inside Account of the Child Star Era*. Dallas: Southern Methodist University Press.

"Catering to Kids: Cable Networks Divide to Conquer." 2010. *Multichannel News*, March 21: 12–13.

"Celebrate Free Comic Book Day, Kicking off Children's Book Week on May 2." 2015. Children's Book Council, April 8. http://www.cbcbooks.org/comic-book-stores-to-kick-off-childrens-book-week-2015/#.WduXFoZrxE4

Chaney, Damien, Mourad Touzani, and Karim Ben Slimane. 2017. "Marketing to the (New) Generations: Summary and Perspectives." *Journal of Strategic Marketing* 25.3: 179–89.

Chávez, Christopher. 2018. "Disney XD: Boyhood and the Racial Politics of Market Segmentation." In *From Networks to Netflix: A Guide to Changing Channels*, edited by Derek Johnson, 209–18. New York: Routledge.

Cheh, Samantha. 2017. "Kid Influencers on YouTube Are Helping Toy Companies Boost Sales." *Techwire Asia*, October 20. http://techwireasia.com/2017/10/kid-influencers-youtube-helping-toy-companies-boost-sales

"Child Badge Policy." 2014. Comic-Con. http://www.comic-con.org/cci/child-badge-policy

"Children's Book Week Celebrates Childhood Literacy." 2009. *Reading Today*, April/May: 34.

Ching, Albert. 2013. "Marvel Reveals SHARE YOUR UNIVERSE." Newsarama.com, July 9. http://www.newsarama.com/18305-marvel-reveals-share-your-universe-live.html

Ching, Albert. 2014. "Axel-in-Charge: In-Depth on 'Avengers NOW!' and New Takes on Captain America, Thor, and Iron Man." *CBR.com*, July 18. http://www.comicbookresources.com/?page=article&id=54183

Christian, Aymar Jean. 2018. *Open TV: Innovation Beyond Hollywood and the Rise of Web Television*. New York: New York University Press.

Colombani, Laurent, and David Sanderson. 2016. "Generation #hashtag: Harnessing the Power of Fans." Bain & Company.

"Comic-Con 2013 Thursday Programs." 2013. Comic-Con. https://www.comic-con.org/cci/2013/thursday

Consalvo, Mia. 2008. "Crunched by Passion: Women Game Developers and Workplace Challenges." In *Beyond Barbie and Mortal Kombat: New Perspectives on Gender and Gaming*, edited by Yasmin Kafai, Carrie Heeter, Jill Denner, and Jennifer Sun, 177–91. Cambridge: MIT Press.

Cook, Daniel Thomas. 2004. *The Commodification of Childhood: The Children's Clothing Industry and the Rise of the Child Consumer*. Durham: Duke University Press.

Copple Smith, Erin. 2018. "Nick Jr.: Co-Viewing and the Limits of Dayparts." In

From Networks to Netflix, edited by Derek Johnson, 188–95. New York: Routledge.

Costello, Rachel. 2015. "Product Testers Wanted—Win Prizes Too!" The Hut. http://www.thehut.com/blog/kids/recruiting-product-testers-win-prizes

Couldry, Nick. 2000. *The Place of Media Power: Pilgrims and Witnesses in the Media Age*. London: Routledge.

Couldry, Nick. 2007. "Pilgrimage in Mediaspace: Continuities and Transformations." *Etnofoor* 20.1: 63–73.

"Co-Viewing for Dollars." 2013. *Kidscreen*, October: 38.

"Co-Viewing with Kids." n.d. WETA. https://weta.org/kids/television/coviewing

Craig, David, and Stuart Cunningham. 2017. "Toy Unboxing: Living in a(n unregulated) Material World." *Media International Australia* 163.1: 77–86.

"Creative England." n.d. Creative England. http://www.creativeengland.co.uk

Crossen, Cynthia. 2007. "It Dawned on Adults After WWII: 'You'll Shoot Your Eye Out!'" *Wall Street Journal*, December 3. https://www.wsj.com/articles/SB119664662089911293

Crossley, Rob. 2014. "NPD: Best-selling US Games of 2013 Revealed." *Computer and Video Games*, January 17. http://www.computerandvideogames.com/445780/npd-best-selling-us-games-of-2013-revealed

Curran, Oisin. 2017. "How Toy Testers Work." HowStuffWorks, November 28. https://money.howstuffworks.com/toy-tester.htm

Curtin, Michael. 1996. "On Edge: Culture Industries in the Neo-Network Era." In *Making and Selling Culture*, edited by Richard Ohmann, 181–201. Hanover: Wesleyan University Press.

Curtin, Michael, and Thomas Streeter. 2001. "Media." In *Culture Works: Essays on the Political Economy of Culture*, edited by Richard Maxell, 225–49. Minneapolis: University of Minnesota Press.

"Customer Service." n.d. Hasbro. https://www.hasbro.com/en-ca/customer-service/faq

D'Acci, Julie. 1994. *Defining Women: Television and the Case of Cagney & Lacey*. Chapel Hill: University of North Carolina Press.

D'Acci, Julie. 1997. "Nobody's Woman? Honey West and the New Sexuality." In *The Revolution Wasn't Televised: Sixties Television and Social Conflict*, edited by Lynn Spigel and Michael Curtin, 72–93. New Brunswick: Rutgers University Press.

"Deluxe Tour." n.d. Warner Bros. Studio Tour Hollywood. https://www.wbstudiotour.com/deluxe-tour

Dickson, Jeremy. 2013. "The Co-Viewing Connection." *Kidscreen*, October: 37.

Dickson, Jeremy. 2014a. "Cartoon Network US Secures Newest Transformers Series." *Kidscreen*, October 7. http://kidscreen.com/2014/10/07/cartoon-network-us-secures-newest-transformers-series

Dickson, Jeremy. 2014b. "Discovery to Rebrand Hub Network as a Family Channel." *Kidscreen*, September 25. http://kidscreen.com/2014/09/25/discovery-to-rebrand-hub-network-as-a-family-channel

Dickson, Jeremy. 2017a. "Study: Majority of Parents Embrace Connected Kids Devices." *Kidscreen*, November 16. http://kidscreen.com/2017/11/16/study-majority-of-parents-embrace-connected-kids-devices/?utm_source=newsletter&utm_

medium=email&utm_campaign=study-majority-of-parents-embrace-connected-kids-devices&_u=%2ffTA5Jevoq0%3d

Dickson, Jeremy. 2017b. "YouTube to Enlist 10,000 Workers to Moderate Content." *Kidscreen*, December 5. http://kidscreen.com/2017/12/05/youtube-to-enlist-10000-workers-to-moderate-content/?utm_source=newsletter&utm_medium=email&utm_campaign=youtube-to-enlist-10000-workers-to-moderate-content&_u=%2ffTA5Jevoq0%3d

Dietcher, Jay. 2013. "Free Comic Book Day: 9 Reasons Your Kids Should Be Reading Comics!" Unleash the Fanboy, April 29. http://www.unleashthefanboy.com/comics/free-comic-book-day-9-reasons-your-kids-should-be-reading-comics/52083

Discovery Toys. 2017. "Home." Facebook. https://www.facebook.com/discoverytoys?fref=ts

"Disney Junior: The New 24/7 Channel Fights to Capture Co-Viewing Audiences This Fall." 2012. *Kidscreen*, October: 94.

D'Orazio, Dante. 2012. "Marvel Reveals Augmented Reality for Comic Books, New 'Infinite' Digital Comics." *The Verge*, March 11. https://www.theverge.com/2012/3/11/2862606/marvel-ar-infinite-augmented-reality-comic-book

Dorfman, Ariel, and Armand Mattelart. 1971/2012. "Introduction: Instructions on How to Become a General in the Disneyland Club." In *Media and Cultural Studies: Keyworks*, 2nd ed., edited by Meenakshi Gigi Durham and Douglas M. Kellner, 110–14. Malden: Wiley-Blackwell.

Downey, Kevin. 2006. "What Children Teach Their Parents." *Broadcasting & Cable*, March 13: 26, 28.

Driscoll, Molly. 2014. "Free Comic Book Day: It's Almost Time." *Christian Science Monitor*, May 2. https://www.csmonitor.com/Books/chapter-and-verse/2014/0502/Free-Comic-Book-Day-It-s-almost-time

Ducard, Malik. 2017. "Op-Ed: Dear YouTube Family Creator Community." *Kidscreen*, December 7. http://kidscreen.com/2017/12/07/op-ed-dear-youtube-family-creator-community/?utm_source=newsletter&utm_medium=email&utm_campaign=op-ed-dear-youtube-family-creator-community&_u=%2ffTA5Jevoq0%3d

Duffy, Brooke Erin. 2016. "The Romance of Work: Gender and Aspirational Labour in the Digital Culture Industries." *International Journal of Cultural Studies* 19.4: 441–57.

Du Gay, Paul. 1996. *Consumption and Identity at Work*. London: Sage.

Dyer-Witheford, Nick, and Greig de Peuter. 2009. *Games of Empire: Global Capitalism and Video Games*. Minneapolis: University of Minnesota Press.

Earls, Stephanie. 2015. "Free Comic Book Day Kicks of Children's Book Week." *Colorado Springs Gazette*, April 27. http://gazette.com/free-comic-book-day-kicks-off-childrens-book-week/article/1550440

Edelman, Lee. 2004. *No Future: Queer Theory and the Death Drive*. Durham: Duke University Press.

Elkington, Trevor. 2009. "Too Many Cooks: Media Convergence and Self-Defeating Adaptations." In *The Video Game Theory Reader 2*, edited by Bernard Perron and Mark J. P. Wolf, 213–37. New York: Routledge.

Fisher, Daniela. 2014a. "Action Toys Transform Hasbro's Second Quarter." *Kidscreen*,

July 21. http://kidscreen.com/2014/07/21/action-toys-transform-hasbros-second-quarter/?utm_source=newsletter&utm_medium=email&utm_campaign=action-toys-transform-hasbros-second-quarter&_u=238834

Fisher, Daniela. 2014b. "Amazon Studios Lines Up Five More Kids TV Pilots." *Kidscreen*, August 25. http://kidscreen.com/2014/08/25/amazon-studios-lines-up-five-more-kids-tv-pilots

Fisher, Daniela. 2014c. "Hasbro Ups Davis to Chief of Content Amid Merger Speculation." *Kidscreen*, November 13. http://kidscreen.com/2014/11/13/hasbro-ups-davis-to-chief-of-content-amid-merger-speculation

Fisher, Daniela. 2014d. "Netflix, Rainbow to Spin Off Winx Club Series." *Kidscreen*, September 25. http://kidscreen.com/2014/09/25/netflix-rainbow-studios-to-spin-off-winx-club

Fisher, Daniela. 2014e. "Netflix, Saban to Bring Popples to New Generation." *Kidscreen*, September 24. http://kidscreen.com/2014/09/24/netflix-saban-bring-popples-to-new-generation

Fisher, Daniela. 2015. "Amazon Rolls Out 2015 Pilot Season." *Kidscreen*, January 6. http://kidscreen.com/2015/01/06/amazon-rolls-out-2015-pilot-season

Fleming, Dan. 1996. *Powerplay: Toys as Popular Culture*. Manchester: Manchester University Press.

Ford, Sam, and Henry Jenkins. 2009. "Managing Multiplicity in Superhero Comics: An Interview with Henry Jenkins." In *Third Person: Authoring and Exploring Vast Narratives*, edited by Pat Harrigan and Noah Waldrip-Fruin, 303–12. Cambridge: MIT Press.

Foster, Elizabeth. 2017a. "Common Sense Media: Mobile is Soaring Among US Kids." *Kidscreen*, October 19. http://kidscreen.com/2017/10/19/common-sense-media-mobile-usage-soars-among-us-kids/?utm_source=newsletter&utm_medium=email&utm_campaign=common-sense-media-mobile-usage-soars-among-us-kids&_u=%2ffTA5Jevoq0%3d

Foster, Elizabeth. 2017b. "Nickelodeon to Launch OTT Channel in Japan." *Kidscreen*, October 18. http://kidscreen.com/2017/10/18/nickelodeon-to-launch-ott-channel-in-japan/?utm_source=newsletter&utm_medium=email&utm_campaign=nickelodeon-to-launch-ott-channel-in-japan&_u=%2ffTA5Jevoq0%3d

Foucault, Michel. 1975. "What Is an Author?" *Partisan Review* 4: 603–14.

"Franchise Index—Brands." 2018. Box Office Mojo. http://www.boxofficemojo.com/franchises/?view=Brand&sort=sumgross&order=DESC&p=.htm

"Franchise Index—Series." 2018. Box Office Mojo. http://www.boxofficemojo.com/franchises/?view=Franchise&sort=sumgross&order=DESC&p=.htm

"Free Comic Book Day." 2014. Free Comic Book Day. http://www.freecomicbookday.com/Home/1/1/27/992

"Free Comics Book Day to Kick Off Children's Book Week." 2015. West Virginia Library Commision. http://www.librarycommission.wv.gov/news/Pages/Free-Comic-Book-Day-to-Kick-Off-Children%27s-Book-Week.aspx

Ganti, Tejaswini. 2012. *Producing Bollywood: Inside the Contemporary Hindi Film Industry*. Durham: Duke University Press.

Gaudiosi, John. 2014. "Disney Powers New Infinity Game with Marvel Super

Heroes." *Fortune*, June 24. http://fortune.com/2014/06/24/disney-infinity-marvel-super-heroes

Geraghty, Lincoln. 2014. *Cult Collectors: Nostalgia, Fandom and Collecting Popular Culture*. New York: Routledge.

Getzler, Wendy Goldman. 2014. "Margaret Loesch Set to Exit Hub Network." *Kidscreen*, June 12. http://kidscreen.com/2014/06/12/margaret-loesch-set-to-exit-hub-network

Getzler, Wendy Goldman. 2015a. "Amazon Readies Six Kids Pilots for Fall Debut." *Kidscreen*, October 16. http://kidscreen.com/2015/10/16/amazon-readies-six-kids-pilots-for-fall-debut

Getzler, Wendy Goldman. 2015b. "Nielsen: Time-shifting, Tablets and Their Transformation of TV." *Kidscreen*, August 27. http://kidscreen.com/2015/08/27/nielsen-time-shifting-tablets-and-their-transformation-of-tv

Giarusso, Chris. 2017. "Our New Poster." Kids' Comic Con. http://www.simmonshereandnow.com/whatido.html

Gibson-Graham, J. K. 1996. *The End of Capitalism (As We Knew It): A Feminist Critique of Political Economy*. Minneapolis: University of Minnesota Press.

Gilmore, James N., and Matthias Stork, eds. 2014. *Super Hero Synergies: Comic Book Characters Go Digital*. New York: Rowman & Littlefield.

Gitlin, Todd. 2000. *Inside Prime Time*. Berkeley: University of California Press.

Gonzales, Jasper. 2013. "Amazing Las Vegas Comic-Con Day 3 (Kid's Day)." Nerdlocker.com, June 18. http://www.nerdlocker.com/comics/amazing-las-vegas-comic-con-day-3-kids-day

Graff, Amy. 2012. "Sad News for Geeky Parents: Comic-Con Introduces Stroller Ban." *Mommy Files* (blog), July 11. http://blog.sfgate.com/sfmoms/2012/07/11/sad-news-for-geeky-parents-comic-con-introduces-stroller-ban

Grenoble, Ryan. 2013. "John St-Onge Barred from Legoland Discovery Center Because He Was Unaccompanied by a Child." *Huffington Post*, July 10. http://www.huffingtonpost.com/2013/07/10/john-st-onge-legoland-senior-age-limit_n_3573608.html

Grossberg, Lawrence. 2011. *Cultural Studies in the Future Tense*. Durham: Duke University Press.

Grossman, Andrew. 2005. "Cartoons Break Barriers." *Multichannel News*, August 19. https://www.multichannel.com/news/cartoons-break-barriers-368700

Guschwan, Matthew. 2012. "Fandom, Brandom, and the Limits of Participatory Culture." *Journal of Consumer Culture* 12.1: 19–40.

Guthrie, Marisa. 2010. "The Hub Joins a Crowded Playground." *Broadcasting & Cable*, October 4: 12.

Halberstam, Judith. 2011. *The Queer Art of Failure*. Durham: Duke University Press.

Hall, Stuart. 1981/2011. "Notes on Deconstructing 'the Popular.'" In *Cultural Theory: An Anthology*, edited by Imre Szeman and Timothy Kaposy, 72–80. Malden: Wiley-Blackwell.

Hanna, Erin. 2019. *Comic-Con Culture: Hollywood, Fans, and the Limits of Exclusivity*. New Brunswick: Rutgers University Press.

Hartley, John. 2013. "Authorship and the Narrative of the Self." In *A Companion to Media Authorship*, edited by Jonathan Gray and Derek Johnson, 23–47. Malden: Wiley-Blackwell.

"Hasbro Expands Storytelling Strategy." 2016. *License Global*, July 13. http://www.licensemag.com/license-global/hasbro-expands-storytelling-strategy

Hauman, Glenn. 2011. "Yet Another Reason for Comics to Go Digital: 40 Is the New 15." ComicMix.com, June 8. http://www.comicmix.com/2011/06/08/yet-another-reason-for-comics-to-go-digital-40-is-the-new-15

Havens, Timothy. 2006. *Global Television Marketplace*. London: BFI.

Havens, Timothy. 2007. "Universal Childhood: The Global Trade in Children's Television and Changing Ideals of Childhood." *Global Media Journal* 6.10. http://www.globalmediajournal.com/open-access/universal-childhood-the-global-trade-in-childrens-television-and-changing-ideals-of-childhood.php?aid=35250

Havens, Timothy. 2018. "Netflix: Streaming Channel Brands as Global Meaning Systems." In *From Networks to Netflix: A Guide to Changing Channels*, edited by Derek Johnson, 321–31. New York: Routledge.

Havens, Timothy, Amanda Lotz, and Serra Tinic. 2009. "Critical Media Industry Studies: A Research Approach." *Communication, Culture & Critique* 2: 234–53.

"Help! My Kid Is a Geek!" 2015. Indy Pop Con. https://indypopcon2015.sched.org/event/6f1f7626cafef1cf79a3404c40552858?iframe=no&w=&sidebar=yes&bg=no#.VZgnIkYqcqM

Hendershot, Heather. 1998. *Saturday Morning Censors: Television Regulation Before the V-Chip*. Durham: Duke University Press.

Hendershot, Heather. 2004. "Nickelodeon's Nautical Nonsense: The Intergenerational Appeal of Spongebob Squarepants." In *Nickelodeon Nation: The History, Politics, and Economics of America's Only TV Channel for Kids*, edited by Heather Hendershot, 182–208. New York: New York University Press.

Hesmondhalgh, David. 2010. "User-Generated Content, Free Labour, and the Cultural Industries." *Ephemera: Theory and Politics in Organization* 10.3: 267–84.

Hesmondhalgh, David, and Sarah Baker. 2011. *Creative Labour: Media Work in Three Industries*. London: Routledge.

"Hey, Marvel Fans!" n.d. Marvel.com. http://marvel.com/ar

Hill, Erin. 2016. *Never Done: A History of Women's Work in Media Production*. New Brunswick: Rutgers University Press.

Hills, Matt. 2002. *Fan Cultures*. London: Routledge.

Hills, Matt. 2012. "*Torchwood*'s Trans-Transmedia: Media Tie-Ins and Brand 'Fanagement.'" *Participations* 9.2: 409–28.

Hilmes, Michele. 2012. *Network Nations: A Transnational History of British and American Broadcasting*. New York: Routledge.

Himberg, Julia. 2013. "Multicasting: Lesbian Programming and the Changing Landscape of Cable TV." *Television & New Media* 15.4: 289–304.

Hipes, Patrick. 2017. "'The Toy Box' Headed for Season 2 on ABC." *Deadline Hollywood*, June 15. http://deadline.com/2017/06/toy-box-renewed-season-2-abc-1202114671

Hjarvard, Stig. 2004. "From Bricks to Bytes: The Mediatization of a Global Toy Industry." In *European Culture and the Media*, edited by Ib Bondebjerg and Peter Golding, 43–63. Bristol: Intellect Books.

Hjarvard, Stig. 2013. *The Mediatization of Culture and Society*. London: Routledge.

Horkheimer, Max, and Theodor W. Adorno. 1944/2012. "The Culture Industry: Enlightenment as Mass Deception." In *Media and Cultural Studies: Keyworks*, 2nd ed., edited by Meenakshi Gigi Durham and Douglas M. Kellner, 53–75. Malden: Wiley Press.

"How It Works." n.d. *Product Testing USA*. https://producttestingusa.com/

Hudson, Laura. 2008. "New York Comic-Con 2008." *Publisher's Weekly*, March 10: 24–25.

Hudson, Laura. 2012. "DC Comics Survey Reports 'New 52' Readership 93% Male, Only 5% New Readers." *Comics Alliance*, February 10. https://comicsalliance.com/dc-comics-readers-survey-reports-new-52-readership-93-male/

Hughes, Kit. 2015. "'For Pete's Sake, I'm Not Trying to Entertain These People': Film and Franchising at International Harvester." *Film History* 27.3: 41–72.

Huizinga, Johan. 1938/2004. "The Nature and Significance of Play as a Cultural Phenomenon." In *The Game Design Reader: A Rules of Play Anthology*, edited by Katie Salen and Eric Zimmerman, 96–121. Cambridge: MIT Press.

Hunting, Kyra, and Jonathan Gray. 2018. "Disney Junior: Imagining Industrial Intertextuality." In *From Networks to Netflix: A Guide to Changing Channels*, edited by Derek Johnson, 197–207. New York: Routledge.

Hutchins, Aaron. 2014. "The Avengers and Hulk Smash into Second Seasons on Disney XD." *Kidscreen*, July 28. http://kidscreen.com/2014/07/28/the-avengers-and-hulk-smash-into-second-seasons-on-disney-xd/?utm_source=newsletter&utm_medium=email&utm_campaign=the-avengers-and-hulk-smash-into-second-seasons-on-disney-xd&_u=238834

"Imagination Center Toy Testing Application." 2018. Mattel Imagination Center. http://www.mattelimaginationcenter.com/assets/img/Imagination_Center_Toy_Testing_Application.pdf

"Information for Parents." 2013. ToyTesters.tv. https://toytesters.tv/Information_for_Parents.aspx

James, Will. 2015. "Emerald City Comic Con 2015 Rundown." *GeekDad* (blog), April 8. https://geekdad.com/2015/04/eccc-2015-rundown

Janoff, Barry. 2011. "David Turns Child's Play into Profits." *Broadcasting & Cable*, June 27: 24.

Jenkins, Henry. 2006. *Convergence Culture: Where Old and New Media Collide*. New York: New York University Press.

Jenkins, Henry, Sam Ford, and Joshua Green. 2013. *Spreadable Media: Creating Value and Meaning in a Networked Culture*. New York: New York University Press.

Jenkins, Henry, Xiaochang Li, Ana Domb Krauskopf, and Joshua Green. 2009. "If It Doesn't Spread, It's Dead (Part Three): The Gift Economy and Digital Culture." *Confessions of an Aca-Fan* (blog). February 16. http://henryjenkins.org/blog/2009/02/if_it_doesnt_spread_its_dead_p_2.html

Johnson, Catherine. 2012. *Branding Television*. London: Routledge.

Johnson, Derek. 2007. "Will the Real Wolverine Please Stand Up? Marvel's Mutation from Monthlies to Movies." In *Film and Comic Books*, edited by Ian Gordon, Mark Jancovich, and Matthew McAllister, 64–85. Jackson: University Press of Mississippi.

Johnson, Derek. 2008. "A Knight of the Realm vs. The Master of Magnetism: Sexuality, Stardom, and Character Branding." *Popular Communication* 6.4: 214–30.

Johnson, Derek. 2009. "Franchise Histories: Marvel, X-Men, and the Negotiated

Process of Expansion." In *Convergence Media History*, edited by Janet Staiger and Sabine Hake, 14–23. London: Routledge.

Johnson, Derek. 2012. "Cinematic Destiny: Marvel Studios and the Trade Stories of Industrial Convergence." *Cinema Journal* 52.1: 1–24.

Johnson, Derek. 2013a. *Media Franchising: Creative License and Collaboration in the Culture Industries*. New York: New York University Press.

Johnson, Derek. 2013b. "Participation Is Magic: Collaboration, Authorial Legitimacy, and the Audience Function." In *A Companion to Media Authorship*, edited by Jonathan Gray and Derek Johnson, 135–57. Malden: Wiley-Blackwell.

Johnson, Derek. 2014a. "Chicks with Bricks: Building Creativity Across Industrial Design Cultures and Gendered Construction Play." In *LEGO Studies: Examining the Building Blocks of a Transmedia Phenomenon*, edited by Mark J. P. Wolf, 81–84. New York: Routledge.

Johnson, Derek. 2014b. "Figuring Identity: Media Licensing and the Racialization of LEGO Bodies." *International Journal of Cultural Studies* 17.4: 307–25.

Johnson, Derek. 2018. "Pop: Television Guides and Recommendations in a Changing Channel Landscape." In *From Networks to Netflix: A Guide to Changing Channels*, edited by Derek Johnson, 3–22. New York: Routledge.

Johnson, Victoria. 2009. "Everything New Is Old Again: Sport Television, Innovation, and Tradition for a Multi-Platform Era." In *Beyond Prime Time: Television Programming in the Post-Network Era*, edited by Amanda Lotz, 114–37. New York: Routledge.

Karmark, Esben. 2009. "Challenges in the Mediatization of a Corporate Brand: Identity-Effects as LEGO Establishes a Media Products Company." In *Media, Organizations, and Identity*, edited by Lilie Chouliaraki and Mette Morsing, 112–28. Basingstroke: Palgrave Macmillan.

Kearney, Mary. 2006. *Girls Makes Media*. New York: Routledge.

Kell, John. 2016. "Toys 'R' Us Wants to Hire a Kid to Professionally Test Toys." *Fortune*, July 26. http://fortune.com/2016/07/26/toys-r-us-kid-test-toys

Kelly, Heather. 2014. "The Bizarre, Lucrative World of 'Unboxing' Videos." CNN Business, February 13. https://www.cnn.com/2014/02/13/tech/web/youtube-unboxing-videos/index.html

Khamis, Susie, Lawrence Ang, and Raymond Welling. 2016. "Self-Branding, 'Microcelebrity,' and Social Media Influencers." *Celebrity Studies* 8.2: 191–208.

"'Kids Day' Activities Highlight Sunday, June 3, at Wizard World Philadelphia Comic Con." 2012. PR Newswire, May 25. https://www.pr.com/press-release/415267

"Kids Rule @ Wizard World Chicago Comic Con on Sunday!" 2015. Wizardworld.com. http://www.wizardworld.com/kiruwiwochco.html

Kinder, Marsha. 1995. "Home Alone in the '90s: Generational War and Transgenerational Address in American Movies, Television and Presidential Politics." In *In Front of the Children*, edited by Cary Bazalgette and David Buckingham, 75–91. London: British Film Institute.

Kline, Stephen. 1995. *Out of the Garden: Toys and Children's Culture in the Age of TV Marketing*. London: Verso.

"Kmart Kids Toy Review Competition." 2017. *Illawarra Mercury*, September 14.

http://www.illawarramercury.com.au/story/4925556/how-would-you-like-to-be-a-kmart-toy-reviewer

Kondolojy, Amanda. 2014. "'Marvel's Avengers Assemble' & 'Marvel's Hulk and the Agents of S.M.A.S.H.' Renewed by Disney XD." *TV By the Numbers*, July 26. http://tvbythenumbers.zap2it.com/2014/07/26/marvels-avengers-assemble-marvels-hulk-and-the-agents-of-s-m-a-s-h-renewed-by-disney-xd/286747/

Kraft, Amy. 2013. "ComiXology: The Changing Face of Comic Book Readers." *GeekMom* (blog), October 10. https://geekmom.com/2013/10/comixology-comic-book-readers

Lambert, Nancy. 2014. "Five Tips for Attending NYC's Comic Con with Kids." TimeOut.com, September 22. https://www.timeout.com/new-york-kids/attractions/five-tips-for-attending-nycs-comic-con-with-kids-arcades-amusements

Lange, Patricia. 2014. *Kids on YouTube: Technical Identities and Digital Literacies*. New York: Routledge.

Lauwaert, Maaike. 2008. "Playing Outside the Box—On LEGO Toys and the Changing World of Construction Play." *History and Technology* 24.3: 221–37.

Leader, Caroline. Forthcoming. "Branding the Disney Princess: Femininity, Family, and Franchising." PhD diss., University of Wisconsin-Madison.

"LEGO Ambassador Network." n.d. LEGO.com. https://www.lego.com/en-us/aboutus/lego-group/programs-and-visits/lego-ambassador

LEGO FORMA. 2018. "LEGO FORMA: Add a Splash of Creativity to Your Day." Indiegogo.com, November 1. https://www.indiegogo.com/projects/lego-forma-add-a-splash-of-creativity-to-your-day#

The LEGO Group. 2013. *Responsibility Report 2013*. https://www.lego.com/r/www/r/aboutus/-/media/aboutus/media-assets-library/progress-report/lego_group_responsibility_report_2013.pdf?la=en-US&l.r=-1861804705

"LEGO Idea House." 2017. Facebook. https://www.facebook.com/pages/LEGO-Idea-House/188949534472560

"LEGO Inside Tour—A Unique LEGO Experience." n.d. *LEGO.com*. https://www.lego.com/en-us/aboutus/lego-group/programs-and-visits/lego-inside-tour

"Legoland Dream Dies for Man, 63, Over Rule That Adults Must Be Accompanied by Kids." 2013. CTVNews.ca, July 8. http://www.ctvnews.ca/canada/legoland-dream-dies-for-man-63-over-rule-that-adults-must-be-accompanied-by-kids-1.1358249

Lemish, Dafna. 2010. *Screening Gender on Children's Television: The Views of Producers Around the World*. New York: Routledge.

Lill, Genevieve. 2017. "Step2 Is Looking for Toy Testers." Simplemost.com. https://www.simplemost.com/step2-looking-families-test-cool-toys

Limbrick, Peter. 2012. "From the Interior: Space, Time, and Queer Discursivity in Kamal Aljafari's The Roof." In *Cinema of Me: The Self and Subjectivity in First Person Documentary Film*, edited by Alisa Lebow, 96–115. London: Wallflower.

Lipmen, Eli. 2016. "A Lesson in How Toys Are Made and Tested." *LA Dads Group* (blog), August 29. https://citydadsgroup.com/la/2016/08/29/lesson-toys-made-tested

Littlejohn, Janice. 2005. "Big Business in Tiny Tots." *Multichannel News*, August 22: 11, 14.

Littleton, Cynthia. 2014. "Shifts in Kids' TV Watching Habits Drives Big Changes to Discovery-Hasbro Partnership." *Variety*, September 25. http://variety.com/2014/tv/news/shift-in-kids-tv-watching-habits-drives-big-changes-to-discovery-hasbro-partnership-1201313387

Livingstone, Sonia, and Kirsten Drotner. 2008. "Editors' Introduction." In *The International Handbook of Children, Media, and Culture*, edited by Sonia Livingstone and Kirsten Drotner, 1–16. Los Angeles: Sage.

"Locations." n.d. LEGO.com. https://www.lego.com/en-us/aboutus/lego-group/locations

"London Toy Fair Report." 2014. BrickFanatics.com, January 21. http://brickfanatics.co.uk/london-toy-fair-report/

Longwell, Todd. 2015. "How Streaming Video Is Changing Kids TV." *Kidscreen*, February 2. http://kidscreen.com/2015/02/02/how-streaming-video-is-changing-childrens-tv

Lopez, Lori Kido. 2009. "The Radical Act of 'Mommy Blogging': Redefining Motherhood Through the Blogosphere." *New Media & Society* 11.5: 729–47.

Lotz, Amanda. 2014. *The Television Will Be Revolutionized*, 2nd ed. New York: New York University Press.

Lotz, Amanda. 2017. *Portals: A Treatise on Internet-Distributed Television*. Ann Arbor: University of Michigan Press.

Lotz, Amanda. 2018. "Spike TV: The Impossibility of Television for Men." In *From Networks to Netflix: A Guide to Changing Channels*, edited by Derek Johnson, 167–75. New York: Routledge.

Luttenberger, David. 2016. "Fighting Words: How 'Unboxing' Videos are Reshaping Consumer Behavior." *Packaging Digest*, March 30. http://www.packagingdigest.com/packaging-design/fighting-words-how-unboxing-videos-are-reshaping-consumer-purchasing-behavior-2016-03-30

Lynch, Jason. 2017. "Mattel Is Teaming Up with ABC for a New Competition Series to Find Its Next Big Toy." *Adweek*, March 26. http://www.adweek.com/tv-video/mattel-is-teaming-up-with-abc-for-a-new-competition-series-to-find-its-next-big-toy

Manning, Shaun. 2013. "Making the Most of a Comic Con's Kids' Day." *CBR.com*, May 7. http://www.comicbookresources.com/?page=article&id=45345

Marsh, Jackie. 2015. "The Discourses of Celebrity in the Fanvid Economy of Club Penguin Machinima." In *Discourse and Digital Practices: Doing Discourse Analysis in the Digital Age*, edited by R. H. Jones, A. Chik, and C. A. Hafner, 193–208. New York: Routledge.

Marsh, Jackie. 2016. "'Unboxing' Videos: Co-Construction of the Child as Cyberflaneur." *Discourse: Studies in the Cultural Politics of Education* 37.3: 369–80.

Martin, Nick. 2015. "Lego Doesn't Care about Your Collection." *FBTB.net*, September 13. https://www.fbtb.net/rants/2015/09/13/lego-doesnt-care-about-your-collection/

"Marvel AR: Intro to Nova by Zack." 2014. Marvel.com. http://marvel.com/videos/watch/3885/marvel_ar_intro_to_nova_by_zack

"Marvel AR: The Kid X-Men." 2014. Marvel.com. http://marvel.com/videos/watch/3171

"Marvel Cinematic Universe." 2018. Box Office Mojo. http://www.boxofficemojo.com/franchises/chart/?id=avengers.htm

Marvel Entertainment. 2013a. "Avengers #8: Sydney and the Hulk—Marvel AR." YouTube, March 20. https://www.youtube.com/watch?v=Xstdws_kkeI

Marvel Entertainment. 2013b. "Nova #4: Sydney's Don't Try This at Home—Marvel AR." YouTube, May 21. https://www.youtube.com/watch?v=6mL2uxqn5jo

Marvel Entertainment. 2013c. "Superior Spider-Man #6—Sydney's Don't Try This at Home—Marvel AR." YouTube, March 22. https://www.youtube.com/watch?v=QTpHjNzzWFU

"Marvel: Share Your Universe." 2013. Marvel.com, July 9. http://marvel.com/news/tv/2013/7/9/20847/marvel_share_your_universe

Marwick, Alice. 2015. "You May Know Me from YouTube: (Micro-)Celebrity in Social Media." In *A Companion to Celebrity*, edited by P. David Marshall and Sean Redmond, 333–50. Malden: Wiley-Blackwell.

Marx, Karl. 1847/2009. "Wage Labor and Capital." In *Essential Writings of Karl Marx*, edited by Lenny Flank, 191–226. St. Petersburg, FL: Red and Black Publishers.

Masters, Kim. 2014a. "DreamWorks Animated Deal Talks Sabotaged by Anonymous Letter." *Hollywood Reporter*, November 19. http://www.hollywoodreporter.com/news/dreamworks-animation-deal-talks-sabotaged-750094

Masters, Kim. 2014b. "How Marvel Became the Envy (and Scourge) of Hollywood." *Hollywood Reporter*, August 1. http://www.hollywoodreporter.com/print/720363

Mattel Imagination Center. n.d. "About." Facebook. https://www.facebook.com/pg/MattelImaginationCenter/about/?ref=page_internal

Mattel Imagination Center. 2018. "Home." Facebook. https://www.facebook.com/MattelImaginationCenter

Mayer, Vicki. 2011. *Below the Line: Producers and Production Studies in the New Television Era*. Durham: Duke University Press.

Mayer, Vicki, Miranda Banks, and John Caldwell, eds. 2009. *Production Studies: Cultural Studies of the Media Industries*. New York: Routledge.

McCracken, Grant. 2009. *Chief Culture Officer*. New York: Basic Books.

McMillan, Graeme. 2013. "Marvel Invites Fans to 'Share Your Universe' with Next Generation." *Hollywood Reporter*, July 9. http://www.hollywoodreporter.com/heat-vision/marvel-invites-fans-share-your-582376

Miège, Bernard. 1987. "The Logics at Work in the New Cultural Industries." *Media, Culture and Society* 9.3: 273–89.

Miège, Bernard. 1989. *The Capitalization of Cultural Production*. New York: International General.

Miller, John Jackson. n.d. "Comic Book Sales by Year." Comichron.com. http://www.comichron.com/yearlycomicssales.html

Miller, John Jackson. n.d. "Comics Sales Records in the Diamond Exclusive Era." Comichron.com. http://www.comichron.com/vitalstatistics/diamondrecords.html

Miller, John Jackson. n.d. "Comics Sales to Comics Shops." Comichron.com. http://www.comichron.com/vitalstatistics/alltime.html

Miller, John Jackson. n.d. "Market Shares of Comics Sold to Comic Shops." Comichron.com. http://www.comichron.com/vitalstatistics/marketshares.html

Miller, John Jackson. n.d. "May 2001 Comic Book Sales to Comic Shops." Comichron.com. http://www.comichron.com/monthlycomicsales/2001/2001-05.html

Millington, Huw. 2010. "What Percentage of LEGO Sales Are to AFOLs?" Brickset.com, March 16. http://brickset.com/article/567

Mills, Brett. 2008. "'My House Was on Torchwood!': Media, Place, and Identity." *International Journal of Cultural Studies* 11.4: 379–99.

"Mission and Vision." n.d. LEGO.com. https://www.lego.com/en-us/aboutus/lego-group/mission-and-vision

Montgomery, Paul. 2013. "Marvel's Next Big Thing: 'Share Your Universe.'" iFanboy.com, July 9. http://ifanboy.com/articles/marvels-next-big-thing-share-your-universe

Morley, David. 1986. *Family Television: Cultural Power and Domestic Leisure.* London: Comedia.

Mozzocco, J. Caleb. 2010. "Batman: The Brave and the Bold Becomes World's Fisch-est." Newsarama.com, August 23. https://www.newsarama.com/5943-batman-the-brave-and-the-bold-becomes-world-s-fisch-est.html

Muñoz, José Esteban. 2009. *Cruising Utopia: The Then and There of Queer Futurity.* New York: New York University Press.

Murphy, Mike. 2015. "'Sesame Street' Is HBO's Gain, Netflix and Amazon's Loss." *SiliconBeat* (blog), August 13. http://www.siliconbeat.com/2015/08/13/sesame-street-is-hbos-gain-netflix-and-amazons-loss

Murray, Simone. 2005. "Brand Loyalties: Rethinking Content within Global Corporate Media." *Media, Culture & Society* 27.3: 415–35.

"Musical Superstar and TV Personality Joey Fatone to Host Hub Network's Original Unscripted Series 'Parents Just Don't Understand.'" 2014. PR Newswire, March 25. https://www.prnewswire.com/news-releases/musical-superstar-and-tv-personality-joey-fatone-to-host-hub-networks-original-unscripted-series-parents-just-dont-understand-252248461.html

Negus, Keith. 1999. *Music Genres and Corporate Cultures.* London: Routledge.

Nelson, Robin. 2007. "HBO Premium: Channeling Distinction Through TVIII." *New Review of Film and Television Studies* 5.1: 25–40.

Nichol, Catherine. 1922. "Children's Book Week." *Educational Research Bulletin* 1.16: 141–43.

Nixon, Helen. 2002. "*South Park*: Not in Front of the Children." In *Small Screens: Television for Children*, edited by David Buckingham, 96–119. New York: Leicester University Press.

"NYCC 2013: Marvel Wants You to Be the Face of Share Your Universe." 2013. Marvel.com, October 9. http://marvel.com/news/tv/2013/10/9/21316/nycc_2013_marvel_wants_you_to_be_the_face_of_share_your_universe.

O'Connor, Jane. 2008. *The Cultural Significance of the Child Star.* London: Routledge.

O'Connor, Jane. 2011. "From Jackie Coogan to Michael Jackson: What Child Stars Can Tell Us about Ideologies of Childhood." *Journal of Children and Media* 5.3: 284–97.

O'Donnell, Chuck. 2009. "North Jersey's Heroes in a Battle for Literacy." *The Record*, February 9: F03.

Ortner, Sherry. 2013. *Not Hollywood: Independent Film at the Twilight of the American Dream*. Durham: Duke University Press.

Ouellette, Laurie. 2018. "MTV: #Prosocial Television." In *From Networks to Netflix: A Guide to Changing Channels*, edited by Derek Johnson, 147–56. New York: Routledge.

Ouellette, Laurie, and James Hay. 2008. *Better Living Through Reality TV: Television and Post-Welfare Citizenship*. Malden: Wiley-Blackwell.

Owczarski, Kimberly. 2008. "Batman, Time Warner, and Franchise Filmmaking in the Conglomerate Era." PhD diss., University of Texas.

Parks, Lisa. 2004. "Flexible Microcasting: Gender, Generation, and Television-Internet Convergence." In *Television After TV: Essays on a Medium in Transition*, edited by Jan Olsson and Lynn Spigel, 133–56. Durham: Duke University Press.

Pecora, Norma Odom. 1998. *The Business of Children's Entertainment*. New York: Guilford.

Pederson, Erik. 2016. "Amazon, PBS Extend & Expand Streaming Deal for Kids Series." *Deadline Hollywood*, July 1. http://deadline.com/2016/07/amazon-prime-pbs-kids-streaming-deal-1201782157

Pereira, Reuben. 2012. "Weekend Box Office: 'The Avengers' Grosses $200 Million in Three Days." *Examiner*, May 7. http://www.examiner.com/article/weekend-box-office-the-avengers-grosses-200-million-three-days

Pesquera, Yvonne. 2007. "They Get Paid to Play with LEGOs." *Christian Science Monitor*, April 24. https://www.csmonitor.com/2007/0424/p18s02-hfks.html

Phegley, Kiel. 2013. "Marvel Annouces 'Share Your Universe.'"CBR.com, July 9. http://www.comicbookresources.com/?page=article&id=46512

Postigo, Hector. 2007. "Of Mods and Modders: Chasing Down the Value of Fan-Based Digital Game Modifications." *Games and Culture* 2.4: 300–13.

Pounsett, Geoffrey. 2005. "Here's Looking Beyond You, Kid . . ." *Kidscreen*, September: 92.

"Product Idea Guidelines." n.d. LEGO Ideas. https://ideas.lego.com/guidelines

Punathambekar, Aswin. 2013. *From Bombay to Bollywood: The Making of a Global Media Industry*. New York: New York University Press.

Reeve, Jackie. 2008. "2008 NY ComicCon Kids Day." *The Orange Room* (blog), April 20. http://www.jackiereeve.com/2008/04/20/2008-ny-comiccon-kids-day

Reeve, Jackie. 2013. "New York Comic Con Has Changed . . . In a Good Way." *GeekMom* (blog), October 19. https://geekmom.com/2013/10/new-york-comic-con-changed-good-way

Reijinders, Stijn. 2011. *Places of the Imagination: Media, Tourism, Culture*. Surrey: Ashgate.

Rheingold, Howard. 1993/2000. *The Virtual Community: Homesteading on the Electronic Frontier*. Cambridge: MIT Press.

Rinaldi, Hannah. 2016. "How to Become a Toy Tester (and Get Free Toys)." *Eat, Drink, and Save Money* (blog), August 29. https://eatdrinkandsavemoney.com/2016/08/29/become-toy-tester-get-free-toys

Robb, David. 2015. "Feds Officially Probing Hollywood's Lack of Female Directors." *Deadline Hollywood*, Ocobter 6. http://deadline.com/2015/10/female-directors-hollywood-federal-investigation-eeoc-1201568487

Robichaux, Mark. 2010. "Parents Welcome." *Multichannel News*, August 2: 8–9.

Rodriguez-Ferrándiz, Raúl. 2013. "Culture Industries in a Postindustrial Age: Entertainment, Leisure, Creativity, Design." *Critical Studies in Media Communication* 31.4: 327–41.

Roesch, Stefan. 2009. *The Experiences of Film Location Tourists*. Bristol: Channel View.

Rose, Jacqueline. 1992. *The Case of Peter Pan, or The Impossibility of Children's Literature*. Philadelphia: University of Pennsylvania Press.

Rusak, Gary. 2010. "Corus Kids Hones in on Co-Viewing." *Kidscreen*, February/March: 24.

Salzinger, Leslie. 2003. *Genders in Production: Making Workers in Mexico's Global Factories*. Berkeley: University of California Press.

Sammond, Nicholas. 2005. *Babes in Tomorrowland: Walt Disney and the Making of the American Child, 1930–1960*. Durham: Duke University Press.

Santo, Avi. 2015. *Selling the Silver Bullet: The Lone Ranger and Transmedia Brand Licensing*. Austin: University of Texas Press.

Schwindt, Oriana. 2016. "ABC Orders Competition Series 'The Toy Box' With Host Eric Stonestreet." *Variety*, October 11. http://variety.com/2016/tv/news/the-toy-box-abc-eric-stonestreet-1201885505

Scott, Suzanne. 2009. "Repackaging Fan Culture: The Regifting Economy of Ancillary Content." *Transformative Works and Cultures* 3. https://journal.transformativeworks.org/index.php/twc/article/view/150/122

Scott, Suzanne. 2013. "Fangirls in Refrigerators: The Politics of (In)Visibility in Comic Book Culture." *Transformative Works and Cultures* 13. https://journal.transformativeworks.org/index.php/twc/article/view/460/384

Scott, Suzanne. 2019. *Fake Geek Girls: The Convergence Culture Industry and the Fan Culture Wars*. New York: New York University Press.

Seidman, Larry. 2014. "Brand Parenting: Defining Your Brand." Dimensions Branding Group.

Seiter, Ellen. 1995. *Sold Separately: Children and Parents in Consumer Culture*. New Brunswick: Rutgers University Press.

Selznick, Barbara. 2018. "Shaking Off the Family Brand within a Conglomerate Family." In *From Networks to Netflix: A Guide to Changing Channels*, edited by Derek Johnson, 219–28. New York: Routledge.

"Share Your Universe!" n.d. Marvel.com. http://marvel.com/comics/list/698/share_your_universe

"Share Your Universe." 2013. Facebook, November 1. https://www.facebook.com/ShareYourUniverse

"Share Your Universe." 2014. Marvel Kids. http://marvelkids.com/activities

Silcoff, Mireille. 2014. "Opening Ceremony." *New York Times Magazine*, August 17.

Simmons, Alex. 2011. "What I Do." *Simmons Here and Now* (blog). http://www.simmonshereandnow.com/whatido.html

Smith, Geoffrey. 2014. "Barbie, Schmarbie—Lego Is Now the World's Top Toymaker." *Fortune*, September 4. http://fortune.com/2014/09/04/barbie-schmarbie-lego-is-now-the-worlds-top-toymaker

Smith, Maureen. 2002. "Watching TV With the Kids." *Broadcasting & Cable*, December 30: 20.

Snook, Raven. 2011. "Kids' Day at New York Comic Con: Geek Out with the Whole Family This Sunday." *Mommy Poppins*, October 12. https://mommypoppins.com/content/kids-day-at-new-york-comic-con-geek-out-with-the-whole-family-this-sunday

Spangler, Todd. 2017. "Disney to End Netflix Deal, Sets Launch of ESPN and Disney-Branded Streaming Services." *Variety*, August 8. http://variety.com/2017/digital/news/disney-netflix-end-acquires-bamtech-espn-ott-services-1202519917

Spigel, Lynn. 1992. *Make Room for TV: Television and the Family Ideal in Postwar America*. Chicago: University of Chicago Press.

Stanhope, Kate. 2017a. "ABC's 'The Toy Box' Renewed for Season 2." *Hollywood Reporter*, June 16. http://www.hollywoodreporter.com/live-feed/toy-box-renewed-season-2-1014170

Stanhope, Kate. 2017b. "ABC's 'The Toy Box' Shakes Up Judges for Season 2." *Hollywood Reporter*, July 25. http://www.hollywoodreporter.com/live-feed/toy-box-season-2-shakeup-1019846

Steel, Emily. 2015a. "Netflix Announces Lineup of Animated Children's Shows." *New York Times*, June 3. https://www.nytimes.com/2015/06/04/business/media/netflix-announces-lineup-of-animated-childrens-shows.html

Steel, Emily. 2015b. "'Sesame Street' to Air First on HBO for Next 5 Seasons." *New York Times*, August 13. https://www.nytimes.com/2015/08/14/business/media/sesame-street-heading-to-hbo-in-fall.html

Steemers, Jeanette. 2010. "The BBC's Role in the Changing Production Ecology of Preschool Television in Britain." *Television & New Media* 11.1: 37–61.

Steinberg, Brian. 2015. "HBO Picks Up 'Sesame Street' as Kids' Viewing Habits Change." *Variety*, August 13. http://variety.com/2015/tv/news/hbo-picks-up-sesame-street-in-five-year-pact-with-sesame-workshop-1201569335

Step2. 2018a. "Home." Facebook. https://www.facebook.com/thestep2company?fref=photo

Step2. 2018b. "Toy Testers Wanted." Facebook. https://www.facebook.com/thestep-2company/app/208195102528120/?ref=woobox

"Step2 Toy Tester Application Spring 2018—Round 1." n.d. Step 2 Toy Tester. https://step2.wufoo.com/forms/step2-toy-tester-application-spring-2018-round-1/.

Stevens, Tim. 2014. "Meet the New Face of Share Your Universe." Marvel.com. May 15. http://marvel.com/news/tv/2014/5/15/22523/meet_the_new_face_of_share_your_universe

Stewart, Lianne. 2006. "Family Channels Co-Viewing Touted as a Selling Point at '06 Kids Upfronts." *Kidscreen*, May: 24.

Stratton, Alexandra. 2017. "Toymakers Are Targeting Your Children Via YouTube Kid Influencers." *Bloomberg Businessweek*, October 18. https://www.bloomberg.com/news/articles/2017-10-18/toymakers-curry-favor-with-precocious-youtube-influencers

"Studio Tours." n.d. Paramount Studio Tour. http://www.paramountstudiotour.com/studio-tours.html

Tate, Lisa. 2014. "5 Reasons Every Mom Should Take Advantage of Free Comic Book Day." *GeekMom* (blog), April 28. https://geekmom.com/2014/04/moms-and-free-comic-book-day

"Terms and Conditions." 2016. ToyTesters.tv. https://toytesters.tv/Terms_and_Conditions.aspx

"Terms & Conditions." 2017. Fisher Price Top Toy Tester. http://fptoptoytester.com/terms/.

"Terms of Service." n.d. YouTube. https://www.youtube.com/static?template=terms

"Terms of Service." 2018. Facebook, April 18. https://www.facebook.com/terms.php

Terranova, Tiziana. 2000. "Free Labor: Producing Culture for the Digital Economy." *Social Text* 18.2: 33–58.

Thielman, Sam. 2015. "The Rise and Fall and Rise of Hasbro's TV Strategy." *Adweek*, February 23. http://www.adweek.com/tv-video/after-rocky-few-years-hasbro-s-tv-strategy-changing-again-163083

"A Third of US Adults, Whether with Kids or Not, Concerned about 'Objectionable' TV Programming." 2000. PR Newswire, September 6.

Thompson, Chris. 2013. "Windsor Lego Fan to Get Free Trip to Legoland." *The Windsor Star*, July 17. http://blogs.windsorstar.com/news/windsor-lego-fan-to-get-free-trip-to-legoland

"Tickets." 2015. New York Comic-Con. http://www.newyorkcomiccon.com/Tickets/.

"The Toy Box." 2017. Facebook. https://www.facebook.com/thetoyboxabc

"The Toy Box: Season 2 Lead Sheet." 2017. ABC.com, August 29. http://www.disney-abcpress.com/abc/shows/the-toy-box/press-releases/

"Toy Box 2017." 2017. MysticArt Pictures. https://www.mysticartpictures.com/mystic/index.php

"Toy Companies." 2013. ToyTesters.tv. https://toytesters.tv/Toy_Companies.aspx

"Toy Fair 2014: Hasbro Marvel Legends Report." 2014. ActionFigurePics.com, February 16. http://www.actionfigurepics.com/2014/02/toy-fair-2014-hasbro-marvel-legends-report

"Toy Testing Solutions." n.d. Intertek.com. http://www.intertek.com/toys/testing/premiums

"Toys R Us Are Looking for Toy Testers." n.d. Extreme Couponing UK. https://www.extremecouponing.co.uk/toyologists

Tran, Allen. 2016. "New LEGO Americas Community Manager Announced." *The Brick Fan*, May 26. https://www.thebrickfan.com/new-lego-americas-community-manager-announced

Trangbæk, Roar Rude. 2012. "LEGO Group Sales Up by 17% in 2011." LEGO.com, March 1. http://www.lego.com/en-us/aboutus/news-room/2012/march/annual-result-2011

Trangbæk, Roar Rude. 2015a. "18 Percent Global Sales Growth in the First Half of 2015." LEGO.com, September 2. http://www.lego.com/en-us/aboutus/news-room/2015/september/interim-result

Trangbæk, Roar Rude. 2015b. "Global Growth Ensures Strong 2014 Result for the LEGO Group." LEGO.com, February 25. http://www.lego.com/en-us/aboutus/news-room/2015/february/lego-group-2014-annual-results

Trenholm, Richard. 2015. "Free Comics! Free Comic Book Day Is this Saturday." CNET, April 28. https://www.cnet.com/news/free-comics-free-comic-book-day-is-this-saturday

Turk, Tisha. 2014. "Fan Work: Labor, Worth, and Participation in Fandom's Gift

Economy." *Transformative Works and Cultures* 15. https://journal.transformative-works.org/index.php/twc/article/view/518/428

"Turner Broadcasting Announces Strategic Changes/Expansions to Its Portfolio of Animation, Kids and Young Adult Networks." 2014. PR Newswire, February 4.

Turow, Joseph. 1998. *Breaking Up America: Advertisers and the New Media World*. Chicago: University of Chicago Press.

"Twitter Terms of Service." 2018. Twitter, May 25. https://twitter.com/en/tos#usWho

Umstead, R. Thomas. 2004. "The Parent Trap." *Multichannel News*, May 17.

Umstead, R. Thomas. 2008. "Nickelodeon Warms to Co-Viewing." *Multichannel News*, September 22: 12.

Umstead, R. Thomas. 2011. "Hub's Primetime Fosters 'Ties.'" *Multichannel News*, March 28: 12.

Umstead, R. Thomas. 2012. "Hub Adds Four New Originals." *Multichannel News*, March 5: 16.

Umstead, R. Thomas. 2016a. "Get 'Em While They're Young." *Multichannel News*, July 25: 6–7.

Umstead, R. Thomas. 2016b. "What's Old Is New Again." *Multichannel News*, April 18: 8–9.

United States Consumer Product Safety Commission. 2010. "Laboratory Tet Manual for Toy Testing." https://www.cpsc.gov//PageFiles/109675/testtoys.pdf

"Universal Studios Hollywood—History Timeline." n.d. The Studio Tour. http://www.thestudiotour.com/ush/chronology.php

Vara, Vauhini, and Ann Zimmerman. 2011. "Hey, Bro, That's My Little Pony! Guys' Interest Mounts in Girly TV Show." *The Wall Street Journal*, November 4. http://online.wsj.com/article/SB10001424052970203707504577012141105109140.html

Vincent, Michael. 2016. "From Unboxing Videos to Millions in Venture Capital: Meet 16-Year-Old Austrialian Ben Pasternak." ABC Premium News, July 12.

"Want to Help Choose the Next Amazon Original Kids' Series?" 2016. Store_news@amazon.com, email, June 17.

Wasko, Janet. 2001. *Understanding Disney: The Manufacture of Fantasy*. Malden: Polity.

Waysdorf, Abby, and Stijn Reijnders. 2017. "The Role of Imagination in the Film Tourist Experience: The Case of *Game of Thrones*." *Participations* 14.1: 170–91.

Wernick, Andrew. 1991. *Promotional Culture: Advertising, Ideology and Symbolic Expression*. London: Sage.

Westcott, Tim, and Anna Stuart. 2015. *Children's On Demand Content Comes of Age*. Cannes: MIPCOM.

Whyte, Alexandra. 2018a. "Only 10% of US Parents Say YouTube Must Deal with Inappropriate Videos." *Kidscreen*, March 1. http://kidscreen.com/2018/03/01/only-10-of-us-parents-say-youtube-must-deal-with-inappropriate-videos

Whyte, Alexandra. 2018b. "So '90s? Netflix Talks Rebooting Content for Today's Kids." *Kidscreen*, June 5. http://kidscreen.com/2017/06/05/so-90s-netflix-talks-rebooting-content-for-todays-kids

Williams, Raymond. 1958/2011. "Culture Is Ordinary." In *Cultural Theory: An Anthology*, edited by Imre Szeman and Timothy Kaposy, 53–59. Malden: Wiley-Blackwell.

Woods, Allan. 2016. "All Play, Some Work Makes Quebec Boy Top Toy Tester for Toys 'R' Us." *The Star*, March 16. https://www.thestar.com/news/canada/2016/03/16/all-play-some-work-makes-quebec-boy-top-toy-tester-for-toys-r-us.html

Yockey, Matt, ed. 2017. *Make Ours Marvel: Media Convergence and a Comics Universe*. Austin: University of Texas Press.

"Your Invitation to Be a VIP Toy Tester on the ToyTesters.tv Summer Tour at Hamley's." 2017. Hamleys.com. http://www.hamleys.com/explore-ToyTesters.irs

Zafirau, Stephen. 2009. "Audience Knowledge and the Everyday Lives of Cultural Producers in Hollywood." In *Production Studies: Cultural Studies of the Media Industries*, edited by Vicki Mayer, Miranda Banks, and John Caldwell, 190–202. New York: Routledge.

Zielinski, Laura. 2016. "Out of Box Experience." *Brand Packaging*, June 1.

Zolides, Andrew. 2017a. "Created By Children: Conceptualising the Child as Media Producer." In *Childhood and Celebrity*, edited by Jane O'Connor and John Mercer, 147–58. London: Routledge.

Zolides, Andrew. 2017b. "Cults of Personality: The Labor of Celebrity in Digital Culture." PhD diss., University of Wisconsin-Madison.

Index

Note: Page references in *italics* indicate illustrations and tables.

ABC, 93, 100, 109
ABC Family, 23
Acland, Charles, 7
A. C. Nielsen, 23, 31
address, transgenerational, 28–29
adult fans of LEGO (AFOLs), 129, 139–40, 146; on LEGO Inside Tour, predominant, 124–25, 142–44, 158; in LEGO market, 136–37
adulthood: boundary of, marketing troubling, 13–14; child labor and, 163, 165; in children's media research, perspective of, 19–22; co-viewing and nostalgic, 45, 50; Disney comics and, 211n1; generative relationship of childhood and, 7; HBO as exclusively, 23; Hub and nostalgic, 40–41, 50; Nickelodeon for, 29; in participatory culture, 10, 204–5; surplus audience of, 18, 124, 127, 157–58
Adult Swim, 39
AFOLs. *See* adult fans of LEGO
age: all-ages comics, 65; boundaries of, adult professionals transgressing, 91–92, 200, 205; categories of, producing, 3–4; categories of, transgressing, 1–2, 9; as co-constitutive, 4; gender, sexuality, and, 8; in LEGO marketing, 135–40; matrix of industry participation and, 9–14; parents transgressing boundaries of, 21; ratings, guidelines for, 1, 63, 67–68, 213n2; transgressing, critical analysis of, 22; transgressing, marketing and, 13–14
Aguila, Rick, 99, 107
Ahmed, Sara, 8, 58, 206–7
Alford, Catherine, 177, 180, 189–90
All-New X-Men (comic book), 65–66, 198
Alonso, Alex, 64
Alters, Diane, 27
amateurism, 3–4, 13
Amazon Prime Video, 44–47
Artsplash, 102, 107, 213n8
authority: in fandom, 59, 90; of father, in superhero sharing, 75–76, 90; heterosexual reproduction and, 17; performance of, at Kidscreen Summit, 111–13, 115; professional, 17–18, 94, 109, 112–15, 117–19; professional, at Kidscreen Summit, 109, 112–15, 117–19. *See also* power
authorship, 59, 104, 119, 198, 202
Avengers (comic), 80, 199, 203
Avengers (film franchise), 62, 72, 135
Avengers Assemble (television series), 63, 78, *79*, 82–83

239

Ball, John, 170
Banet-Weiser, Sarah, 11, 28, 128
Banks, John, 166, 213n1
Banks, Miranda, 95, 98, 208, 213n6
Baym, Nancy, 176
Being Elmo (film), 91
Beyond the Brick (film), 148–49
Big (film), 161–63, *162*, 194–95
Billund, Denmark, 124, 143–44, *145*, 149–50, 154, 167
boomers, 3, 7
boundaries: age, adult professionals transgressing, 91–92, 200, 205; age, marketing troubling, 13–14; age, parents transgressing, 21; child media labor and, 120–21, 163–65, 171, 195; consumption and production, transgression of, 2; reflexive work of, 213n4; in *Toy Box*, work of, 99–100, 102–3, 106–9; in toy testing, participation, 175–76, 186
brand/brand culture: family television, 23; general entertainment, 27; in identity, 128; LEGO management of, fandom and, 124, 127–30, 156–57, 159, 201; network television, 28; surplus audience and management of, 129; SYU, 78, 80–81, 86
Breevort, Tom, 67–68
Bryant, J. Alison, 12, 97
Buckingham, David, 5, 10–11; on adult professionals, children and, 97, 213n5; on children, cultural segregation of, 13, 211n7
Buckley, Dan, 77, 84–85, 88
Bulut, Ergin, 166
Burbidge, Émile, 176, 178

cable. *See* television, cable
Caldwell, John, 11; on deep texts and rituals, 95, 126, 208, 213n2, 213n4; on para-industry, 111
capitalism: digital, gift economy and, 171; labor in, 165, 208; power in, 10; reproductive futurity and, 8–9; transgenerationalism in, 7–10

Captain Marvel (comic), 66–67
Cartoon Network, 30, 111–13, 115, 117
Chen, Julie, 91–93, 115
childhood: adulthood and, generative relationship of, 7; boundary of, marketing troubling, 13–14; consumer subjectivity of, 10; Cook on, 10, 211n3, 211n6; in participatory culture, 10, 162, 204–5; as queer, 211n2
child labor. *See* labor
child media production, 168
children: Buckingham on, 13, 97, 211n7, 213n5; at comic book conventions, days for, 17, 71–76, 121–22; competent and vulnerable, 211n4; in co-viewing, parents bonding with, 35–36; in digital era, viewing habits of, 47–48; Disney comics and, 211n1; extra-commercium status of, 11–12, 18–19, 129–30, 178, 200; FCBD targeting, 70–71, 89; at Kidscreen Summit, identity of, 115–17; LEGO Group strategy focusing on, 135–40, 142–44, *145*, 154, 167; in Marvel AR, 207; Nickelodeon as exclusive to, 23, 28–29, 39, 49; in production studies, consumer, 96; as professionals, 91–92, *162*, 162–63; on *Toy Box*, as judges, 100, 103–6, *106*, 108, 109, 120
Children's Book Week, 69
children's programming: on HBO, 16, 47–48; on streaming television, 44–50; subscription and, 48–49
The Children's Television Community (book), 12
Christian, Aymar Jean, 26
Christiansen, Ole Kirk, 147
Chumsky, Sarah, 114, 120
Clark, Lynn Schofield, 27
Clash, Kevin, 91–92, 94, 115
co-evaluation, 46
Cohn, Marjorie, 38–39, 112–13
comic book conventions: for children, days of, 17, 71–76, 89, 121–22; New York, 71–73, 83–84, 87; parents at,

69–76; professionalism at, 121–22; San Diego, 72–73, 83–84, 142; SYU at, 83, 87

comic books, 206; aging readership of, 61–64, 204; all-ages, 65; DC, 56, 60–61, 64–65, 69–70; digital distribution of, 61; Disney, 211n1; fandom of, inheriting, 16–17, 55, 76, 80, 85–87, 89–90, 203; FCBD, 17, 53, 55, 69–71, 75–76, 89–90; identity work of, 16–17; market for, 59–60; in transmedia industry structures, 56–57, 61–65

Comic-Con Kids Days, 17, 55, 73–76, 89–90, 121–22

Comixology, 61, 197

communities, imagined, 12

communities, industrial: children's media as, 96–97; children's television, as distinct, 97; gender in, 121, 202; Kidscreen Summit and, 112–13

competition, 202; Kidscreen Summit and, 118; on LEGO Inside Tour, 150–52, *153*; *Toy Box* and, 100, 104; toy testing as, 183–85

consumption/consumer culture: digital, participatory culture and, 165–71; of LEGO Group, transgenerational, 20–21; in LEGO Inside Tour, professionalized, 149–59, *153*; LEGO Inside Tour and adult, 124–25, 134; motherhood in, 11; nonconforming, 206; power of, responsibility and, 59; production and, 2, 4; in production studies, child, 96; subjectivity of, childhood and, 10; toy influencers of, 169–70, 179, 201

Cook, Daniel Thomas, 10, 11, 97–98, 211n3, 211n6

co-subscribers, 49–50

Couldry, Nick, 130

co-viewing, 200–201; cable television and, 29–31, 38–41, 50, 212n6; child-parent bonds in, 35–36; co-evaluation and, 46; co-subscribers and, 49–50; of Discovery Family, 43; of Disney, 34–35, 39; family and, 24–25, 30, 32, 206; franchise extensions and, 36–37; futurity and, 51–52; of Hub, 25, 40–43, 50; legacy media industries and, 23–25, 50; as market opportunity, 33–36, 203; market segmentation and, 37–39; of Nickelodeon, 29, 34–36, 38–39, 41; of sports, 50–51; of streaming television, 24–26, 31–33, 44–46, 49–50; subscription and, 49–50; television, post-network, 24–29, 37–38, 43, 51, 203; television industry discourse of, 15–16, 25, 29–30, 50–51; transformation and, 25–26; transgenerational address of, 28–29

Craig, David, 168, 183, 192

critical media industry studies, 8–9, 14–15, 126, 208

Cullen, Sean, 119

culture industries: LEGO Group in, 125–26, 134; physical and screen media in, 15; toy testing in, 165–66

Cunningham, Stuart, 168, 183, 192

Curtin, Michael, 27, 50, 125

Cyclops (comic), 66

DC Comics, 56, 61, 64; all-ages comics of, 65; in FCBD, 69–70; market share of, 60

deep texts and rituals, 95, 208, 213n2; reflexive boundary work of, 213n4; in tourism, 126; on *Toy Box*, 121

DeVillier, Lauren, 111–12

Diamond Comic Distributors, 60, 69–70

Dietcher, Jay, 71

digital economy, free labor in, 165–66

digital media: celebrities of, 168, 176, 192, 214n2, 215n6; comic books distributed through, 61; generation gaps bridged by, 31–32; legacy media industries competing with, 32–33, 203–4; television disrupted by, 203–4

digital platforms: commodified labor on, 176–77; toy manufacturers on, 166, 170–71

Digital Video Recorders (DVR), 31
Discovery Family, 43
Discovery Kids, 39–40
Discovery Toys!, 191–92
Disney: comics of, adulthood and, 211n1; co-viewing of, 34–35, 39; family television brands disaggregated by, 23; franchise extensions of, 36; at Kidscreen Summit, 111–12; Marvel under, 55–57, 62; media tourist industry sites of, 131–32; television, child market differentiation of, 30–31
Disney Infinity (game), 63
Disney Junior, 37, 212n6
Disneyland (television series), 213n7
Disney theme parks, 131
Disney XD, 81–83, *82*, 89
Dorfman, Ariel, 8, 211n1
Drotner, Kirsten, 19–20, 211n4
Ducard, Malik, 33
DVR. *See* Digital Video Recorders

Edelman, Lee, 8
EvanTubeHD, 180, 192
extra-commercium status, 11–12; prize economy and, 19; professionalization and, 18–19, 129–30, 178, 200; toy testing and, 18–19, 178

Facebook: LEGO Idea House on, 148; SYU on, *82*, 82–86, 88; *Toy Box* on, 100, 103; toy testing and, 173, 188–92
family: co-viewing and, 24–25, 30, 32, 206; neo-network television and, 27–28; post-network television and, 23, 28; SYU and, 83–84; television as medium for, 27; YouTube and, 32
Family Game Night, 41
fandom, 20, 53–54; adult, SYU and, 16, 76, 78, 80–88; authority in, 59, 90; in brand management, 128–29; gift economy of, 58–59, 80; labor of, 57–59; LEGO, branded management of, 124, 127–30, 156–57, 159, 201; Marvel, as transgenerational, 66–69, 80, 87; responsibility of, 58–59
Fantastic Four (comic franchise), 67–68, 86, 198
fantasy: in *Big*, 162; in LEGO Inside Tour, 18, 124, 135, 141, 150–51, 154, 158–60; in media industry tourism, 131–33; in *Toy Box*, 94, 102, 110; in *Willy Wonka and the Chocolate Factory*, 123–24
FCBD. *See* Free Comic Book Day
feminism, 9, 98, 122, 213n6
FF (comic), 67–68, 86, 198
Fisch, Sholly, 65
Fisher Price, 184
Fitzpatrick, Terry, 32
Fleming, Dan, 212n10
Forces of Destiny, 20
Ford, Sam, 171
Foucault, Michel, 59
Fraction, Matt, 67–68
framework, transgenerational, 4; legacy media industries in, 5–6; Marvel reframing, 65–68; transmedia, 6, 57, 204
franchising. *See* media franchising
Free Comic Book Day (FCBD), 17, 53, 55; children targeted by, 70–71, 89; as literacy promoter, 69; as marketing event, 69–70; parents and, 70–71, 75–76, 90
Freeform, 23
future/futurity, 73, 84–85, 88, 124, 128, 147; co-viewing and, 51–52; reproduction and, 8–9, 201–2, 204, 206–9

Game of Thrones (television series), 48–49, 131
gamification, 185–86, 202
GeekDad blog, 75
GeekMom blog, 71
Geek My Kids podcast, 74
gender: age, industrial investment in, and, 8; in industrial communities, 121, 202; in industry lore, 113–14; at Kidscreen Summit, discourse of,

112–15, 117–19; LEGO Group and, 140, 155–56; in Marvel AR, 198–99, 202, 209; Marvel Dad reproducing, 17, 55, 85–87, 89; Marvel Mom, 86–87; pediocularity, race, and, 98; in production studies, 98, 213n6; race, sexuality, and, 98, 122, 129, 205, 209, 214n10; in superhero sharing, 75–76, 83–84, 90; in SYU, 83–86, 88–89
general entertainment, 27, 44, 48–49
generation: as co-constitutive, 4; co-viewing and closing gap of, 35; digital media bridging gaps of, 31–32; in industry lore, 7, 212n5; millennial, 7, 35–36; post-millennial, 112, 170; in reproduction, 7
Generation #hashtag, 31–32
Generation X, 7
Generation Z, 170
gift economy, 164; of fandom, 58–59, 80; toy testing as, 171–73, 180, 184–86
GI Joe, 39–40
Gorman, Michelle, 108–9
Green, Joshua, 171

Halberstam, Jack, 8, 211n2
Harry Potter (book franchise), 2
Hartley, John, 59
Hasbro, 166, 168–70; Hub and, 39–43; Marvel properties licensed by, 64; streaming services and, 43; toy testing for, 175
Havens, Timothy, 11–12, 27, 95; on critical media industry studies approach, 14; on industry lore, 213n1; on Netflix, 48; on production studies, 212n8
HBO, 15–16, 23, 47–49
HBO Now, 15, 26, 47–50
Hendershot, Heather, 5, 28–29
Hesmondhalgh, David, 58, 166, 182
heteronormativity, 8–9, 206–8; *FF* critiquing, 67; in Kidscreen Summit, 119; Marvel Dad and, 17
Hilmes, Michele, 6

Himberg, Julia, 16
Hjarvard, Stig, 212n9
The Hub: co-viewing of, 25, 40–43, 50; Discovery Kids relaunched as, 39–40; Hasbro and, 39–43
Hughes, Kit, 126
Huizinga, Johan, 166
Hulu, 26
Hulyan (toy reviewer). *See* Maya and Hulyan
The Hut, 172–73, 184–85, 189

identity: branding in, 128; capitalist labor as site of, 208; child, at Kidscreen Summit, 115–17; parent, at Kidscreen Summit, 117–19
identity work, 1–2; of comic book companies, 16–17; of Marvel Dad, 17; pediocular, 93, 97–98; professional, 12–13, 91–93, 97, 120; SYU, 16–17
imagined communities, 12
industrial communities. *See* communities, industrial
industry lore, 96; gender in, 113–14; generations in, 7, 212n5; Havens on, 213n1; in Kidscreen Summit, 94, 111–14, 117, 121; Kids' Day campaigns and, 122
influencers: LEGO Inside Tour and, 157; Marvel AR and, 199; in toy industry, consumer, 169–70, 179, 201; in toy testing, adult, 187, 189–90
inheritance, 51, 205, 207, 209; of comic book fandom, 16–17, 55, 76, 80, 85–87, 89–90, 203; fan, gift economy of, 58–59, 80; queer theory on, 8–9

James, Will, 75
Jenkins, Henry, 6, 171
Johnny DC, 65
Johnson, Catherine, 26, 28, 128
Johnson, Vicki, 51

Kanter, Nancy, 37
Katsafanas, Constance, 87–88

Kearney, Mary, 11, 211n5
Kids Comic Con, 72, 122, 214n10
Kidscreen Summit: authority performed in, 111–13, 115; child identity in, 115–17; gender roles discourse in, 112–15, 117–19; industry lore in, 94, 111–14, 117, 121; parent identity in, 117–19; professionalism and, 93–94, 109–14, 118–19; professionalism in, pediocular, 17–18, 115–17, 120–21; ritual space of, 94, 110–11, 113–15, 119–21
Kids Day. *See* Comic-Con Kids Days
KidToyTesters, 169, 179–80, 193–94
Kinder, Marsha, 5, 28–29

labor, 161–62, *162*, 172, 209; under capitalism, 165, 208; child, gift economy of, 164; child, popular discourse around, 163; child media, boundaries and, 120–21, 163–65, 171, 195; child media production, 168; co-creative, of LEGO, 139–41, 149–52, 156; co-creative, play as, 166; commodified, on digital platforms, 176–77; creative, *Toy Box* and, 101, 104, 107, 109; employee, in LEGO Inside Tour, 124, 146–48, 154–56, 158; extra-commercium status and, 11–12, 18–19, 129–30, 178, 200; of fandom, 57–59; free, of participatory culture, 57–58, 165–66, 213n1; gamification of, 185–86; gift economy of, 58, 164; parent, commodified, 183; prize economy and, 181–83; relational, digital as, 176, 183; in *Willy Wonka and the Chocolate Factory*, 123–24
LA Dads Group, 191
Lambur, Joan, 118
legacy media industries: co-viewing and, 23–25, 50; digital media competing with, 32–33, 203–4; reproduction of, 204–7; transgenerational framework for, 5–6
LEGO: AFOLs, 124, 129, 136–37, 139–40, 142–44, 146, 158; *Beyond the Brick* documentary of, 148–49; branded fan management of, 124, 127–30, 156–57, 159, 201; co-creative labor of, 139–41, 149–52, 156; critical media industry studies and, 126; marketing of, age in, 135–40; in media industry tourist culture, 127–30, 134; as mediatization site, 125–26; Memory Lane archive of, 147, *148*, 149; online, moderating, 152–54; pediocularity and, 18, 128; production studies and, 126, 208; queer theory and, 206; social media of, 148, 157; surplus audience, adult, and, 124, 127, 157–58; tour group makeup of, 141–43; transnational brand culture and, 127
LEGO.com, 152–53
LEGO Employee Store, 158
LEGO Foundation Cultures of Creativity project, 138–39
LEGO Friends, 140, 155–56
The LEGO Group: in Billund, Denmark, 144, *145*; child attractions of, 135; child-centric strategy of, 135–40, 142–44, *145*, 154, 167; in culture industries, 125–26; gender and, 140, 155–56; Marvel and DC superheroes licensed by, 64; as media company, 15; play and, 124, 127, 134–41, 159; *Responsibility Report* of, 127, 138, 140, 142, 144, 155; toy testers for, 175; transgenerational consumption of, 20–21; transmedia, 63, 125–26, 135–36
LEGO House, 149–50, 157
LEGO Idea House, 147–49, 154
LEGO Ideas, 139
LEGO Inside Tour, 201; adult consumers and, 124–25, 134; AFOLs dominating, 124–25, 142–44, 158; child-centric culture in, 146–47, 154; competition in, 150–52, *153*; consumers professionalized in, 149–59, *153*; deep texts and rituals in, 126;

employees in, 124, 146–48, 154–56, 158; fantasy in, 18, 124, 135, 141, 150–51, 154, 158–60; gender in, 155–56; human resources recruiters in, 154–56; pediocularity and, 18, 128; play in, 143–44, 150–51
LEGOLAND, 135, 142–45, 184
LEGOLAND Discovery Center, 135
LEGOLAND Hotel, 141, 143, 151
LEGO Marvel Super Heroes (game), 63, 125
The LEGO Movie (film), 135–36
Lelash, Curtis, 117
Lima, Melissa, 187
Livingstone, Sonia, 20, 211n4
Loesch, Margaret, 35, 40–43
LOL Surprise!, 169–70
Lotz, Amanda, 28; on critical media industry studies approach, 14; on post-network era, 24, 26, 37–38, 212n1; on production studies, 212n8
Lowe, Nick, 198
Lund, Søren, 149–50

Maker Studios, 192, 215n6
management: as authority and labor, 19, 104, 109, 119; brand, 117, 127–29; industrial, future and, 9, 73; of LEGO, branded fan, 124, 129–30, 156–57, 159, 201; transgenerational, 93, 99, 125, 183, 187, 192–93, 201, 203–4, 207
marketing/promotion, 3; adulthood boundary troubled by, 13–14; FCBD as, 69–70; Hasbro and Hub, failures of, 42–43; of LEGO, age in, 135–40; of LEGO, gender in, 140; of toys, through television, 213n7
market segmentation, 37–39
Martin, Nick, 137
Marvel: adult sharing cultivated by, 54–55, 69, 75–76, 206; all-ages comics of, 65; comics, market share of, 60; under Disney, 55–57, 62; on Disney XD, 81–83, *82*, 89; fandom of, transgenerational, 66–69, 80, 87; films of, 56–57, 61–62; letters columns of, 66–68, 86–87; online, 55, 81–86, *82*, 88, 197–98, 203; television series of, SYU and, 78, *79*, 81–82, *82*; toy merchandising of, 64; transgenerational reframing of, 65–68; transgenerational success of, 62–63; transmedia success of, 56–57, 61–65; video games of, 63–64, 125. *See also* comic books; "Share Your Universe"; superheroes
Marvel AR, 203–4, 207; gender in, 198–99, 202, 209; professionalism and, 197–200, 202
Marvel Dad: adult sharing of, 17, 53–55, 66–68, 80, 85–87, 89; gender relations reproduced by, 17, 55, 85–87, 89; identity work of, 17; in letters column, 66–68; on SYU Facebook page, 85–86
Marvel Mom, 86–87
Marvel Studios, 56, 62
Marwick, Alice, 214n2
matrix, discursive, 10
matrix, transgenerational, 9–14
Mattel, 170–71; *Toy Box* and, 93, 101–4, 107, 109, 213nn7–8; toy testing of, 168, 172, 186–89, 191
Mattelart, Armand, 8, 211n1
Mattel Imagination Center, 172, 186, 188, 191
Matthias, Stacey, 114, 120
Maya and Hulyan (toy reviewers), 192–93
Mayer, Vicki, 95, 208
McCracken, Grant, 113, 214n9
media franchising, 36, 57; as extension, 20, 36–37, 45, 56, 212n7; specific franchises and, 16, 25, 39–42, 45, 50–51, 59, 62–63, 65, 68, 80, 122, 202
media industries. *See specific topics*
mediatization: LEGO as site of, 125–26; of play, 15, 212n9
MGA Entertainment, 169–71
micro-celebrity, 168, 214n2
millennials, 7, 35–36

246 *Index*

MIPCOM, 97
MIP Jr. trade show, 97
moderating, online, 152–54, 214n3
mommy blogging, 71, 75, 183
motherhood, 11
Mr. Rogers' Neighborhood (television series), 92
Muñoz, José, 8, 206
My Little Pony (television series), 39–40, 43

narrowcasting, 23, 28–29, 42, 44, 51
Netflix: cable channels and, 43–44; children's programming on, 44–45, 48; co-viewing of, 24, 26, 31–33, 44–45; family and, 23; as general entertainment brand, 27; as portal, 26; *Winx* franchise expansion on, 45, 212n7
New York Comic-Con, 71–73, 83–84, 87
Nick at Nite, 38
Nickelodeon: child market differentiation of, 30–31; for children exclusively, 23, 28, 39, 49; co-viewing of, 29, 34–36, 38–39, 41; franchise extension of, 36; at Kidscreen Summit, 111–13, 116–17
NickMom, 38
Nixon, Helen, 13–14
Noah (*Toy Box* judge), 105–6, *106*
Nova, 199, 202

orientation, 8, 20
Ortner, Sherry, 213n3

para-industry, 111
Paramount, 132–34
parents: age boundaries transgressed by, 21; at comic book conventions, 69–76; commodified labor of, 183; in co-viewing, children bonding with, 35–36; as fans, 20; FCBD and, 70–71, 75–76, 90; at Kidscreen Summit, identity of, 117–19; Kids' Day programming for, 74; kids' television sharing of, 32–33; Marvel Mom, 86–87; media as reference point for, 27; millennial, co-viewing by, 35–36; mommy blogger, 71, 75, 183; mother, as adult consumer category, 11; NickMom programming for, 38; in superhero sharing, authority of, 75–76, 90; toy testing and, 172–73, 186–91, 195–96, 206; toy testing and, on YouTube, 192–94
Parents Just Don't Understand (television series), 42
participation/participatory culture: adults in, 10, 204–5; of Amazon Prime, 45–46; childhood in, 10, 162, 204–5; digital consumer, toy testing and, 165–71; free labor of, 57–58, 165–66, 213n1; gift economy of, 171; play in, 205–6; subjectivity in, 10–11; in toy testing, boundaries of, 175–76, 186; transgenerational matrix of, 9–14
PBS. *See* Public Broadcasting System
pediocularity, 12; in *Big*, 161–62, *162*; gender, race, and, 98; identity work of, 93, 97–98; in Kidscreen Summit, 17–18, 115–17, 120–21; of media industry tourism, 18, 128; in professionalism, 17–18, 98, 104, 115–17, 120–21, 201, 203; of *Toy Box*, 99, 101, 103–4, 108–9
peer reviews, 169–71, 203–4
Phineas and Ferb (television series), 29–30, 35
Pitt, Adina, 111–13, 115, 118
play: as co-creative labor, 166; LEGO Group and, 124, 127, 134–41, 159; on LEGO Inside Tour, 143–44, 150–51; mediatization of, 15, 212n9; participatory, 205–6
portals, 26, 212n3
post-millennials, 112
post-network television. *See* television, post-network
power, 209; for consumers, responsibility and, 59; in critical media industry studies, 14; inheritance and, 58; market, 10; media, of culture indus-

tries, 134; viewer, in post-network television, 26, 212nn1–2
prize economy: extra-commercium ideologies and, 19; gamification in, 185–86; labor and, 181–83; of toy testing, 165, 181–87, 189, 195, 201
production, consumption and, 2, 4
production culture: children's media industries in, 92–93; media, as imagined community, 12
production studies, 209, 212n8; child consumer in, 96; children's media professionals and, 95–96; critical media industry studies and, 14–15, 208; deep texts and rituals in, 95, 208; feminist, 98, 213n6; LEGO and, 126, 208
professional/professionalism, 206; adult, age boundaries transgressed by, 91–92, 200, 205; adult, Buckingham on children and, 97, 213n5; amateurism converging with, 3–4, 13; authority of, 17–18, 94, 109, 112–15, 117–19; boundary work of, 99; child, 91–92, *162*, 162–63; of children's media performers, 91–92; at comic book conventions, 121–22; extra-commercium status and, 18–19, 129–30, 178, 200; identity work of, 12–13, 91–93, 97, 120; at Kidscreen Summit, pediocular, 17–18, 115–17, 120–21; Kidscreen Summit and, 93–94, 109–14, 118–19; in LEGO Inside Tour, consumer, 149–59, *153*; Marvel AR and, 197–200, 202; media industry tourism and, 130–34; participatory subjectivity in, 11; pediocular, 17–18, 98, 104, 115–17, 120–21, 201, 203; production studies and, 95–96; of *Sesame Street* performers, 91–92; on *Toy Box*, parodied, 104–6, *106*; *Toy Box* and, 18, 93–94, 99, 102–3, 107–9, 120; of toymakers, 93; in toy testing, 177–79, 194–96; transgenerational subjectivity in, 12–13; in unboxing videos, 179, 187

Public Broadcasting System (PBS), 16, 46–48
Pyle, Ellie, 199

queer, childhood as, 211n2
queer theory, 8–9, 206
Quesada, Joe, 85

race, 98, 122, 129, 205, 209, 214n10
reframing, transgenerational, 65–68
reproduction: fandom and cultural, 58; futurity of, 8–9, 201, 206, 209; generation in, 7; heteronormativity and, 8–9, 17, 206–8; labor and, 209; of legacy media industries, 204–7; Marvel AR and media, 209; by Marvel Dad, gender, 17, 55, 85–87, 89; orientation and, 8, 20; SYU and, 87–88
retail, 42, 64, 161, 170, 193; comics, 56, 60–61; FCBD and, 66–71; LEGO, 149, 158, 168; reviewing economies of, 167–68, 175–76, 180; toys, 101–02, 109, 136, 164, 172, 184, 189, 203; Toys "R" Us, 169, 178
ritual, 122; in Kidscreen Summit, space of, 94, 110–11, 113–15, 119–21; space of, 93; trade show as, 95, 118. *See also* deep texts and rituals
Rivera, Melissa, 108
Rivers, Joan, 92–93
Rogers, Fred, 92

Sammond, Nicholas, 10–11
San Diego Comic-Con, 72–73, 83–84, 142
Santo, Avi, 182
Scott, Suzanne, 18, 58, 129–30
segment-making media, 27–29, 212n4. *See also* market segmentation
Seidman, Larry, 117
Seiter, Ellen, 5
Sesame Street (television series), 16, 47–48, 91–92, 94
sexuality, 8, 205, 209; at Kidscreen Summit, 112; Marvel Dad and, 17, 55

"Share Your Universe" (SYU) (marketing campaign): adult fandom and, 16, 76, 78, 80–88; branding of, 78, 80–81, 86; at comic book conventions, 83, 87; as family experience, 83–84; gender in, 83–86, 88–89; identity work of, 16–17; Katsafanas in, 87–88; launch of, 76–78; Marvel television series and, 78, 79, 81–82, 82; online, 81–86, 82, 88; reproduction and, 87–88; samplers of, 78, 79; social media and, 55, 82, 82–86, 88; Spider-Man in, 78, 79; as transmedia strategy, 76–78, 79, 80–82, 82, 88–89; *Uncanny Avengers* linkage with, 80–81

sharing, 74; adult, Marvel cultivating, 54–55, 69, 75–76, 206; adult, Marvel Dad, 17, 53–55, 66–68, 80, 85–87, 89; in FCBD, transgenerational, 70–71; gender in superhero, 75–76, 83–84, 90; parental, in children's television, 32–33, 51–52

Simmons, Alex, 72, 122

Snyder, Stuart, 30

social media, 32, 36, 100, 103; Kidscreen Summit and, 112; LEGO, 148, 157; SYU and, 55, 82, 82–86, 88; toy testing and, 163–64, 168, 170, 173, 176, 188–92. *See also* influencers

society-making media, 27, 212n4

Sophia Grace (*Toy Box* judge), 105–6, 108

South Park (television series), 13

Spagnuolo, Marguerite, 98–99

Spider-Man, 58–59, 78, 79, 198

Spider-Man (films), 61–62

SpongeBob SquarePants, 29

sports, 50–51

Sprout, 31

Star Wars (franchise), 20, 122

Step2, 173, 190

Stewart, Ryan, 102, 107

Stonestreet, Eric, 100–101, 105, 108–9

St-Onge, John, 135

streaming. *See* television, streaming

Stuart, Anna, 48

subject/subjectivity, 205; of labor, 208; nonconforming consumer, 206; participatory, 10–11; in professionalism, transgenerational, 12–13

subscription, 48–50

superheroes: Marvel, inheriting fandom of, 80, 87; Marvel, transmedia success of, 61–63; sharing of, gender in, 75–76, 83–84, 90; sharing of, parental authority in, 75–76, 90; toys of, 64; transgenerational reframing of, 65–68

surplus audience: adults as, 18, 124; adults as, LEGO Inside Tour and, 124, 127, 157–58; brand management and, 129

SYU. *See* "Share Your Universe"

Tate, Lisa, 71

television, 205; children's, as discrete sector, 12, 97; children's, parental sharing in, 32–33, 51–52; co-viewing discourse of, 15–16, 25, 29–30, 50–51; disrupted, digital video economy and, 203–4; as family medium, emergence of, 27; Marvel series, SYU and, 78, 79, 81–82, 82; narrowcasting, 23, 28–29, 42, 44, 51; neo-network, family and, 27–28; network, brand culture of, 28; portals of, 26, 212n3; toys marketed through, 213n7

television, cable: child market differentiation of, 30–31; for children, 25–26; for children, advertising revenue and, 33–34; co-viewing and, 29–31, 38–41, 50, 212n6; streaming services and, 43–44, 48

television, post-network: co-viewing in, 24–29, 37–38, 43, 51, 203; family and, 23, 28; Kidscreen Summit and, 94; as networked, 26, 212n2; viewer power in, 26, 212nn1–2

television, streaming: cable television and, 43–44, 48; children's programming on, 44–50; co-viewing of, 24–26, 31–33, 44–46, 49–50; Genera-

tion #hashtag and, 31–32; Hasbro and, 43
Terranova, Tiziana, 165–66
Thomas, Jake, 199
Tinic, Serra, 14, 212n8
TiVo, 31
tourism, industry: deep texts and rituals in, 126; of film production studios, 132–34; LEGO in, 127–30, 134; pediocularity of, 18, 128; as pilgrimage, 130, 133; professionalism and, 130–34; theme parks, in media industry, 131–32
The Toy Box (television series): ABC and, 100, 109; boundary work in, 99–100, 102–3, 106–9; child judges of, 100, 103–6, *106*, 108, 109, 120; contestants of, 98–99, 106–9; creative labor and, 101, 104, 107, 109; deep texts and rituals in, 121; fantasy in, 94, 102, 110; Mattel and, 93, 101–4, 107, 109, 213nn7–8; pediocularity of, 99, 101, 103–4, 108–9; professionalism and, 18, 93–94, 99, 102–3, 107–9, 120; professionalism parodied in, 104–6, *106*; in reality competition genre, 100, 104; Toys "R" Us and, 93, 102, 213n8
toys: consumer influencers of, 169–70, 179, 201; in critical media industry studies, 15; Fleming on, 212n10; industry of, disruption faced by, 169, 204; makers of, as professionals, 93; manufacturers of, on digital platforms, 166, 170–71; mediatization of, 15; peer reviews of, 169–71, 203–4; superhero, 64; television marketing, 213n7
Toys "R" Us, 169; *Toy Box* and, 93, 102, 213n8; toy testing and, 176, 178, 190–91
toys-to-life, 63, 125
ToyTesters.tv, *176*, 179; as exchange-based practice, 173–75; prize economy and, 185–86
toy testing: as competition, 183–85; in culture industries, 165–66; as exchange-based practice, 171–72, 176–78, 180, 191–95; as exchange-based practice, ToyTesters.tv and, 173–75; extra-commercium status and, 18–19, 178; as gift economy, 171–73, 180, 184–86; influencers in, 169–70, 189–90; influencers in, adult, 187, 189–90; in manufacturing, 166–67, 181, 215n5; Mattel, 168, 172, 186–89, 191; online, 163, 165–68, 172–73; parents and, 172–73, 186–91, 195–96, 206; parents and YouTube, 192–94; participation in, boundaries of, 175–76, 186; participatory culture, digital, and, 165–71; popular discourse around, 163, 181; prize economy of, 165, 181–87, 189, 195, 201; professionalization of, 177–79, 194–96; recruiting, application for, 172, 175–78, *176*, 184, 190–91, 196, 214n3; restrictions of, 186–88; social media and, 163–64, 168, 170, 173, 176, 188–92; Toys "R" Us and, 176, 178, 190–91; as transgenerational, 182, 188–95; unboxing videos, 19, 167–69, 172, 179–80, 186–87, 190, 192; value of, 163, 166; on YouTube, revenue from, 179–80, 193–94, 214n4. *See also* labor
trade show: MIP Jr., 97; as ritualized, 95, 118
trans- (prefix), 3
transformation: co-viewing and, 25–26; transgenerational, 160–63, 194
Transformers, 39–40, 43
transgenerational industries. *See specific topics*
transgression: by adult professionals, age boundary, 91–92, 200, 205; of age categories, 1–2, 9; of age categories, by parents, 21; of age categories, critical analysis of, 22; of age categories, marketing and, 13–14; by nonconforming consumer subjects, 206; of production and consumption boundary, 2

transmedia: comic books in, 56–57, 61–65; LEGO Group as, 125–26, 135–36; Marvel success with, 56–57, 61–65; SYU as strategy of, 16–17, 76–78, *79*, 80–82, *82*, 88–89; transgenerational framework for, 57, 204; transgenerational framework influenced by, 6
transnationalism, 6, 127
Turow, Joseph, 27, 212n4
Twitter. *See* social media

unboxing videos, 167; adults and, 187, 190, 192; professionalization of, 179, 187; on YouTube, 19, 168–69, 172, 179–80, 186–87, 192
Uncanny Avengers (comic), 80–81
Universal Studios resorts, 131–32
Unleash the Fanboy blog, 71

video games, 63–64, 125, 166, 213n1

Warner Bros., 56, 65, 132–34
Westcott, Tim, 48

Willy Wonka and the Chocolate Factory (film), 123–24, 158–59
Winx Club WOW: World of Winx (television series), 45, 212n7
Wizard World Kids' Days, 73–74, 121–22

X-Men (comic franchise), 21, 80, 86; *All-New X-Men*, 65–66, 198; *Cyclops*, 66; films, 61–62

Yeatman, Andy, 45
YouTube: family and, 32; influencers on, 169–70; moderation of, 214n3; toy testing on, parents and, 192–94; toy testing on, professionalization of, 179; toy testing on, revenue from, 179–80, 193–94, 214n4; unboxing videos on, 19, 168–69, 172, 179–80, 186–87, 192; user-generated data exploited by, 58

Zafirau, Stephen, 96, 117
Zarghami, Cyma, 31, 35, 38–39
Zolides, Andrew, 182